get cooking.

get co

oking.

150 SIMPLE RECIPES TO GET YOU STARTED IN THE KITCHEN

MOLLIE KATZEN

with photographs by the author

harperstudio

An Imprint of HarperCollinsPublishers

To Sam and Eve

HarperCollins books may be purchased for educational, business, or sales promotional use. For information please write: Special Markets Department, HarperCollins Publishers, 10 East 53rd Street, New York, NY 10022.

For more information about this book or other books from HarperStudio, visit www.theharperstudio.com.

FIRST EDITION

Designed by Janet M. Evans

Library of Congress Cataloging-in-Publication Data has been applied for.

ISBN 978-0-06-173243-0

09 10 11 12 13 ID/QWT 10 9 8 7 6 5 4 3 2 1

contents

also by Mollie Katzen

Moosewood Cookbook

The Enchanted Broccoli Forest

Still Life with Menu

Vegetable Heaven

Sunlight Café

Eat, Drink, and Weigh Less (*with Walter Willett, M.D.*)

The Vegetable Dishes I Can't Live Without

Pretend Soup and Other Real Recipes

Honest Pretzels

Salad People and More Real Recipes

acknowledgments

One of the best parts of my job is that I get to work with some of the funniest, nicest, smartest, most food-passionate/knowledgeable people on the planet. Number one in all of these categories is the inimitable Steve Siegelman, who helps me organize my thinking about the broader project, and then zooms into the micro with his brilliant sense of language. A huge thank-you to Steve for his comprehensive support—in every sense.

Christi Swett is my recipe test accomplice, and Lorraine Battle, my food styling partner. Could I do it without you? Maybe. But it wouldn't be nearly as good, and it definitely would be a whole lot less fun.

Major thanks to Beth Shepard for being here for me, always—for the big, medium-sized, and little pictures, all of them important and insistent.

To Janet M. Evans, graphic designer extraordinaire: I have loved sitting with you at the computer for umpteen hours, and I am thrilled with the results. You are a true example of artistic talent minus the temperament! There should be more of you in the world, but for now, I'll settle for just one. And thanks to Philip Rolph Scanlon for feeding us.

To my wonderful mother, Betty Katzen: Thank you for everything-in-general, and for your brisket recipe in particular.

To my children, Sam Black and Eve Shames: Thank you for your inspiration and advice, and for your great taste in food (and in everything else). And thanks to my terrifi-cally helpful, unofficial focus group for your great input: Steve Troha, Sarah Goodin, David Havelick, Becca Hunt, Laura Mead, and Cooper Reaves.

To Ted Mayer and everyone at Harvard University Dining Services, and to all the many incredible Harvard students who have so generously shared meals, stories, and helpful feedback over the past number of years: Much appreciation for the honor of collaboration and friendship.

Thanks to Ken Swezey for providing consistently excellent pragmatic support; to Will Schwalbe for your generosity of spirit and your dead-on sense of context; and to Robert MacKimmie for being my garden-and-photo guru and champion.

Bob Miller is a publishing visionary, and a one-man cheerleading squad who has helped me stay buoyant throughout the past more than a dozen years. Big thanks to Bob, and to the gang at HarperStudio: Debbie Stier, Sarah Burningham, Julia Cheiffetz, Katie Salisbury, Kim Lewis, Nikki Cutler, Lorie Young, Leah Carlson-Stanisic, Doug Jones, and Mary Schuck (cover maven). You're the best!

Much appreciation to Kathie Ness, who is a most "respectfully submitted" copy editor, and to Elizabeth Parson for building the index.

Special thanks to Lara Gish and the Kashi Company for their support of get-cooking.com, and for their impressive work in making healthy products taste singularly delicious. However you do it, please keep it up.

get cooking.

We all love food, and we all know what we like. But for many people—sadly, frustratingly—the love of food doesn't necessarily translate into happy, good eating on a daily (or even weekly or monthly or any kind of regular) basis. Somehow, as our options have increased—from restaurants and take-out to more and more frozen heat-and-eat options of every kind—the fine, ancient craft of cooking has become something of a lost art. Why it that? What bridge is out?

I truly believe the missing link is pure knowledge: learning how to cook—for real—and then falling in love with it so much that we find ourselves making the time for it. Over and over. And then it becomes part of our lives.

Here's the irony: *Interest* in cooking is at an all-time high. We love everything from watching cooking shows and competitions on TV to blogging about where to get the best *banh mi* sandwich. But that's not what I'm talking about. I mean, I wonder how many people are munching junk food (or just plain not-very-good food) while watching gourmet cooking on a screen. We've kind of become a nation of nutrient- and flavor-challenged food voyeurs. Let's change that. I'm here to help.

For starters, I'm exceedingly happy to present you with 150 delicious, doable recipes that even the most inexperienced person can walk into any kitchen right now and make for dinner tonight. The "cuisine" is what I like to call "Big Tent," accommodating a broad base of tastes and needs, vegetarian and meat-loving and everything in between. I'm talking about soup-from-scratch, pastas that are light and well seasoned, salads you can make quickly and well, classic meat dishes with vegetable and potato sides to round them out, and plenty of vegetarian recipes (many of them vegan) that will please just about everyone. You'll find this food to be boldly seasoned—there's absolutely no need for "beginning" to mean "bland"—with lots of ethnic influences and flavors to keep things interesting.

These recipes are written in a way that I hope you can grasp in a single read-through, with a list of ingredients that isn't overwhelming and step-by-step instructions that really walk you through the process. The key phrase is "read-through," which I hope you'll take literally, as a thorough grasp of the tasks at hand will make all the difference between driving the boat and drifting around at sea. I want to stand beside you (in spirit and in information, if not in person) as you cook, letting you know what to expect and what things should look like as your meal goes from idea to reality.

Along with the recipes, I have also included many handy skills for learning how to cook the food you love in your own (possibly first) kitchen—in your own way and often. I hope these recipes and advice will give you both the knowledge and the confidence to find the link between your appreciation of food and your ability to prepare it with your own two hands. Joy and pleasure and fun (and a newborn sense of accomplishment) can be yours all along the learning curve.

IS THIS YOU?

Does this sound familiar? You find yourself eating pizza or fast food more nights a week than you wish. Higher-end takeout is an occasional option, but it's expensive. You regularly crave a home-cooked meal at the end of the day instead of that slab of pizza. You'd really rather be eating a healthier, tastier, and more balanced diet. You're curious about flavor combinations and interesting cuisines (ethnic and otherwise), and you'd like to experiment. You'd also like to know what the heck you're doing in the process. And most of all, you'd like to have what you really enjoy, rather than settling for someone else's idea of what's good.

You'd like to think of yourself (and have your friends and family think of you) as someone who knows how to cook.

You'd like to share the pleasure of food and drink with your friends, without spending a ton of money at a restaurant. You fantasize about everyone getting together to shop, cook, eat, and hang out till all hours at your place without using up your entire month's entertainment budget in a single evening.

But you're not sure where to begin. You leaf through cookbooks, surf the web, pick up a food magazine at the grocery store—and end up reading it in bed rather than cooking from it (or not reading it at all because it's too slick, and you're sure it's been written for someone else).

YOUR NEW COOKING LIFE

Having taught many people how to make a lot of good food in the course of my life, I can tell you that, if any or all of the above sounds like you, what you need are three things: good, reliable recipes for the kind of dishes you actually like; just enough advice on how to navigate them; and most important, the desire and confidence to *get cooking*. Not someday, not when you move into that place with the nice kitchen. Tonight. And thereafter.

This book, and its companion website, get-cooking.com, are going to give you plenty of the first two things—the recipes and the advice. The desire and the confidence, of course, are going to come from you. But trust me, the more you cook, the more that will happen on its own.

Learning to cook real food for yourself and the people you love is life-transforming. You'll gain skills you can rely on forever. You'll discover a whole new way to be creative, healthy, and focused, as well as popular. And who knows? Cooking might just become your favorite hobby—replete with benefits.

Once you've made these recipes your own (and started adding the *get creative* touches suggested throughout the book), you might find that you're not so much following recipes as using them as springboards to invent new dishes that reflect who you are and what you love. You'll be eating better, spending less, and feeling good about it. And, best of all, you'll really *get* cooking in a whole new way.

Getting Started

So where to begin? Well, before you do anything in the kitchen, the best advice I can give you is to read—and I mean *really* read—each recipe well, visualizing everything as you do so. And don't do this as you're rolling up your sleeves to get started, but much earlier, at the point when you're deciding what to make and laying out a game plan.

Studying the recipe will give you a sense of what ingredients you need to buy, whether you have all the right equipment, and how long the whole process will take. In these recipes, I've given you a heads-up each time something needs to be done in advance (especially when there is a waiting period for something to cool down, chill, or warm up to room temperature). Take the time to familiarize yourself with a recipe before you start, and you'll be cooking from the driver's seat instead of by the seat of your pants.

I strongly recommend that you get all the ingredients for each recipe completely prepped and ready before you start the actual cooking. Lay everything out (having a lot of containers helps) in an organized fashion near the stove.

Get your tools handy, too. In most recipes I've been pretty specific about the best tools to use, so again, if you read through first, you'll find embedded set-up information. The better set up you are, the more fun you're going to have once you turn on the stove.

There's another really important streamlining habit I strongly encourage you to develop: Try to clean up as you go. This is especially helpful if your kitchen is small. After you're done prepping the ingredients and you have them all lined up in their respective containers by the stove, clean the knife and cutting board, and put away anything you're finished using. Wipe down the counters, wash your hands, and take a deep breath. Now, proceed to the cooking phase.

What about the big, possibly overwhelming *uber*-cleanup awaiting you at the other end? Try to minimize it by keeping a tub of warm, soapy water in the sink. As soon as you're done with a dish or a utensil, just clear it of debris (compost bin, anyone?) and slip it into the tub. The exception is sharp knives, which should be kept separate so you won't accidentally slice your hand under the suds. Rinse the stuff later; just get it soaking for now. It will make a big difference.

Get the Gear

Equipping a kitchen for good, basic, fun cooking is less daunting than you might think. Start with the essentials, and go slow accumulating the rest. Remember that you don't need to buy the newest and the fanciest tools—or even anything new at all. Scour garage sales and thrift shops. And let all your relatives and friends know that you are in the exciting process of setting up a serious(ly fun) kitchen, so that they will keep you at the top of their hand-me-down list whenever they upgrade. Remind them, also, of your birthday, and promise to invite them often for dinner. That should help. Here's a starter list that should pretty much get you through every recipe in this book.

KNIVES

Chef's knife: This is where it all begins. You can—and should—do most of your slicing, dicing, chopping, and mincing with a single knife. It's known as a chef's knife or utility knife, and has a blade that's 6 to 8 inches long, without serrations. A good knife is one that feels comfortable in your hand, heavy enough to let you chop assertively but light enough to work with easily. There are many styles and options, and you need to find the one that feels right to you, but this is a good place *not* to scrimp, so visit a cookware store and get some advice.

Paring knife: You will also want a sharp paring knife (also straight-bladed, not serrated), which is way smaller than the chef's knife and thus invaluable for cutting diminutive things (like shallots) or doing fine work (like peeling and seeding fruit and vegetables).

Honing steel: High-quality knives will last you a lifetime if you maintain them properly. To that end, you'll want to invest in a knife-honing steel. This is a long rod with a handle. Here again, get advice at the cookware store, and ask for a demonstration. Use the steel to hone your knife frequently, and if you notice that the blade is getting dull and the steel isn't helping, take your knives to a professional sharpener. It's a good idea to do this once or twice a year, depending on how much of a workout your knives get.

Bread knife: A long-bladed serrated bread knife is good to have for slicing bread. A high-quality bread knife will stay sharp for years. It can't be honed on a steel, but you can have it sharpened professionally. And speaking of serrated knives, you might also want to have a smaller one on hand for cutting citrus and tomatoes.

CUTTING BOARDS

Buy a few wood or plastic cutting boards—you can't have too many, and they take up very little space. I recommend having a dedicated one for onions, garlic, and shallots, as these flavors are difficult to get rid of and tend to keep imparting themselves to other things that get cut on the board long after the fact. That's okay for vegetables, but really frustrating when your fruit salad is inadvertently seasoned with a hint of garlic. You should also have a separate plastic board for raw meat, poultry, and seafood to avoid cross-contamination with other foods. Make sure you clean it with soap and hot water—and thoroughly dry it—after each use.

SOUP POT OR DUTCH OVEN WITH A LID

You will use this a lot! Let it double as a pasta cooking pot to save cupboard space. The pot and its handles and lid need to be ovenproof;

you will often start a recipe on the stovetop, and then cover the pot and put it in the oven. Since you'll often be browning things in this pot as a first step, it's essential that it have a heavy bottom. (A thin metal pot will scorch food rather than browning it evenly.) Look for a substantial pot, such as one made of enameled cast iron, and treat it with respect, using wooden utensils to avoid scratching its surface.

SKILLETS

A 10- or 12-inch skillet is likely to be one of the most used pieces of equipment in your kitchen, so here again buying a good one matters. That doesn't mean it needs to be expensive. A cast-iron skillet will work well. If your skillet comes with a lid, all the better. If it doesn't, look for a heavy lid that will fit it (garage sales and thrift stores are sure to have a selection). A 6- to 8-inch skillet is handy for cooking eggs and small amounts of food. It's good to have both sizes.

OTHER POTS AND PANS

You will need a medium-sized (around 2-quart) saucepan with a tight-fitting lid and a heavy bottom, a 9- by 13-inch baking pan (metal or glass), and a few good, heavy baking trays.

WAFFLE HEAT ABSORBER

This is a small, round, corrugated metal insulation pad, also known as a Flame Tamer or heat diffuser, that you can put under a pot on the burner. It allows your lowest setting on the stove to become even lower for long simmering of foods, like rice and soup, that you want to cook through very slowly without burning them on the bottom.

OVEN MITTS AND POT HOLDERS

Keep these near the stove, in a drawer or hanging from a hook—and make sure they stay dry. If they get wet, they'll conduct heat and this will painfully (to you) defeat their purpose.

BOWLS

Collect various sizes from large to small—and various shapes (deep and shallow) for marinating, tossing, beating, combining, and serving. Nesting sets are nice for space-saving. And in general, when it comes to bowls, between holding ingredients, mixing, and serving, you can't have too many.

COLANDER

Your colander should be large enough to drain a batch of pasta. You might also want to have a smaller one for washing and draining small amounts of vegetables, fruit, herbs, or other ingredients—or use a strainer for this purpose.

STRAINER

A medium-mesh strainer is useful for everything from sifting powdered sugar over foods to draining and rinsing a can of beans.

WOODEN SPOON SETS

These are very inexpensive and effective. Usually these sets come with several wooden spoons and a few wooden spatulas. I use them all the time. It's handy to keep them in a pitcher or vase by the stove for easy grabbing. Keep some whisks, tongs, and other frequently used items in there as well.

RUBBER SPATULAS

They're cheap, so get a few of various dimensions. Invest in heatproof ones, which cost a bit more but won't melt into your scrambled eggs.

THIN-BLADED METAL SPATULA

This tool is indispensable for when you want to loosen and then flip a burger or other skillet food and don't want to leave any of the crisp parts in the pan.

WHISKS

Get yourself a set of whisks—small, medium, and large—and you'll be able to handle anything from whipping cream to whipping up a salad dressing.

TONGS

Spring-loaded tongs that you can use with one hand are indispensable. Watch any professional cook in action, and you'll see why.

SCISSORS

Buy a pair to use just for food and keep them in your kitchen drawer. You will be surprised at how much these will get used—from snipping chives and other herbs to cutting fish and poultry. Like your knives, your kitchen scissors will last longer and perform better if you have them professionally sharpened from time to time.

LADLE

Get a 4- to 6-ounce ladle for soups and stews and for ladling pasta water from the pot into a sauce.

GARLIC PRESS

When you see a recipe that calls for minced garlic in this book, you can either mince it with a knife or press it through a garlic press, which saves time.

BOX GRATER

A good, heavy-duty box grater is indispensable for grating everything from vegetables and potatoes to cheese.

MICROPLANE GRATER

These ultrasharp graters, sold in cookware stores, are fabulous for fine-grating citrus zest and ginger, hard cheeses like Parmesan, and chocolate (for sprinkling on desserts or drinks as a garnish).

PASTRY BRUSH

Useful for spreading olive oil on baking trays or brushing food with oil or melted butter.

VEGETABLE PEELER

Look for a good, sturdy one, either Y-shaped or straight. A cheap, flimsy peeler will slow you down and won't do as thorough a job.

INSTANT-READ THERMOMETER

If you will be cooking meat or chicken, this is your "when is it done?" insurance policy (see pages 149–50).

MEASURING SPOONS

Treat yourself to a nice, heavy-duty set. Actually, treat yourself to two. I find that having two sets really helps when you are measuring both dry and wet ingredients in one go-round and you want to keep them separate.

DRY MEASURING CUPS

These are used to measure dry ingredients, such as flour, and have flat edges, so that you can fill them and then scrape the excess off with the back of a knife blade. This gives you a more accurate measure for dry ingredients than a liquid measuring cup (see below).

LIQUID MEASURING CUPS

These are usually made of glass with measurement lines on the side. Get two heatproof glass ones with spouts for pouring—one 2-cup and one 4-cup capacity. These can be used both for measuring and for heating/melting ingredients (like milk or butter) in the microwave.

OTHER HELPFUL TOOLS AND GADGETS

- Salad spinner
- Dish towels
- A heavy-duty apron or two
- Citrus juicer or reamer
- A hardworking peppermill

ELECTRICAL APPLIANCES

- Blender and/or immersion blender (see pages 2–3)
- Hand-held electric mixer
- Toaster oven
- Microwave

FOR STORAGE

Containers: Collect food containers with tight-fitting lids in various sizes (store them stacked, with covers in a shoebox on the side). This is better for the environment than using plastic bags and plastic wrap. Also, save those plastic tubs with tight-fitting lids—the ones left over from when you binged on a bulk cookie purchase at the club store. They're great for storing grains, beans, nuts, and dried fruit, and they stack well for space-saving.

Jars with lids: Wash and save jars. Small ones are great for storing all your brilliant homemade salad dressings. Larger ones are perfect for keeping dried fruit and nuts, or beans, lentils, and grains.

Resealable plastic bags: Lay in a supply of freezer-weight and regular-weight bags in various sizes. (If this goes against your environmental values, just stick with the leftover containers, above.)

Plastic bags: If the ones you brought home from the produce section or the farmers' market are clean and dry, keep them for further use.

Large coffee cans: Clean them out when the coffee is gone, and use them to store those plastic bags you saved.

Permanent markers: Keep a few around for labeling whatever you are storing, with both the item name and the date. You might think this is overkill, but you will later thank yourself for doing this, I promise.

Aluminum foil and plastic wrap: These take turns being indispensable.

Shoeboxes: These are great for storing small bags of spices bought in bulk (which reminds me to recommend that you look for specialty food stores that sell spices in bulk, by the ounce, which will save you lots of money over time).

SPECIALTY FOODS

I will often suggest small touches of certain special ingredients—often as *get creative* additions to the recipes. Note that these are "special" and not "essential." Here's some useful information about them, so you can stock up to the degree that your wallet allows.

But first, before we get to the fun part, a few words about oil.

You will be cooking with oil a *lot* throughout this book. Your standard, everyday workhorse oils will, in most cases, be olive oil (choose a not-too-expensive extra-virgin) plus a second, more neutral-tasting oil, to use when olive flavor is incompatible with the dish. For this second oil, I recommend canola, soy, or peanut oil. Occasionally, but not often, I will also include some butter (which vegans can simply omit). So these are your daily heavy lifters. Onward to the flavoring ones.

High-quality olive oil: There are many, many imported and domestic olive oils on the market these days, ranging from "pure" to "extra-virgin." As I mentioned above, I recommend using a not-too-expensive extra-virgin for everyday cooking and salad dressings, and keeping an extra-extra special one around for special-occasion finishing and drizzling (recommended throughout the book). A small drizzle can have a large and good effect, so you can use this economically.

Toasted sesame oil: This dark Chinese flavoring oil is sold in the Asian foods section of supermarkets. All I want to say is "please get some"—it's that good, and that important an ingredient.

Other roasted nut and seed oils: These profoundly flavorful seasoning oils (which include walnut, almond, hazelnut, pistachio, and pumpkin seed oils) are not for cooking, but rather for drizzling onto your cooked food as a "flavor finish" or to supplement the olive oil in salad dressings. You can also use them as a dunk for fresh bread to create an exquisite appetizer, soup accompaniment, or quick snack.

Keep all oils stored in a cool, dark place—or in the refrigerator. This is especially true for the "gourmet" ones, so they will stay good over the period of time you are parceling them out.

Pure maple syrup: No imitations, now or ever, or you will go to culinary jail. Actually, I'm only somewhat kidding. If you love maple syrup impersonators on your pancakes, I won't tell you to stop using them there. But please don't cook or bake with them.

Vinegars: Store these in your cupboard (they keep indefinitely): cider vinegar; a decent, moderately priced balsamic; red wine vinegar; seasoned rice vinegar (make sure the label says "seasoned"). From there, you can experiment with fancier varieties, such as sherry, raspberry, and so on.

Pomegranate molasses: This sweet-tart-tangy syrup made from reduced pomegranate juice is available at Middle Eastern food shops and in the imported foods section of many grocery stores. It keeps forever in your cupboard, and a little bit goes a long way, adding flavor and bright color to Middle Eastern dishes and all kinds of other foods, from salads and grilled chicken to yogurt and cheese.

Dried fruit: Keep a supply of dried apricots, prunes, figs, dates, cherries, cranberries, and blueberries (as well as other, more exotic dried fruit, such as pears, papayas, and chili-dusted mango) on hand to liven up salads, grains, entrées, and desserts.

"Designer" salts: Fancy salts harvested from the sea and mined from the land are becoming more popular all the time. As an alternative to ordinary table salt, kosher salt has a pure, clean flavor and somewhat coarse grains, and it's a great multipurpose choice that goes anywhere, including the rim of a margarita glass. Sea salt tends to have a more assertive flavor than kosher salt and can be fine or coarse. Specialty salts, like *fleur de sel,* gray salt, black salt, and pink salt, tend to have a coarse, crunchy texture, which makes them a good choice for "finishing"—that is, sprinkling on dishes like salads or vegetables at the very last minute, so their texture and intense hit of saltiness stand out. Then there are flavor-infused options, like smoked salts and truffle salts. And of course, there's only one way to know which of any of these you'll like: buy a few and start experimenting.

Get Preppy

Most cooking involves an initial preparation phase, in which you cut stuff up. Check out the prep videos at get-cooking.com for quick lessons in the best way to handle most vegetables. And in the meantime, on pages xvii–xx is a quick reference guide to basic prep techniques you'll be using to make the recipes in this book.

VEGETABLE CHOPPING GUIDE

As you become increasingly comfortable and adept at chopping, cooking will feel more and more fluid, like a dance. (Go ahead and put on some music!) Be sure to use a very sharp knife (see page xi), go slow, and pay careful attention while you work. (Don't try to motor your way through at the speed of light, as some of the cool chefs seem to do on TV. Please!) Always maneuver whatever item you are cutting into the most stable position on the cutting board (for example, flat side down after an initial cut—or just plain hold it very steady with your noncutting hand), in order to keep things safe. (An escaping morsel can lead to your slicing your hand instead!) For vegetables not covered in this guide, use the same principles as those on the following pages. This process will become familiar to you soon enough. Have fun!

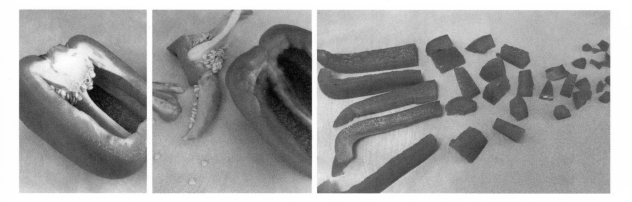

BELL PEPPER   Cut in half lengthwise • Cut out and discard stem, seeds, and inner membranes • Slice lengthwise into strips (thicker for diced; thinner for minced) • Cut across the strips to dice or mince

BROCCOLI   Cut off and discard base (bottom inch or so) • Use peeler to shave tough skin from remainder of stem • Cut on slight diagonal into stalks and florets • For chopped broccoli, cut across stalks and florets into smaller pieces

CARROT Peel • Cut off and discard stem end • Cut across into 2-inch sections • Slice sections lengthwise into flat, wide pieces • Slice each piece lengthwise into strips • Cut across the strips to dice

. . . and this is how to just plain slice one

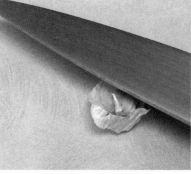

GARLIC Separate bulb into cloves • Lay clove on its side and smack with side of knife to loosen skin • Remove and discard skin • Slice into thin strips and then cut across the strips (and/or every which way) to mince

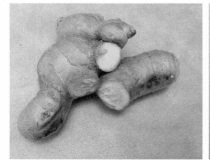

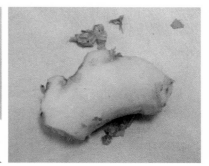

GINGER Scrape off and discard skin • Slice lengthwise into wide, thin pieces • Cut pieces into thin strips • Cut across the strips (and/or every which way) to mince

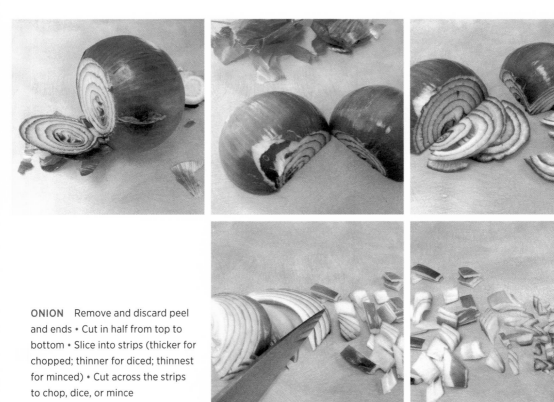

ONION Remove and discard peel and ends • Cut in half from top to bottom • Slice into strips (thicker for chopped; thinner for diced; thinnest for minced) • Cut across the strips to chop, dice, or mince

PARSLEY/CILANTRO   Remove and discard large stems • Chop the rest, picking out and discarding any larger stem remnants as you go (okay to leave in smaller stems)

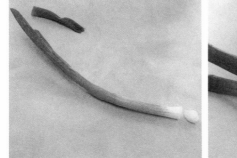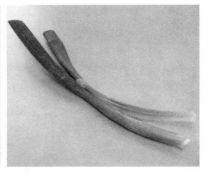

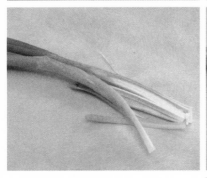

SCALLION   Remove and discard ends and any limp or damaged greens • Slice the white part lengthwise two or three times • Cut across to mince

For rounds or ovals, skip the lengthwise cuts, and make thin slices across (diagonal for the greens)

soups.

HOMEMADE CHICKEN NOODLE SOUP 6   CARAMELIZED BALSAMIC-RED ONION SOUP WITH CHEESE-TOPPED CROUTONS 8   CREAMY TOMATO-BASIL SOUP WITH PARMESAN FRICOS 11   CUBAN BLACK BEAN SOUP 14   CORN CHOWDER 16   WHITE CHEDDAR MASHED POTATO SOUP 18   HOT AND SOUR SOUP WITH FRESH SHIITAKE MUSHROOMS 20   CREAM OF SPINACH AND BROCCOLI SOUP 22   NORTH AFRICAN RED LENTIL SOUP 24   ROASTED BUTTERNUT SQUASH AND APPLE SOUP 26

The How of Soup

If you want to master the art of making a good home-cooked meal for yourself and the people in your life, soup is a perfect place to start.

Soup fills your home with the welcoming smell of good things simmering, and in most cases it practically cooks itself, once you do a bit of initial ingredient prep. Why not just open a can? Well, when you're pressed for time, there's nothing wrong with that. But a little time making soup from scratch is a great investment that beats canned soup hands down. Why?

• It's tastier because you're in control of the ingredients and the seasonings, and you can choose what's fresh and in season for the raw materials.

• It's cheaper, especially when you consider that a big pot of soup can last for several meals or feed a crowd.

• It's likely to be healthier, because the ingredients are freshly prepared and less chemically "enhanced."

• It generally freezes and reheats well.

• It's filling and soul-satisfying.

• And, best of all, it's something wonderful you can take pride in having created—often from next to nothing.

Soup is, generally speaking, ingredients simmered with water or broth—sometimes puréed, sometimes not—served hot (or sometimes cold). It's about that simple. So, if you have a large heavy pot, a ladle, and something to purée with, even the tiniest apartment can be home to a great soup kitchen.

READ BEFORE YOU LEAP

There's no single way to make soup, and some recipes involve a little more advance preparation than others. That's why it's important to read through any recipe in this chapter (and really, any recipe at all) before you start cooking—and especially before you decide to make it for the first time. That way, you'll be able to gauge the timing, check what ingredients you need, and decide if this is one for tonight or something to try next weekend.

PURÉEING SOUP

Many soups are made by cooking ingredients like potatoes or vegetables in broth or water until they're soft, and then puréeing them to achieve a thick, smooth consistency. A regular stand blender works well for the purpose, but an immersion blender is even better. Whichever way you go, before you purée any soup, let it cool down a bit so you don't get burned if any accidentally spills or splashes.

Blender Ladle some of the soup into the blender, filling it no more than two-thirds full so the steam doesn't blow the lid off when you turn on the motor. Put the lid on the blender, and then fold a kitchen towel in half and drape it over the lid (another very helpful safety measure to keep hot soup from splattering you). Put one hand on the towel and hold the lid down firmly before you turn on the motor. With the other hand, turn the blender on, setting it to its lowest speed (cranking it to "high" right away will probably pop the lid). Then increase the speed gradually to the highest setting.

After a few seconds, turn off the blender and check to see if you've reached the consistency you're looking for. If you want a chunky soup, it's usually best to purée some of the soup completely and then combine that with the remaining unblended soup. (You can also simply purée all of the soup, "pulsing" the motor on and off a few times so the soup doesn't get completely liquefied.)

Because you're puréeing in batches, you'll need a large container, bowl, or a second soup pot to hold the blended soup as you work. When you're done, pour everything back into the original cooking pot to reheat the soup; or for cold soups or ones you're making in advance, let the soup cool in the container and then cover it and chill it in the refrigerator.

Immersion blender   Immersion blenders (also known as stick blenders) are among a handful of game-changing kitchen tools. So if you're liking the idea of making soup a more regular part of your life, I highly recommend you rush out and buy one. They're not that expensive, and they have several advantages over a conventional blender: There's no second bowl or pot to dirty up, because the puréeing happens right in the soup pot. They're easy and fast to use, because you don't have to work in batches. They allow you to see just how puréed everything is getting, so you can stop the minute you've achieved the texture you want. And they're easy to clean and don't take up much space. Convinced?

To use an immersion blender, take the pot off the stove and set it somewhere stable. Submerge the business end of the immersion blender completely into the soup, holding it straight up with the base flat against the bottom of the pot. To avoid splattering and overblending, turn on the motor to the lowest setting and then gradually increase the speed. Then simply move the blender around, always keeping the base flush with the bottom of the pot and the blade submerged.

Food processor   You can use a food processor fitted with the steel blade attachment to purée some soups, but for very liquidy ones it really doesn't do as good a job as a blender or immersion blender. If you do use one, work in batches and avoid filling the bowl of the processor more than two-thirds full.

Potato masher   Yes, the lowest-tech option of all works quite nicely when you want a somewhat puréed but still fairly chunky texture. Just mash (gently, to avoid splashing) until you like what you see.

GET THIS   **SOUP SUPPLIES**

Keep these staples around so you can make soup any time by rounding up a few good vegetables:

- Broth in boxes (various vegetable broths, plus maybe some chicken)
- Bouillon cubes
- Canned beans
- Canned tomatoes
- Tomato paste
- Dried thyme, oregano, cumin, and red pepper flakes
- Olive oil
- Garlic and onions
- Soy sauce
- Toasted sesame oil
- Parmesan cheese
- Rice
- Soup pasta (such as orzo or little stars)

STOCK OPTIONS

When a soup calls for stock or broth, I recommend using the kind that comes in boxes because it tastes much better than canned. Look for a good organic brand. They're all quite different, so shop around until you find one you like. For those emergencies when you run out of broth, keep some bouillon cubes on hand.

STORING SOUP

To store soup, let it cool, transfer it to an airtight container, and put it in the refrigerator. Stored in this way, most soups will keep for 3 to 4 days.

Most soups also freeze well. A handy way to do this is to let the soup cool and then put individual portions in resealable plastic freezer bags. That way you can put one in the refrigerator to thaw in the morning (never thaw soup, or anything, at room temperature—it's not safe, bacteriologically speaking) and it will be ready to heat up when you come home from work. Press most of the air out of each bag and lay it flat in the freezer until it has frozen solid.

You can also freeze soup in plastic containers with airtight lids. Liquids expand when they freeze, so leave about half an inch of space at the top. Always label bags or containers with the kind of soup and the date (permanent markers work best). If a soup has lived in your freezer for more than 6 months, throw it out.

Soups that tend to be freezer-challenged are those made with dairy, eggs, and/or lots of puréed potatoes. Freezing tends to make them break apart and take on a mealy or watery consistency. So don't freeze these.

STYLE IT

The aesthetic and psychological impact of a simple garnish can't be overstated. Set aside some of the herbs used in making a soup to top each serving. Or add a dollop of sour cream, yogurt, crème fraîche, or salsa, or a drizzle of good olive oil. Grated Parmesan or crumbled feta or goat cheese works well with many soups. And for crunch, sprinkle a few croutons or crumbled tortilla chips on top.

**ROUNDING OUT
A SOUP MEAL**

Soup can definitely be a one-bowl meal. But depending on your appetite and your mood, you might want to add a little something to round out the menu.

- **SALAD** Match the dressing to the style of the soup. I've given you some recommendations with the recipes (kind of like wine-and-food pairings, except it's soup-and-salad pairings), and you can take it from there.

- For a filling, nutritious, and inexpensive dinner, simply ladle some soup over a bowl of cooked rice.

- A vegetable or potato side dish

- **SLICED TOMATOES** Drizzle with olive oil, feta, olives, and herbs.

- **GREAT BREAD** Warm or toast a few slices of crusty bread or cornbread—store-bought or homemade (see page 101).

- Sliced deli meats

- Some good cheese

roasted garlic paste

A GREAT INGREDIENT FOR SOUP

Makes 6 tablespoons

This recipe is vegan.

Roasting garlic completely transforms its flavor. It's still pungent, but the sharpness is greatly softened. Use Roasted Garlic Paste for mashing into soups, potatoes, sauces, or dressings—also for spreading on crackers or little toasts as an appetizer; topping grilled chicken, fish, or steak; or tossing into cooked vegetables. This will keep well (packed into a small, tightly covered container and topped with a slick of olive oil) for up to 3 weeks in the refrigerator—or indefinitely in the freezer. (Never store it at room temperature—it needs to stay cold.)

3 whole heads
   of garlic

3 tablespoons
   olive oil, plus a
   little extra

1. Adjust the oven rack to the center position (if using a full-size oven) and preheat the oven (or toaster oven) to 375°F. Line a small baking pan with foil.

2. Slice off and discard the very topmost tips of each garlic head. Stand the heads, cut side up, on the foil. Carefully pour about 1 teaspoon of the olive oil onto the cut surface of each head. Roast for 30 to 40 minutes, or until the bulbs feel soft when gently pressed. (Larger bulbs will take longer.)

3. When cool enough to handle, break each bulb into individual cloves and squeeze the pulp onto a plate. Use a fork to mash the garlic, gradually adding the remaining olive oil as you mash. Use right away, or refrigerate or freeze with a little olive oil until use.

homemade chicken noodle soup

Makes 4 to 5 servings

Canned chicken noodle soup is about to become a thing of your past. This straightforward version is all about making (and keeping) it real: big chunks of chicken, wide noodles, plenty of carrots and celery. For the broth, go for the kind sold in boxes, and choose a good-quality brand, preferably organic. To make this soup even easier, you can replace the chicken breasts with some leftover rotisserie chicken or other cooked chicken meat. Just shred enough to make about 2 cups and add it to the soup along with the noodles.

2 tablespoons olive oil

1 medium red or yellow onion, minced

¼ teaspoon salt

2 medium carrots, sliced ¼-inch thick

2 stalks celery, sliced ¼-inch thick

8 cups (2 quarts) chicken broth

2 medium boneless, skinless chicken breasts

¼ pound wide egg noodles

Freshly ground black pepper

A handful of chopped flat-leaf parsley

1. Place a soup pot or a Dutch oven over medium heat. After about a minute, add the olive oil and swirl to coat the pan. Add the onion and salt, and cook, stirring occasionally, for about 5 minutes, or until the onion softens.

2. Add the carrots and celery and continue cooking, stirring occasionally, for another 5 minutes.

3. Pour in the broth and bring to a boil. Add the chicken breasts and turn the heat all the way down to the lowest possible setting. Cover and simmer gently for 8 to 10 minutes, or until the chicken is no longer pink in the center. (You can check by cutting into the meat with a sharp knife.) Use a slotted spoon or tongs to remove the chicken from the broth. Put it on a plate and let it rest for about 5 minutes, or until it is cool enough to handle comfortably.

4. Meanwhile, using a large spoon, skim off and discard any foamy residue that might have shown up on the surface of the soup. Bring the soup back to a gentle boil over high heat, and add the noodles, stirring to keep them from sticking together. Cook for 5 to 8 minutes, or until the noodles are tender.

5. While the noodles are cooking, shred the chicken (use two forks, a small knife, or your fingers) into bite-sized pieces.

6. When the noodles are tender, add the shredded chicken to the soup and season to taste with a few grinds of black pepper. Serve hot, topped with a sprinkling of parsley.

GET CREATIVE

- For a nostalgia-laced simple dinner, pair this soup with a green salad dressed with Homemade Ranch Dressing (page 37), and garnish the salad with very sweet cherry tomatoes.

- Squeeze some fresh lime juice into the soup just before serving, or serve with wedges of lime on the side for people to add at the table.

- To take the soup in a Latin direction, in addition to adding lime juice, you can garnish each serving with chopped cilantro plus some crispy tortilla strips (or crumbled tortilla chips) and a dollop of your favorite salsa.

- Love matzo ball soup? Buy a package of matzo meal, follow the directions for making matzo balls (you can even make them a day or two ahead of time), and add them to the soup instead of the noodles.

caramelized balsamic–red onion soup with cheese-topped croutons

Makes 6 servings

Try this sweeter, simpler take on traditional French onion soup, topped with toasted cheese croutons. You can use any kind of mustard—Dijon, spicy brown, or even plain old yellow. Make the croutons while the soup is simmering, so everything can be ready at about the same time.

Make this vegan by omitting the butter and leaving the cheese off the croutons.

¼ cup olive oil

1 tablespoon butter (optional)

6 large red onions
    (4 to 5 pounds), thinly sliced

2 teaspoons salt

¼ cup balsamic vinegar

2 tablespoons soy sauce

2 tablespoons prepared mustard

6 cups water

⅛ teaspoon freshly ground black
    pepper

Cheese-Topped Croutons
    (recipe follows)

1. Place a soup pot or a Dutch oven over medium heat. After about a minute, add the olive oil and swirl to coat the pan. Toss in the butter, if desired, and swirl until it melts into the oil.

2. Stir in the onions and salt, and reduce the heat to medium-low. Cook, stirring occasionally (and more often as the onions darken), for about 30 minutes, or until the onions become deep golden brown and very soft.

3. Add the vinegar, soy sauce, and mustard, and cook, stirring occasionally, for 5 minutes longer.

4. Pour in the water and bring to a boil. Then turn the heat all the way down to the lowest possible setting, partially cover, and simmer gently for 15 minutes.

5. Season with black pepper, then ladle the soup into bowls. Top each steaming bowlful with a crouton, and serve right away.

GET CREATIVE

- A good salad partner for this soup is Original-ish Waldorf Salad (page 52).

- Use scissors to snip some fresh chives on top of each serving.

- Use the croutons to top other kinds of soup, too. They're particularly good with the Roasted Butternut Squash and Apple Soup (page 26).

- Put some extra grated Swiss cheese at the bottom of each soup bowl, then ladle in the soup and top with a crouton.

cheese-topped croutons

Makes 6 large croutons

You can make these with any kind of Swiss cheese, but the flavor will be much better if you use one of the higher-end ones, like Gruyère or Emmentaler. (And if you don't have any of these cheeses handy, you can use bleu cheese, or any grating cheese with assertive flavor.) This works well with day-old bread, so it's a great way to use up what's left of a baguette.

Six ½-inch-thick slices French bread
    baguette, cut on the diagonal

¾ cup (packed) grated Swiss cheese

1. Preheat the oven or a toaster oven to 350°F.
Line a baking tray with foil.

2. Arrange the bread slices on the prepared tray.
Place the tray in the center of the oven and bake
for about 5 minutes, or until the bread is lightly
toasted. (Keep an eye on it, so it doesn't burn.)

3. Remove the tray from the oven, and change
the setting to "broil." Divide the grated cheese
evenly among the tops of the toasts. Then place
the tray under the broiler for about 3 minutes, or
until the cheese melts and is just beginning to
turn brown. (Again, pay close attention.) Remove the tray from the broiler and set it aside
until you're ready to serve the soup.

creamy tomato-basil soup with parmesan fricos

Makes 4 servings

Imagine the flavor of grilled cheese and tomato soup—all in a single bowl. This super-easy soup is all about tomato flavor. And the fun little Parmesan Fricos add a cheesy crunch that takes the whole thing over the top. Some canned tomatoes are saltier than others, so start by adding the ½ teaspoon salt, then taste the soup and see if you think it needs more. Make sure you have prepared some Roasted Garlic Paste ahead of time.

Make this vegan by using plain soy milk instead of the regular milk and skipping the fricos.

One 28-ounce can crushed tomatoes

2 tablespoons Roasted Garlic Paste (page 5)

15 to 20 large basil leaves, roughly torn

1½ cups milk

½ teaspoon salt (or more, to taste)

Freshly ground black pepper

Parmesan Fricos (recipe follows)

1. Combine the tomatoes, garlic paste, basil, and milk in a soup pot or a Dutch oven, and place it over medium-high heat. Bring to a boil, and then immediately turn the heat to low and let the soup simmer for 10 minutes. Turn off the heat and let the soup cool for a few minutes.

2. Use a blender or immersion blender (see page 3) to purée the soup until it is smooth.

3. Heat the soup gently over medium heat, stirring occasionally, until it is hot but not boiling.

4. Season with the salt and black pepper to taste. Serve with Parmesan Fricos on the side.

GET YOUR FRICO ON

Once you master the simple technique of frico-making, you'll find all kinds of uses for them. They're great with soups, they're a nice alternative to chips, and you can serve them with olives and salami and call it an antipasto platter. They also make a perfect garnish for Caesar Salad (page 44) in addition to, or in place of, the traditional croutons. To make them, you'll need the kind of grated Parmesan that's shredded, not powdered. You can buy it pre-grated or make your own from a piece of cheese, using the medium holes of a grater. If you're DIY-inclined, you might enjoy playing with different frico sizes and shapes. You can make them huge, or shape them by draping them inside cups, around a rolling pin, or whatever else you think of, as soon as they come out of the pan. As they cool, they'll keep that shape, and then you can fill them with a little salad or just use them as an extra-cool garnish.

parmesan fricos

Makes 14 to 16 fricos

1 cup Parmesan cheese, shredded

1. Set a large skillet over medium heat. Drop 1-tablespoon heaps of Parmesan directly in the pan, and working fairly quickly, use the back of a spoon to spread each heap into a round of cheese about 3½ inches in diameter. (They should look lacy, with a bit of the pan showing through between the shreds.) Make sure to leave a little space in between fricos, so you'll have room to get in there with your spatula.

2. Cook for 4 to 5 minutes, or until the underside is golden and stays stiff when prodded. When the top surface of the cheese goes from melty to somewhat dry looking, the fricos are ready to flip. Use a thin-bladed metal spatula to turn them over gently, and cook on the second side for about 2 minutes, or until golden and crisp all over. Transfer to a rack or platter to cool and finish crisping.

GET CREATIVE

- Drizzle some high-quality olive oil onto each serving.

- If you like your tomato soup a little on the sweet side, add 1 to 2 teaspoons honey or brown sugar before the final simmer.

- Garnish with additional minced fresh basil.

- This soup pairs well with Caesar Salad (page 44).

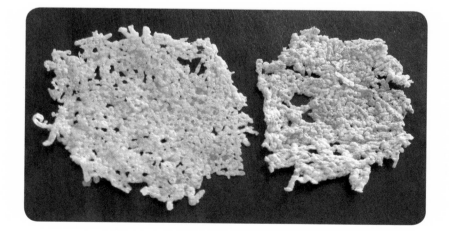

cuban black bean soup

Makes 4 to 5 servings

R eal, hearty black bean soup with a tangy edge of lime can be yours in under an hour (most of which is just the soup simmering while you do something else). The silver bullet here is canned beans, which, generally speaking, are perfect for soups and simmered dishes. To make a heartier meal, serve this soup spooned over rice.

This soup is vegan.

- 2 tablespoons olive oil
- 1 medium red or yellow onion, minced
- 2½ teaspoons ground cumin
- Half a medium red bell pepper, minced
- 1 tablespoon minced or crushed garlic (about 3 good-sized cloves)
- 1½ teaspoons salt
- Three 15-ounce cans black beans (approximately 4 cups cooked beans)
- 3 cups water
- 1 to 2 tablespoons fresh lime juice
- A big handful of cilantro leaves
- Freshly ground black pepper
- Red pepper flakes
- Lime wedges, for garnish

1. Place a soup pot or a Dutch oven over medium heat. After about a minute, add the olive oil and swirl to coat the pan. Add the onion and cumin, and cook, stirring occasionally, for about 5 minutes, or until the onion softens.

2. Add the bell pepper, garlic, and salt, and reduce the heat to medium-low. Cook, stirring occasionally, for about 15 minutes, or until the vegetables are very soft.

3. Meanwhile, set a colander in the sink and pour in the beans; give them a quick rinse and allow them to drain.

4. Add the beans and the water to the soup pot, and bring to a boil. Then turn the heat all the way down to the lowest possible setting, partially cover, and simmer gently, stirring occasionally, for 15 minutes.

5. Use a potato masher or the back of a slotted spoon to mash about half of the soup so it thickens. The soup will become somewhat chunky,

GET CREATIVE

• Pair this soup with Wilted Spinach Salad with Hazelnuts, Goat Cheese, and Golden Raisins (page 56).

• Top each serving with sour cream or yogurt, and/or a whole cilantro sprig.

• Garnish with a sprinkling of toasted cumin seeds (see page 25).

• Garnish with tortilla chips or plantain chips.

• Top with a bit of diced mango, fresh or frozen.

• Sprinkle some diced red onion and/or chopped hard-boiled egg (see page 34) over each serving. (Very Cuban!)

• If you like things hot and smoky, add a minced canned chipotle chile along with the bell pepper in step 2.

• Finely chop a fresh jalapeño chile and sprinkle a bit on each serving. (Regarding both this point and the previous one, be sure to wash the knife, the cutting board, and your hands with warm water and soap after handing any hot chiles.)

• Top with a spoonful of your favorite salsa.

• Serve with warm flour or corn tortillas.

not completely smooth. (You can also purée it, if you like, with a blender or immersion blender—see page 3.) If at any point it seems to have gotten too thick, it's okay to add a little extra water (about ¼ cup at a time) until it's a consistency you like.

6. Add a tablespoon of the lime juice, and then taste to see if you think it needs the second tablespoon. Use scissors to snip in the cilantro (it's okay if the pieces are a bit rough). Add about 8 grinds of black pepper and a pinch of red pepper flakes, and then simmer and stir for another minute or two to let the flavors blend. Serve hot, with the lime wedges alongside.

corn chowder

Makes 4 to 5 servings

Classic, comforting corn chowder is simple to make—especially if you use frozen corn kernels. Look for sweet corn or a blend of sweet and yellow. You can defrost it by putting it in a large strainer or colander and rinsing it under running water. And if fresh sweet corn is in season, by all means use it. Just peel off the husks and silks, stand an ear on a cutting board, and holding the ear firmly, use a paring knife to cut the kernels off. You'll need 3 to 4 ears to make the 3 cups called for in this recipe. Use either milk or heavy cream for the final enrichment, but not half-and-half, which curdles when heated.

2 tablespoons butter

1 medium red or yellow onion, minced

1 stalk celery, minced

1 teaspoon minced garlic
  (about 1 good-sized clove)

1½ teaspoons salt

4 cups water

2 or 3 medium-small waxy potatoes
  (about ¾ pound),
  cut into ¾-inch dice

1 pound frozen corn kernels
  (about 3 cups), thawed

½ cup milk or heavy cream
  (or a combination)

Freshly ground black pepper

GET CREATIVE

- Pair Corn Chowder with a green salad featuring a very sweet red bell pepper and dressed with Raspberry-Shallot Dressing (page 35).

- For a smokier flavor and a bit more substance, at the beginning of step 1 replace the butter with 2 slices of bacon, cut into thin strips. When the bacon is lightly browned, add the onion and proceed as directed.

- Stir a small handful of chopped flat-leaf parsley into the soup just before serving for a little extra color.

- Use scissors to snip some chives and/ or cilantro over each serving, and/or garnish with a sprig of cilantro or flat-leaf parsley.

- Serve with crusty sourdough or any rustic-style bread.

- Turning this soup into Clam Chowder is easy. Just reduce the corn to ½ pound and add two small (6.5-ounce) cans chopped clams, with their juice, when you add the corn.

1. In a soup pot or a Dutch oven, melt the butter over medium heat. Add the onion, celery, garlic, and salt. Cook, stirring occasionally, for about 5 minutes, or until the onion and celery begin to soften.

2. Add the water and the diced potatoes. Bring to a boil, then turn the heat all the way down to the lowest possible setting. Partially cover and simmer gently for about 15 minutes, or until the potatoes become completely soft. (It's okay to err on the side of their becoming falling-apart tender.)

3. Add the corn and simmer for 5 minutes. Stir in the milk or cream and heat the soup very gently for a minute longer. Season to taste with pepper, ladle into bowls, and serve.

white cheddar mashed potato soup

Makes 5 to 7 servings

I f you're fond of the flavor of rich, cheesy baked potatoes, this creamy soup will be right up your alley. For a soup made with this much potato, use russets rather than a waxy variety, which can turn gluey when puréed. A medium-sharp white Cheddar is the perfect complement to the potatoes, but you can use any kind of Cheddar or jack cheese.

2 tablespoons olive oil

1 medium yellow onion,
    chopped

1 tablespoon ground cumin

1 tablespoon minced garlic
    (about 3 good-sized cloves)

1½ teaspoons salt

3 cups water

4 medium-large russet potatoes
    (about 3 pounds),
    cut into small chunks

1½ cups milk

¾ cup (packed) grated white
    Cheddar cheese

Red pepper flakes

Freshly ground black pepper

1. Place a soup pot or a Dutch oven over medium heat. After about a minute, add the olive oil and swirl to coat the pan. Add the onion and cumin, and cook, stirring occasionally, for about 5 minutes, or until the onion softens.

2. Stir in the garlic and the salt. Reduce the heat to medium-low, partially cover the pot, and cook, stirring occasionally, for another 10 minutes.

3. Add the water and the potatoes. Bring to a boil, then turn the heat all the way down to the lowest possible setting. Partially cover, and simmer gently for about 15 minutes or until the potatoes become completely soft. (It's okay to err on the side of their becoming falling-apart tender.) Turn off the heat, stir in the milk, and let the soup sit, uncovered, to allow it to cool down a bit.

4. Use a blender or immersion blender (see page 3) to purée the soup until it is smooth. (If it seems too thick, add a little extra water.)

5. Reheat the soup very slowly over medium-low heat, being careful not to let it boil. When it is hot, stir in the cheese and season to taste with red pepper flakes (a pinch or two) and black pepper (6 to 10 grinds). Serve hot, passing around the pepper mill and extra red pepper flakes.

- For a hearty soup-and-salad supper, serve this with All-American Three-Bean Salad (page 38).

- Add up to 3 tablespoons Roasted Garlic Paste (page 5) along with the fresh garlic.

- Top each serving with some salsa (any kind you love), some extra grated cheese, and/or a scattering of roughly chopped flat-leaf parsley.

- Garnish each serving with a dollop of sour cream and some thinly sliced scallion greens or snipped chives.

- Cook a few strips of bacon (see page 233, figuring on one strip per serving), let cool, crumble, and sprinkle over each serving.

hot and sour soup with fresh shiitake mushrooms

Makes 4 to 5 servings

You'll be amazed at how doable this classic Chinese restaurant soup can be—in your own kitchen, and with no fancy technique or mysterious ingredients. Fresh shiitake mushrooms are easy to find these days, and very rewarding to cook with. You only need a few to get a major flavor and texture impact. Same with the toasted sesame oil: Here's your front-row seat to witness how a mere teaspoon works exponential magic, infusing an entire batch of soup with its inimitable flavor.

Make this vegan by omitting the eggs.

2 eggs

10 medium-sized (about ½ pound) fresh shiitake mushrooms

2 tablespoons canola, soy, or peanut oil

1¼ teaspoons salt

¼ teaspoon red pepper flakes

5¼ cups water

¼ cup cider vinegar

2 tablespoons soy sauce

¼ pound firm tofu, cut into thin strips

1 to 2 tablespoons light brown sugar (optional)

1 teaspoon toasted sesame oil

Freshly ground black pepper

1½ tablespoons cornstarch

1 scallion, green part only, very thinly sliced on the diagonal

A handful of cilantro leaves, torn or coarsely chopped

1. Lightly beat the eggs in a small bowl until you no longer see any bits of egg white. Leave the bowl on the counter or somewhere warm, so the eggs can come to room temperature while you make the soup.

2. Clean the mushroom caps by wiping them with a damp paper towel. Use a paring knife or scissors to cut off the stems. Discard the stems, and then thinly slice the caps and set them aside.

3. Place a soup pot or a Dutch oven over medium heat. After about a minute, add the oil and swirl to coat the pan. Add the sliced mushrooms, ½ teaspoon of the salt, and the red pepper flakes. Cook, stirring occasionally, for about 10 minutes, or until the mushrooms are golden brown.

4. Add the remaining ¾ teaspoon salt, 5 cups of the water, and the vinegar, soy sauce, tofu, and, if desired, a tablespoon of the brown sugar. (Then taste the soup, and if you think it needs more sweetness, add the second tablespoon of brown sugar.) Bring to a boil, then turn the heat all the way down to the lowest possible setting. Partially cover, and simmer gently for 10 minutes.

5. Add the sesame oil and about 10 grinds of black pepper, and stir to combine.

6. Put the cornstarch in a small bowl with the remaining ¼ cup water, and mix until smooth. Stir the cornstarch mixture into the hot soup. Continue simmering for a minute or two, stirring once or twice. The soup will become glossy and will thicken slightly.

7. Slowly drizzle the beaten eggs into the simmering soup, stirring as you go. Cook for just 1 minute longer, until the eggs are set. Serve hot, topping each bowl with a scattering of scallion greens and cilantro leaves.

GET CREATIVE

- Pair this soup with Chinese Chicken Salad (page 54) for a great little dinner.

- Use chicken or vegetable broth in place of some or all of the water for a richer-tasting soup. Taste before adding the salt in step 4; you may not need it all.

- Add ½ cup frozen peas, thawed under running water in a strainer, at the end of step 4.

- Add 8 uncooked peeled, deveined prawns in step 4. They will cook directly in the soup.

- Add 1 cup of cooked chicken, cut into strips, in step 4.

- Add an 8-ounce can of sliced water chestnuts, an 8-ounce can of sliced bamboo shoots, and/or a 15-ounce can of straw mushrooms at the end of step 4. (Drain and discard the liquid from any of these.)

- Garnish each serving with a few drops of additional toasted sesame oil.

- Pass some chile oil or additional red pepper flakes at the table.

cream of spinach and broccoli soup

Makes 4 to 6 servings

A bright green soup belongs in every cook's repertoire, and I hope this one will become yours. Garlic appears twice in this recipe, in two forms—fresh and roasted. This adds layers of flavor that make the soup multidimensional (a good thing in a soup—or in anything you cook, for that matter). Peeling the potato is optional; if the skin looks fresh and tight and the potato is organic, you can simply give it a rinse and a quick scrub with a vegetable brush. The peel will then add some nice subtle texture to the soup. Prewashed spinach, packed in a bag or box, makes this easy. You can also use frozen chopped spinach (defrost it first), but avoid using frozen broccoli—its flavor just won't come close to fresh here.

2 tablespoons olive oil

2 teaspoons butter

1 medium red or yellow onion, chopped

2 teaspoons salt

2 teaspoons minced garlic (about 2 good-sized cloves)

4 cups water

1 medium russet potato, cut into small dice

10 ounces fresh baby spinach (can also be frozen, defrosted)

3 heaping cups chopped broccoli

1 heaping tablespoon Roasted Garlic Paste (page 5)

¾ cup milk

30 basil leaves, minced (about ¼ cup)

Freshly ground black pepper

1. Place a soup pot or a Dutch oven over medium heat. After about a minute, add the olive oil and swirl to coat the pan. Toss in the butter, and swirl until it melts into the oil. Add the onion and salt, and cook, stirring occasionally, for 8 to 10 minutes, or until the onion becomes translucent. Stir in the fresh garlic, reduce the heat to medium-low, and cook for 5 minutes longer.

2. Add the water and the diced potato. Bring to a boil, then turn the heat all the way down to the lowest possible setting. Partially cover, and simmer gently for about 15 minutes, or until the potato becomes completely soft. (It's okay to err on the side of its becoming falling-apart tender.)

3. Add the spinach, broccoli, and garlic paste. Bring to a boil, then turn the heat all the way down to the lowest possible setting. Simmer, stirring occasionally, for about 10 minutes, or until the broccoli is very tender.

4. Add the milk, remove the pot from the heat, and let it sit until the soup cools down to a comfortable puréeing temperature.

5. Use a blender or immersion blender (see page 3) to purée the soup until it is smooth. When you're finished blending, stir in the basil.

6. Reheat the soup gently over medium-low heat, being careful not to let it boil (which would cook it further and alter its flavor). Add a few grinds of black pepper to taste, and serve hot.

GET CREATIVE

• Pair this with Taco Salad (page 58) for a very satisfying—and unexpected— soup-salad combo dinner.

• Top each serving with a dash of nutmeg. (It will be more aromatic and flavorful if you grate it from a whole seed, which also makes for a nice serving touch at the table.)

• Garnish each serving with a dollop of sour cream or yogurt and/or a small sprig of basil or a sprinkling of minced chives.

• *Make this vegan by omitting the butter and using plain soy milk instead of the regular milk.*

north african red lentil soup

Makes 6 to 8 servings

This is one of those remarkable dishes that manages to be both quick and complex-tasting at the same time—and with just a few ingredients. The key lies in cooking the lentils first, and then adding sautéed onion, carrot, and garlic toward the end of the cooking process, so you really taste their full flavor in every spoonful. Look for red lentils in the bulk section near the brown lentils. (They're actually orange, not red, and turn a deep golden yellow when cooked. For some reason, they're confusingly labeled.)

This soup is vegan.

2 cups red lentils

8 cups water

2 tablespoons olive oil

1 medium red or yellow onion, chopped

1 large carrot, diced

2 teaspoons ground cumin

1 tablespoon minced garlic (about 3 good-sized cloves)

1½ teaspoons salt

Freshly ground black pepper

Lime wedges, for garnish

1. Combine the lentils and water in a soup pot or a Dutch oven. Bring to a boil, then turn the heat all the way down to the lowest possible setting. Partially cover, and simmer gently for 20 to 30 minutes, or until the lentils are completely soft.

2. Meanwhile, place a large (10- to 12-inch) skillet over medium heat. After about a minute, add the olive oil and swirl to coat the pan. Add the onion, carrot, cumin, garlic, and 1 teaspoon of the salt. Cook, stirring occasionally, for about 15 minutes, or until the onion is golden and very soft and the carrot is tender.

3. Transfer the onion mixture to the cooked lentils, and add the remaining ½ teaspoon salt. Bring to a boil, then turn the heat all the way down to the lowest possible setting. Partially cover, and simmer gently, stirring occasionally, for about 10 minutes, or until the flavors are well blended.

4. Grind in a generous amount of black pepper (about 10 or more turns), and stir to blend. Serve hot, with a lime wedge on the side.

GET CREATIVE

- Add a Greek Salad (page 46) and a wedge or two of toasted pita, and you've got yourself a seriously rib-sticking dinner.

- Drizzle some high-quality olive oil onto each serving.

- Sprinkle some lightly toasted whole cumin seeds (up to 2 teaspoons total; see below) onto each serving, or mix them into the soup just before serving.

- Brown a spicy lamb or chicken sausage or two in a skillet while the soup simmers. Slice, and stir into the finished soup.

- Garnish each serving with a dollop of sour cream or yogurt, and a sprig of flat-leaf parsley or cilantro.

TOASTING SEEDS

Toasting mellows and deepens the flavor of cumin seeds, sesame seeds, and many other seeds and spices. It's as easy as spreading the seeds in a shallow layer on the tray of a toaster oven (or on a baking tray, if you're using a regular oven) and toasting them at 200°F for about 5 minutes (give or take) until they're lightly browned and aromatic. You can also toast them on the stovetop in a dry cast-iron skillet over medium-low heat. Either way, shake the tray or the pan frequently, and hover. If you turn away for too long, the seeds can suddenly go from toasty to scorched.

roasted butternut squash and apple soup

Makes 4 to 5 servings

You are probably expecting something sweet and cinnamon-y, but that's not what you're going to get. This soups heads in another, very refreshing direction, opting for tart over sweet (or, to be more accurate, a playful tension between both sweet and tart) and it chooses the mysterious savory presence of sage over the more predictable (and in my opinion, overused) pumpkin-pie family of spices (cinnamon, nutmeg, allspice, cloves). Ix-nay on those this time around! It's time for something entirely different—and quite utterly great-tasting.

Unless you give it a little help, squash can be bland. Roasting it in chunks at a high temperature intensifies its natural sugars, bringing out a wonderfully sweet, toasty flavor. You can roast the squash in advance. If you do, let it cool and then store it in an airtight container in the refrigerator for up to 3 days; let it come to room temperature (or warm it in the microwave) before making the soup.

1 tablespoon olive oil

2 medium (about 4 pounds) butternut squash

2 tablespoons butter

1 medium red or yellow onion, chopped

1½ teaspoons salt

2 medium Granny Smith apples, peeled and thinly sliced

½ teaspoon crumbled dried (or rubbed) sage

¼ teaspoon dried thyme

4 cups water

Up to 1 tablespoon fresh lemon juice, as needed

Up to 1 tablespoon brown sugar (light or dark), as needed

1. Adjust the oven rack to the center position, and preheat the oven to 400°F. Line a baking tray with foil and drizzle it with the olive oil.

2. Use a sharp heavy knife to cut the squash in half lengthwise. (Do this very carefully. Safest technique: Insert the point of the knife first, and use a gentle sawing motion to initiate the cutting.) Use scissors to cut loose the strands of pulp around the seeds, and then scrape the seeds away with a spoon. Discard the seeds or reserve them to toast (see page 28). Use a sturdy vegetable peeler to peel the squash halves. Then cut the flesh into 1-inch pieces, once again being careful with your knife because the squash can be both very hard and very slippery. (The shape and uniformity of the chunks do not matter, since it will all get puréed.)

3. Arrange the squash chunks in a single layer on the prepared tray, and roast in the center of the oven for 20 to 30 minutes, or until the pieces are fork-tender and turning golden around the edges. (Shake the tray a few times during the roasting to keep the pieces from sticking.) Remove from the oven and set aside.

4. While the squash is roasting, melt the butter in a soup pot or a Dutch oven over medium heat. When the butter foams, swirl to coat the pan, and then add the onion and salt.

Cook, stirring occasionally, for about 5 minutes, or until the onion begins to soften.

5. Add the apple slices, along with the sage and thyme, and continue to cook, stirring occasionally, for about 10 minutes, or until the apples are very tender.

6. Add the roasted squash and the water to the onion-apple mixture. Turn up the heat and bring the soup to a boil, then turn the heat all the way down to the lowest possible setting. Cover, and simmer gently for 10 minutes.

7. Remove the pot from the heat, uncover, and let it sit until the soup cools down to a comfortable puréeing temperature. Use a blender or immersion blender (see page 3) to purée the soup until it is smooth.

8. Time for the taste test: If the soup tastes good, you're there. If it seems too sweet, add some or all of the lemon juice. If it's tarter than you like, add brown sugar to taste.

9. If necessary, reheat the soup gently over medium-low heat, being careful not to let it cook or boil. Serve hot.

TOASTING SQUASH SEEDS

The next time you cook a butternut or acorn squash (or carve a pumpkin), save the seeds for toasting. They make a tasty little snack and a crunchy garnish for soups and salads. Preheat the oven or a toaster oven to 300°F. Put the seeds in a colander and rinse them under cold water, discarding any bits of stringy squash. Drain the seeds, dry them with paper towels or a clean tea towel, and then spread them on a foil-lined baking tray or toaster oven tray. Sprinkle on a little olive oil and salt, and toss to coat well. (You can also add a bit of seasoning, like chili powder or cumin.) Roast the seeds for 10 to 15 minutes, stirring them once during that time, until they're golden brown and just starting to pop open. Let the toasted seeds cool; you can store them in an airtight container at room temperature for a week or more. Or just snack on them right away.

- This soup goes particularly well with Old-Fashioned Iceberg Wedges with Luxurious Bleu Cheese Dressing (page 50).

- Top each serving with a dollop of sour cream or yogurt.

- Top with a sprinkling of fresh apple, minced or grated on the large holes of a grater.

- Garnish each serving with a sprinkling of toasted squash seeds (see preceding note).

- Top with a few toasted sliced almonds or chopped toasted pecans.

- Garnish with a fresh sage leaf or a sprig of fresh thyme.

- Garnish with a scattering of pomegranate seeds or a drizzle of pomegranate molasses (see page xvi).

- *Make this vegan by replacing the butter with canola, soy, or peanut oil.*

salads.

A Salad a Day

A salad should be a thing of beauty, not duty. Salads can be colorful, filled with flavor, easy and inexpensive to make, and, generally speaking, a brilliant vegetable delivery system.

I'm about to teach you how to make a stellar tossed green salad—beautifully and often. In addition, I've included in this chapter some popular standards (pasta salad, potato salad, cole slaw, three-bean) that you can enjoy for picnics (outdoors on a Saturday in the spring, or at your desk on a winter Wednesday) or as easy dinners, supplemented with soup and bread. Many of these keep well and can be made in advance and eaten over a period of days as meals or snacks.

Think of these recipes as templates to which you can add other ingredients to fit your taste and appetite. Salads are a great place to experiment with becoming a more improvisational cook, because you really can't go wrong. Also, most, if not all, of these recipes welcome the addition of cooked meat or strips of omelet or tofu, so they can be elevated easily to main-dish status.

TOSSED GREEN SALAD BASICS

I want to say, right out of the gate, that there is no excuse (and no need)—ever—for bringing a package of plain salad greens to the table along with a bottle of dressing. If you think this is a real way to serve green salad, a wonderful upgrade awaits you in these pages.

Homemade dressing can be so much better than the bottled kind that it's almost a different category of food altogether. And there is no comparison between a plate of limp greens with an indiscriminate puddle of dressing simply dumped on and a carefully tossed, perfectly and evenly coated plateful of crisp leaf-heaven.

ABOUT SALAD DRESSINGS IN GENERAL

For some reason, many people are blocked when it comes to making salad dressing. Hence the wild success of the bottled stuff, which is always ridiculously overpriced and, in my opinion, never great. Once you whip them up (and as you'll see, that's not hard to do), homemade dressings can be kept in jars in the refrigerator, so they're just as convenient as store-bought ones. They keep for months and take up very little space. So start saving little jars—like the ones mustard comes in—to use for mixing and storing salad dressing.

In this chapter, in addition to the Five Most Wanted dressings, many of the recipes list the dressing ingredients separately—so if you like, you can make one of those dressings on its own and keep it on hand to use with your own combinations of salad ingredients. Also try these dressings as sauces on warm cooked vegetables, on cold leftover cooked vegetables, or on plain cooked chicken or fish.

The ratio of dressing to salad in these recipes is on the generous side. Add most, but not all, of the dressing to begin with. Then toss and taste. You might want to stop right there, or add more, or pass extra dressing at the table so people can add as much as they like.

About mayonnaise   If you want to use reduced-fat mayo, look for a good brand, one that is not full of sugar. I prefer full-fat regular mayo made with no added sugar. I tend to lighten it by mixing it with low-fat or nonfat yogurt in a ratio of about 3 or 4 parts yogurt to 1 part mayo. This scheme works very nicely, and is fresher tasting and better for you than "lite" mayo.

About buttermilk   Buttermilk is another secret ingredient that adds a subtle creaminess to various dressings (like Bleu Cheese, Creamy Balsamic, and more). It's very much like a liquid yogurt—a cultured low-fat product that contributes both heft and tang without adding much fat.

About yogurt   As I mentioned above, I like to use yogurt in conjunction with mayonnaise. This brings out the best traits of both and keeps things light. I use plain nonfat yogurt, spooning out just the thick part and leaving behind any liquid (whey) that has separated out. You can also whisk the whey back in, and then the yogurt will be a little thinner. Either approach is fine.

HOW TO SHOP FOR GREEN SALAD INGREDIENTS

Buy only the freshest greens available. Avoid yellow wilted leaves or anything that appears wet or slimy (or that looks like it's even thinking of becoming wet or slimy). Small young leaves tend to be tender; old overgrown leaves are usually tough.

Lettuce, salad mix, and spinach   Packaged salad mix often comes in 5-ounce bags and is also frequently available loose, in bulk. You can substitute baby spinach for some of it.

When you get it home, use it as soon as possible, but if you need to store it, keep it very dry and wait until just before making the salad to wash it. Tired-looking-but-still-okay leaves can usually be perked up by soaking them in cold water for 5 minutes and then drying them in a salad spinner.

Wash salad greens in cold running water in the basket of your salad spinner, a colander, or in a sinkful of cold water. Dry them as thoroughly as possible in a salad spinner. The drier the leaves, the better their relationship with the dressing will be. If the greens are really water-soaked when you get them home (owing to overactive misters in the produce aisle), spin them dry before storing them.

Remove and discard any damaged leaves, and store the good leaves in any of the following ways:

- In plastic bags with almost all the air squeezed out of them (the greens need to be very dry for this).

- Directly in the salad spinner in the refrigerator, if you have room (the greens can be a little wet).

- In a food storage container with a tightly fitting lid, with a folded paper towel in the bottom of the container (the paper towel helps absorb excess moisture and the covered container helps keep excess air out).

Bunches of herbs can be stored like bouquets in glasses partially filled with water (at room temperature if it's only for a day or so, in the refrigerator if storing for longer).

If lettuce leaves need to be made smaller, try to accomplish this, as noted food authority Harold McGee says, "with the least possible physical pressure." Cutting swiftly with a very sharp knife just before assembling the salad is a good idea, as is simply tearing greens gently with your hands.

Okay, enough about the technicalities of leaf life span. Let's get to the fun part. What do you put in a green salad, and what's the best way to assemble it all?

THE GREENS

Of course you can use any kind of lettuce. Beyond that, try baby spinach, arugula, watercress (stems and leaves), chicories (including radicchio, which has a slightly bitter flavor and white-veined dark red leaves, and Belgian endive, those tight little pale-green elongated heads). A good place to start if you're less familiar with any of these is a prepared salad mix (also known as "mesclun" or "field greens").

ADD-INS

You can add any vegetables you think you might enjoy raw. Just cut them small and thin, and toss them into the mix. These might include:

- Carrots (chopped, sliced, or grated)
- Cabbage (finely sliced or grated)
- Bell peppers (go for the brightly colored ones)
- Red onion
- Scallions
- Celery
- Cucumber
- Cauliflower
- Mushrooms (very fresh, clean domestic ones only)
- Radishes
- Beets (peeled and grated)
- Sugar snap peas
- Thin "French" green beans (*haricots verts*)

You can also include vegetables and other ingredients that are better cooked (and cooled down or chilled) before adding. Cut these small, too.

- Broccoli
- Squash
- Potatoes
- Beets (peel after cooking)
- Thicker green beans
- Cooked beans (canned or homemade)
- Leftover cooked grains

Small amounts of torn, minced, or snipped (with scissors) fresh herbs are a lovely touch and add deeper flavor to salads.

- Flat-leaf parsley
- Basil

- Cilantro
- Thyme
- Mint
- Savory
- Dill
- Chives

Fruit can be wonderful in a green salad. Add fresh fruit to a salad just before serving—or even at the table, so all stays fresh and unbroken, and sogginess is avoided. Try:

- Apple or pear slices
- Citrus sections
- Chopped fresh cranberries (super-tart)
- Pomegranate seeds
- Berries (whole smaller ones; sliced larger ones)
- Watermelon (really, give it a shot), in 1-inch chunks
- Dried fruit, in small pieces

ADD-ONS

Some ingredients should be cut at the very last minute and added as a garnish. These include:

- Avocados (for more on these, see page 225)
- Tomatoes (cherry or larger ones, sliced)

More accoutrements to consider sprinkling on top include:

- Grated or crumbled cheese (goat cheese, bleu cheese, feta)

- Chopped hard-boiled egg (see page 34)
- Olives
- Capers
- Crumbled bacon (see page 233)
- Canned tuna (flaked)
- Lightly toasted nuts or seeds
- Sprouts
- Freshly ground black pepper (keep a filled pepper mill at the table)

tossed green salad

EASY ASSEMBLY INSTRUCTIONS

- Your greens are very clean, dry, and cold.
- You have figured on approximately ¼ pound—about 2 large handfuls— per person.
- Your dressing is made and handy.
- Your add-ins and add-ons are ready.
- You have a nice big bowl (large enough to toss your salad with abandon and have it stay in the bowl) and salad servers or tongs in front of you.

1. The greens go in the bowl, along with whatever "add-in" items you've chosen. Toss gently to combine.

2. Shake or whisk the dressing to reincorporate all the ingredients, which will have separated into layers while it sat around. (If the oil in the dressing has hardened from the cold of the refrigerator, give it a few extra minutes to soften back up again and/or shake or whisk the dressing a bit longer.) Add about 1 tablespoon

dressing per serving, tossing it in and mixing the greens from the bottom of the bowl.

3. Taste a sample leaf to see if the salad needs more dressing.

4. Top the bowlful of greens with your chosen "add-ons," or plate the salads individually and top each serving with them.

5. Serve right away.

NOT-SO-HARD-BOILED EGGS

You may not think you need these instructions, but chances are you do. For many people (even experienced cooks), cooking and peeling hard-boiled eggs can be a real pain.

Sometimes (often) the shell just doesn't want to come off and you end up throwing away half the egg. Here's a technique that truly works.

Place the eggs in a pot that fits them comfortably, and fill it with enough cold water to completely cover them. Bring it to a boil, and then immediately lower the heat to a simmer. Cook very gently for 1 minute. Then remove the pot from the heat, and let it stand for 15 minutes. Drain, and refresh the eggs—right in the pot—in several changes of cold water, pouring it off each time. Then leave the eggs in the pot, put the lid on, and shake it vigorously like a big percussion instrument, banging the eggs together to crack their shells. Finally, peel the eggs under cold running water. The peel will practically fall off!

the big five: america's most wanted salad dressings

Make one, some, or all of these on a regular basis. They keep well for weeks—even months—if stored in tightly lidded containers in the refrigerator, where they will take up very little space. And they work well as a sauce on cooked vegetables, meats, and tofu, too.

In any of these recipes, some or all of the olive oil can be a high-quality type, for more intense flavor. At the very least, it should be extra-virgin olive oil.

ABOUT SHALLOTS

Great for salad dressings, shallots look like small pink onions and taste like a lively cross between onion and garlic, slightly sweeter than either. Use a very sharp paring knife and mince them tiny, tiny.

ABOUT HONEY

In general, the lighter the color, the milder the flavor. So unless you want a strong presence, choose light-colored honey. (The lighter ones also tend to be less expensive.)

raspberry-shallot dressing

Makes a generous ½ cup,
enough for 4 to 5 servings of salad

The fruitiness of raspberry vinegar and the sweetness of shallots are a fine match. This versatile vinaigrette goes with pretty much any kind of greens, and it's great on grilled chicken.

This dressing is vegan.

1 tablespoon finely minced shallot

3 tablespoons raspberry vinegar

2 teaspoons sugar

Heaping ¼ teaspoon salt

⅓ cup olive oil

Combine the shallot, vinegar, sugar, and salt in a smallish bowl. Whisk until thoroughly combined, then continue whisking as you drizzle in the olive oil. When all the olive oil is incorporated, the dressing is ready to serve—or to refrigerate until use. (Alternatively, you can put all the ingredients in a small jar with a tight-fitting lid and just shake it emphatically until thoroughly combined.) Immediately before using, shake well or stir from the bottom.

GET CREATIVE

- Substitute roasted walnut oil or roasted pecan oil for half of the olive oil.

- Add 1 tablespoon minced mint or basil leaves.

- After adding the olive oil, stir in up to ½ cup raspberries (fresh or unsweetened frozen). If using frozen, let them defrost directly in the dressing, and they will give off lovely raspberry juices in the process.

- Add 1 to 2 tablespoons pomegranate molasses (see page xvi) before whisking in the oil.

creamy balsamic-honey dressing

Makes about ¾ cup,
enough for about 6 servings of salad

Sometimes you want a vinaigrette with a little creaminess. Buttermilk makes this one luxurious and rich-tasting. If your honey is stiff, place the jar (without the lid) in a microwave for about 15 seconds, to get it more liquefied. (Don't try this with a plastic honey bear or squeeze bottle, however, which can easily overheat and melt. Instead, spoon the honey into a microwavable bowl and heat it in that.)

2 tablespoons balsamic vinegar
¼ cup buttermilk
2 tablespoons honey
¼ teaspoon salt
1 tablespoon finely minced shallot
5 tablespoons extra-virgin olive oil

Combine the vinegar, buttermilk, honey, salt, and shallot in a smallish bowl. Whisk until thoroughly combined, then continue whisking as you drizzle in the olive oil. When all the olive oil is incorporated, the dressing is ready to serve—or to refrigerate until use. (Alternatively, you can put all the ingredients in a small jar with a tight-fitting lid and just shake it emphatically until thoroughly combined.) Immediately before using, shake well or stir from the bottom.

GET CREATIVE

- Use yogurt instead of buttermilk for a thicker, tangier dressing.
- Try this as a dressing on broccoli slaw and/or shredded cabbage and carrots.

honey-mustard dressing

Makes about ½ cup,
enough for 4 to 5 servings of salad

This recipe calls for Dijon mustard. You can also try it with other fancy types. It's wonderful on a spinach salad.

3 tablespoons sherry vinegar
   or balsamic vinegar
2 tablespoons Dijon mustard
1 tablespoon honey
½ teaspoon minced garlic (about 1 small clove)
¼ teaspoon salt
6 tablespoons olive oil

Combine the vinegar, mustard, honey, garlic, and salt in a smallish bowl. Whisk until thoroughly combined, then continue whisking as you drizzle in the olive oil. When all the olive oil is incorporated, the dressing is ready to serve— or to refrigerate until use. (Alternatively, you can put all the ingredients in a small jar with a tight-fitting lid and just shake it emphatically until thoroughly combined.) Immediately before using, shake well or stir from the bottom.

- Spread a bit of this dressing on the bread when making a grilled cheese sandwich or a ham sandwich. It's a classic combo.

- Any time you're making a salad with bacon in it, this dressing will be right at home.

- Drizzle this over fish or chicken.

homemade ranch dressing

Makes 1 cup,
enough for about 8 servings of salad

"Ranch" flavor lands at the top of many people's list of faves. Problem is, most commercially prepared dips and dressings can be loaded down with unhealthy fats and ingredients not found in nature, much less on a ranch. Here's a way to make your own very satisfying version with clean, real ingredients. You can use it as a dressing for salad or as a dip for vegetables, chips, or crackers.

⅓ cup mayonnaise
⅔ cup buttermilk
2 teaspoons cider vinegar
¼ teaspoon salt
½ teaspoon onion powder
¼ teaspoon garlic powder

Place all the ingredients in a medium-sized bowl and whisk until smooth. Cover and chill until serving time.

GET CREATIVE

- Serve this dressing drizzled over a wedge of iceberg lettuce, as directed in Old-Fashioned Iceberg Wedges (page 50).

- Drizzle the dressing over a plate of juicy ripe tomato slices.

russian dressing

Makes about ¾ cup,
enough for about 6 servings of salad

Way more than the sum of its humble parts, this classic can multitask as a dip for raw vegetables, a topping for hard-boiled eggs (a really great little quick lunch), and a terrific sandwich spread.

½ cup mayonnaise
⅓ cup ketchup

Combine the mayonnaise and ketchup in a medium-sized bowl and whisk until smooth. Cover and chill until serving time.

GET CREATIVE

- For some zing, add a tablespoon of prepared horseradish.

- You could replace all or some of the ketchup with chili sauce or cocktail sauce.

- For some crunch and an extra layer of flavor, add 1 to 2 tablespoons very finely minced shallot.

- Add a tablespoon or two of minced pickles or pickle relish to make Thousand Island Dressing.

all-american three-bean salad

Makes 4 to 6 servings

So not-high-end, so retro, and yet so good. I couldn't believe I was using a canned green vegetable, but I wanted to get this as close as possible to the American picnic classic of my youth, and canned green beans (which I always have secretly liked anyway) are the authentic choice. Also, in keeping with the not-fancy theme, you might be pleased (and a few pennies richer) to know that regular yellow mustard works best for this, so put away that Dijon or grainy type for now. And just this once, in a pinch, you could substitute ½ cup good-quality bottled Italian dressing or vinaigrette (such as Newman's Own) for your own brilliant homemade batch. That's "could," not "should."

This salad is vegan.

One 15-ounce can chickpeas
(about 1½ cups cooked chickpeas)

One 15-ounce can red kidney beans
(about 1½ cups cooked beans)

One 15-ounce can green beans
(about 1½ cups cooked beans;
see *get creative*)

¼ cup olive oil

¼ cup red wine vinegar

1 teaspoon sugar

1 teaspoon yellow mustard

¾ teaspoon salt

⅛ teaspoon freshly ground black pepper

1 stalk celery, diced

Half a small red bell pepper, minced

¼ cup minced red onion

1. Set a colander in the sink and pour in the contents of the three cans of beans. Give them a quick rinse and allow them to drain.

2. In a large bowl, whisk together the olive oil, vinegar, sugar, mustard, salt, and pepper.

3. Add the drained beans, celery, bell pepper, and onion to the dressing, and toss well to mix. Cover the bowl tightly, and let the salad marinate for at least 1 hour at room temperature or overnight in the refrigerator. Stir (or shake) occasionally to marinate evenly. Serve cold.

GET CREATIVE

• To make this with fresh green beans, put a medium-sized pot of cold water over high heat, add a pinch of salt, and bring to a boil. Place a colander in the sink. Meanwhile, trim and discard the stem ends from ¼ pound green beans, and cut the beans into 1½-inch-long pieces. When the water boils, turn the heat down to low and add the beans. Simmer for 5 to 7 minutes, or until the beans are done to your liking. Drain them in the colander, and then rinse with cold water and drain again. Pat dry with paper towels or a clean, dry dish towel, and add to the salad.

potato salad, basic and beyond

Makes 4 servings (possibly more, if you add a lot from the *get creative* list)

This is a very, very basic recipe. The salad tastes great in its pure form, and I've given you many ideas to spruce it up. The best potatoes for this are the waxy varieties (Yukon Gold, Yellow Finn, small red "creamers"). A combination of colors is guaranteed to be beautiful. You can even use red, white, and blue potatoes for a Fourth of July picnic. Peeling is easiest after the potatoes are cooked. Even easier is *not* peeling, which adds flavor, color, and nutrients. This salad needs time to chill completely, so you might want to make it a day ahead.

Make this vegan by replacing the mayonnaise and yogurt with eggless vegan mayonnaise.

Salt for the cooking water

1½ pounds potatoes
(about 2-inch diameter),
scrubbed

⅓ cup mayonnaise

⅓ cup plain yogurt

¼ teaspoon salt (possibly more)

⅛ teaspoon freshly ground black
pepper (possibly more)

¼ cup finely minced red onion

1. Put a medium-sized pot of cold water over high heat, add a teaspoon of salt, and bring to a boil. Place a colander in the sink. When the water boils, turn the heat down to low, add the potatoes, and cook for 15 to 20 minutes, or until very tender (easily pierced with the tip of a sharp knife—you don't want the potatoes to be at all crunchy). Drain them in the colander, and then dry them by patting them with paper towels or a clean, dry dish towel.

2. While the potatoes are simmering, whisk together the mayonnaise, yogurt, salt, and pepper in a medium-large bowl. Add the onion, and mix well.

3. When the potatoes are cool enough to handle, you can peel and discard the skins (use your fingers or a sharp knife) or leave the skins on (especially if you want the red of red potatoes, since their insides are white). Cut the potatoes into 1-inch chunks, and transfer them to the bowl containing the other ingredients. Toss gently until everything is well combined, then cover the bowl tightly and chill until cold.

4. If the potatoes seem to have soaked up too much of the dressing while chilling, add a tablespoon more each of the mayonnaise and the yogurt. Season to taste with additional salt and pepper, if needed, and serve.

GET CREATIVE
(THIS IS THE "BEYOND" PART)

Add any of the following when tossing the potatoes and dressing together:

- 2 hard-boiled eggs (see page 34), diced

- 1 stalk celery, diced

- 1 tablespoon minced parsley

- 1 scallion, minced

- Half a small red bell pepper, minced

- Half a small green bell pepper, minced

- 1 small carrot, coarsely grated

- Minced bread-and-butter pickles, dill pickles, or pickle relish (about ¼ cup)

- A few sliced or diced radishes

- 1 teaspoon mustard (yellow, Dijon, or your favorite kind)

- A handful of toasted cashews, almonds, or sesame seeds

- Crumbled bacon (see page 233)

- Sprouts (any kind) for heaping on top

mostly classic cole slaw

Makes 6 to 8 servings

"ostly" refers to the non-classic addition of yogurt, which has become standard in my repertoire. Cole slaw is always best if made at least a day ahead, packed into a container with a tight-fitting lid, and refrigerated until serving time. Given this melding time, the cabbage softens and packs down, and all the flavors bond and unify as a team. This will keep for up to a week in a tightly covered container in the refrigerator. To save time, you can buy pre-shredded cole slaw mix in a bag.

Make this vegan by replacing the mayonnaise and yogurt with eggless vegan mayonnaise.

2 pounds cabbage
(purple and/or green),
shredded

1 large carrot, coarsely grated

½ cup very finely minced red onion

¾ teaspoon salt

¼ cup olive oil

⅓ cup cider vinegar

¼ cup mayonnaise

¼ cup plain yogurt

1 to 2 tablespoons sweetener
(white or brown sugar,
pure maple syrup, or a
light-colored honey)

1. Combine the cabbage, carrot, and onion in a very large bowl. Sprinkle with the salt, toss to combine, and set aside.

2. In a second, smaller bowl, combine the oil, vinegar, mayonnaise, yogurt, and 1 tablespoon of the sweetener, and whisk until smooth. Pour this into the cabbage mixture, and toss to mix well. Taste to see if it's sweet enough for you, and if not, add the other tablespoon of sweetener. Transfer to a container with a tight-fitting lid, cover, and refrigerate. (It will pack down quite a bit.) Serve cold.

- Add a pinch of celery seed (old-fashioned, and really nice here; buy a small jar just to use for cole slaw).

- Add up to 2 cups chopped pineapple—either fresh or canned (packed in water or juice), drained.

- Add up to ½ cup dried cranberries or ¼ cup minced fresh cranberries.

- Slice a Bosc pear (the crunchy brown kind), drizzle it with a little lemon juice, and gently mix it in just before serving.

- Top the slaw with up to 1 cup chopped roasted peanuts or toasted walnuts.

- Substitute packaged broccoli slaw for some or all of the cabbage.

- For a richer dressing, substitute sour cream for some of the mayonnaise or yogurt.

- Garnish with lemon wedges for squeezing on at the table.

- In addition to serving this as a side, try packing it into your favorite sandwich.

caesar salad with its own from-scratch dressing

Makes 2 to 3 large dinner-sized salads, or 4 to 6 smaller side salads

Too many restaurants serve mediocre Caesar salads, and that's a shame. This homemade version, with just the right amount of scratch-made dressing lightly coating crisp romaine and croutons made from a real baguette, can go head to head with any restaurant or bottled-dressing Caesar.

This recipe calls for 1 pound of romaine lettuce. If you're buying hearts of romaine (they come packaged, with the larger outer leaves already removed), buy a pound and use it all. But if you're buying the entire head, try to get one that weighs slightly more than a pound, so you will have a pound left after removing any imperfect outer leaves.

Coarsely shredded Parmesan works better here than the fine, powdery stuff. If you're making your own croutons, simply follow the recipe on page 9, omitting the cheese (or replacing it with Parmesan). You can prepare the croutons a few hours (and up to a day) ahead and store them in a sealed plastic bag or a tightly lidded container.

You can make the dressing up to 3 days ahead of time, and store it in a tightly covered container in the refrigerator. For best results, put the salad together just before serving.

caesar dressing

1 tablespoon fresh lemon juice

1 tablespoon Worcestershire sauce

1 teaspoon Dijon mustard

¼ teaspoon minced garlic
(about half a small clove)

⅛ teaspoon salt

2 tablespoons shredded Parmesan cheese

¼ cup olive oil

3 tablespoons mayonnaise

salad

1 pound romaine lettuce
(a large head or "hearts")

⅓ cup shredded Parmesan cheese

Freshly ground black pepper

Croutons (store-bought or homemade—
see page 9)

GET CREATIVE

- You can add whole anchovies to the salad, or up to 1 tablespoon anchovy paste to the dressing. If using either, omit the salt.

- Top each serving with strips or chunks of Pan-Grilled Boneless Chicken Breasts (page 154) or chunks of Poached Salmon (page 160). Both are great hot, warm, or cold.

- Toss in some torn or coarsely chopped flat-leaf parsley, or sprinkle it on top.

- For a fun change of pace, Parmesan Fricos (page 13) can replace both the Parmesan in the salad and the croutons.

- Top each serving with a still-warm, freshly poached egg.

1. To make the dressing, combine the lemon juice, Worcestershire sauce, mustard, garlic, salt, and Parmesan in a bowl (a small one if you are making the dressing ahead of time, or the salad bowl itself if you are making this just before serving). Whisk until thoroughly combined, then continue whisking as you drizzle in the olive oil. When all the olive oil is incorporated, stir in the mayonnaise until completely blended.

2. Separate the romaine leaves, and then wash them in very cold water and spin them very dry. (If you have purchased hearts of romaine in a sealed pack, you can skip the washing; just cut off the stems and separate the leaves.)

3. Shortly before serving, transfer the entire batch of dressing to the salad bowl (a wide, shallow one works very well for this). Break or cut the romaine leaves into bite-sized pieces, and add them to the dressing in the bowl. Begin turning the leaves with salad servers or tongs, sprinkling in the Parmesan cheese as you turn. The leaves will begin to get coated with the dressing. When they are mostly coated, grind in a generous amount of black pepper, then continue turning until everything is nicely combined. Toss in the croutons at the very end, and serve.

greek salad with oregano-laced vinaigrette

Makes 2 to 3 large dinner-sized salads,
or 4 to 6 smaller side salads

The quintessential Greek salad: fresh greens tossed with Greek olives, onions, bell peppers, tomatoes, cucumbers, and feta cheese, in a delicious vinaigrette. The salad greens can be a packaged salad mix or your favorite lettuces—on their own or combined with baby spinach leaves and some arugula. Spinach fans, try this with all baby spinach leaves. The dressing keeps for weeks in a tightly lidded jar in the refrigerator and is wonderful on any kind of cooked vegetables, especially broccoli and green beans.

oregano-laced vinaigrette

- 3 tablespoons red wine vinegar
- ¼ teaspoon minced garlic (about half a small clove)
- 1 teaspoon Dijon mustard
- 1 teaspoon dried oregano
- Heaping ⅛ teaspoon salt
- 5 tablespoons olive oil

salad

- 1 pound salad greens, washed and thoroughly dried (or use three 5-ounce packages)
- About 12 cherry tomatoes, halved
- 1 medium cucumber, peeled, seeded, and sliced
- 1 medium bell pepper (any color), diced
- 1 medium red onion, thinly sliced
- 1 cup crumbled feta cheese
- About 12 Kalamata olives
- Freshly ground black pepper

1. To make the dressing, combine the vinegar, garlic, mustard, oregano, and salt in a smallish bowl. Whisk until thoroughly combined, then continue whisking as you drizzle in the olive oil. When all the olive oil is incorporated, set the dressing aside. (Or you can put all the ingredients in a small jar with a tight-fitting lid and just shake it emphatically.)

2. Combine the salad greens, tomatoes, cucumber, bell pepper, onion, and ½ cup of the feta in a large bowl, and toss to mix well.

3. Just before serving, whisk the dressing—or shake it, if it's in a jar—to recombine, and add about half of it to the salad. Toss to coat, and give it a taste. You might want to add the rest of the dressing right now, or bring it to the table (along with the pepper mill) for people to add more to their own portions. Top with the remaining ½ cup feta, the olives, and a few grinds of black pepper, and serve immediately.

GET CREATIVE

- Use high-quality olive oil in the dressing.

- Make the dressing with a fancier variety of wine vinegar (such as sherry vinegar or Spanish Moscatel vinegar).

- Toss in a few tablespoons of chopped mint leaves.

- Use a "designer" flavored mustard in the dressing.

- Serve with toasted pita wedges.

- Drape a few whole anchovies over the top of the assembled salad.

- Top the assembled salad with some flaked canned tuna (especially good with tuna packed in olive oil).

- Toss in a handful or two of canned black beans, white beans, or chickpeas (rinsed and drained).

- Top with a scattering of chopped lightly toasted walnuts.

- *Make this vegan by omitting the feta cheese.*

best pasta salad

Makes 4 servings (possibly more, if you add a lot from the *get creative* list)

Pasta salad is perfect party or picnic food, and it packs well for bag lunches, too. While the pasta cooks, put the other ingredients together, so they're ready to dress the pasta as soon as it's cooked and drained. The heat from the pasta will slightly cook the garlic and onion, and will partially melt the cheese, causing it to stick to the pasta (which adds a layer of texture beyond what you'd get if you just sprinkled cold cheese onto cold pasta). After the dressed pasta has cooled down, you add an assortment of diced vegetables, and possible other goodies, and then either serve it at room temperature or chill it (in a tightly covered container for up to 3 days) and serve it cold. So factor in cooling and possible chilling time when you make this dish.

Salt for the pasta water

¾ pound fusilli (corkscrew), small penne, or orecchiette ("little ears") pasta

5 tablespoons olive oil

¾ teaspoon minced garlic (about 1 medium clove)

¾ cup very finely minced red onion

⅓ cup grated Parmesan cheese

3 tablespoons red wine vinegar

¾ teaspoon salt

⅛ teaspoon freshly ground black pepper

1 medium bell pepper (any color), diced

Half a medium cucumber, peeled, seeded, and diced

1. Put a large pot of cold water to boil over high heat, and add a tablespoon of salt. Place a large colander in the sink. When the water boils, add the pasta, keeping the heat high. Cook for the amount of time recommended on the package, tasting a piece of pasta toward the end of the suggested time to be sure it is not getting overcooked. When it is *just* tender enough to bite into comfortably but not yet mushy, dump the water-plus-pasta into the colander. Shake emphatically to drain.

2. While the pasta is cooking, combine the olive oil, garlic, onion, Parmesan, vinegar, salt, and black pepper in a large bowl (a wide, shallow one works well) and whisk to blend. As soon as the hot pasta is thoroughly drained, add it to the bowlful of dressing, stirring to coat all the pasta. Set aside to cool to room temperature.

3. Add the bell pepper and cucumber, and mix gently but thoroughly. Serve at room temperature, or chill and serve cold.

GET CREATIVE

- Use other pasta shapes (bowties, campanelle, shells) in place of some or all of the fusilli. Or try rainbow fusilli (a mix of white, red, and green; often sold in bulk bins) for extra color.

- Make this with high-quality olive oil.

- Whisk a teaspoon or two of mayonnaise into the olive oil mixture.

- Just before serving, toss in a generous handful of chopped flat-leaf parsley and/or about 25 basil leaves, cut into strips.

- When adding the bell pepper and cucumber, toss in any of the following:

    - Up to 1 cup tiny cherry tomatoes (or regular-sized ones, cut in half)

    - Up to ½ cup small pitted olives (any kind you like)

    - Up to ½ cup grated or minced carrot, celery, or radishes, for crunch

    - Up to 1 cup raw or leftover cooked vegetables (such as zucchini, green beans, or peas)

    - Up to ¼ cup minced scallion (white and tender green parts)

    - ¼ cup lightly toasted pine nuts or chopped toasted walnuts

    - Cubes of mild cheese (fontina, mozzarella)

    - Crumbles of crumbly cheese (feta, goat cheese, ricotta salata)

- *Make this vegan by using eggless noodles and omitting the Parmesan cheese.*

old-fashioned iceberg wedges with luxurious bleu cheese dressing

Makes 4 to 6 servings

Once upon a time, iceberg lettuce (the clownishly round, very pale green variety) was the only salad green on most American dinner plates. Then for years it seemed to have been banished from all venues except for low-end salad bars and Mexican combo platters. But even though more fashionable species of deeper-hued, smaller, shapelier salad greens replaced it in discriminating culinary circles, in recent years iceberg has made a major comeback as the uber-cool wedge, its mildness offset with a big-flavored bleu cheese dressing. It's nice to serve this on individual salad plates. It's even nicer if you chill the plates first (everything about this dish should be cold) by stacking them in the refrigerator at least 30 minutes before serving time.

With a very simple dressing and minimal lettuce prep, this is a good recipe for beginners. When shopping for iceberg lettuce, buy the tightest, greenest head you can find. You can use any kind of bleu cheese. Some are saltier and more pungent than others, and prices vary widely. Try different kinds until you find your favorite. The dressing can be made up to 5 days ahead and stored in a tightly covered container in the refrigerator until just before serving.

luxurious bleu cheese dressing

1 cup buttermilk

⅓ cup mayonnaise

½ cup crumbled bleu cheese

salad

1 large head (about 1 pound) iceberg lettuce, chilled

Freshly ground black pepper

GET CREATIVE

• Sprinkle the top with chopped lightly toasted pecans.

• In addition to the pecans, you can add some sliced or diced apple and/or a scattering of dried cranberries.

• Cut some very sweet tomatoes in half and scatter a few on each plate. Tomatoes are hugely compatible with bleu cheese, and the color will perk this up greatly! Sprinkle on some chopped parsley or snipped chives for even more color.

• Cook 2 strips of bacon (see page 233), cool, and crumble over each serving.

• Try serving iceberg wedges with other dressings, including Homemade Ranch (page 37) or the Oregano-Laced Vinaigrette from the Greek Salad (page 46).

1. To make the dressing, combine the buttermilk and mayonnaise in a medium-sized bowl, and whisk until blended. Continue whisking as you sprinkle in the bleu cheese. Continue to mix, mashing the cheese a bit. The cheese will mostly, but not completely, blend into the mixture. There will be some small lumps. You want them there. It's part of the charm.

2. Peel off and discard any wilted or damaged outer leaves from the head of lettuce. Stand the lettuce on the stem end and use a sharp knife (choose one with a blade about as large as the head of lettuce) to cut the entire head in half. Cut each half from top to stem into two or three wedges. If the core looks tough, use a paring knife to trim it off each wedge.

3. Stand one wedge (resting on its outer-leaf side looks cool) on each serving plate, and spoon a generous amount of dressing over the top, letting it drip down to the plate if it wants to. Serve right away, passing a pepper grinder at the table.

original-ish waldorf salad

Makes 4 to 5 servings

It may seem old-school, but give it a try and you'll see why this classic apple-celery-walnut salad has never gone out of style. The addition of yogurt makes this version a bit tangier and more multidimensional than the original. It's nice to use a variety of apples for this. I like to combine tart green ones, such as Granny Smiths, with a medium-sweet variety, like Galas, and something sweet and crunchy, like Honeycrisps, Fujis, or Pink Ladies. Cut the apples right before assembling the salad; otherwise they'll turn brown.

4 medium-sized apples, chopped into roughly ½-inch chunks (unpeeled)

1 stalk celery, minced

¼ cup (packed) raisins (dark or golden)

1 cup plain yogurt

¼ cup mayonnaise

½ cup chopped walnuts, lightly toasted

1. Combine the apples, celery, and raisins in a medium-large bowl.

2. In a second, smaller bowl, whisk together the yogurt and mayonnaise until smooth. Pour this mixture over the apples, and stir gently until everything is evenly coated. Serve topped with the walnuts.

- Serve with lemon wedges for squeezing over each serving.

- For a lighter result, you can use all yogurt and leave out the mayo.

- If you like a sweeter Waldorf, add up to 1 tablespoon honey or real maple syrup.

- For a richer salad, you can swap in some sour cream for some or all of the mayonnaise and/or yogurt.

- Add up to ½ cup crumbled bleu cheese when combining the yogurt and mayo. Add some diced chicken to make this a main dish for lunch. The chicken and the bleu cheese go very well together.

- Toss in up to ½ cup halved seedless grapes.

- Mash half a ripe avocado until it's smooth, and whisk this into the yogurt-mayo mixture.

- Garnish with fresh orange or tangerine sections (seedless or seeded by you) or drained canned mandarin oranges (if you *really* want to go old-school).

- You can swap in pecans or almonds for the walnuts.

- Mix in some diced or thinly sliced carrot.

- Other dried fruit (chopped dates, sliced figs, dried blueberries, cranberries, or cherries) can sub for the raisins; or use a mix of black and golden raisins.

- *Make this vegan by replacing the mayonnaise and yogurt with eggless vegan mayonnaise.*

TOASTING NUTS

Toasting brings out the flavor of nuts and gives them a delightful crispness. It's an easy process that makes a huge difference, especially when you're going to be tossing nuts into a dish like a salad or pasta (or even if you just want to have them around to snack on).

To toast nuts, adjust the oven rack to the center position and preheat the oven to 300°F. Spread the nuts in a single layer on a baking tray, and bake them for 7 to 12 minutes, or until they are fragrant and just beginning to turn brown. (I recommend setting a timer for 7 minutes and then checking the nuts every minute or two after it goes off.) Remove the nuts from the oven, and let them cool on the tray for at least 5 minutes. (You can also do this same process in a toaster oven.)

chinese chicken salad with soy-ginger-sesame vinaigrette

Makes 2 to 3 large dinner-sized salads, or 4 to 6 smaller side salads

The next time you're contemplating Chinese takeout, try this big, colorful, crunchy main-dish salad. You can make it with Pan-Grilled Boneless Chicken Breasts (page 154), which you'll need to make ahead of time (as much as 3 days in advance) so they can cool. If you're in a big hurry, cook the chicken, slice it, spread the slices out on a plate, and put the plate in the refrigerator while you make the dressing and put the rest of the salad together. In 15 minutes or so, the chicken should be cool enough to toss into the salad. Or use leftover roast chicken (made using the recipe on page 156; or store-bought rotisserie chicken; or even better, roast chicken—or even duck—from a Chinese deli).

The dressing keeps for weeks in a tightly lidded jar in the refrigerator; shake it well before serving. This recipe calls for seasoned rice vinegar, which is a commonly available version of rice vinegar that contains a little salt and sugar. In a pinch, you can substitute plain rice vinegar or even cider vinegar. If you do, increase the quantity of sugar to 1 tablespoon and the salt to ¼ teaspoon.

Don't stress about stemming the cilantro. Just tear off the longer stems so you have mostly leaves, and you're good to go.

soy-ginger-sesame vinaigrette

- 3 tablespoons seasoned rice vinegar
- ¼ teaspoon minced garlic (about half a small clove)
- 1 teaspoon finely minced fresh ginger
- 1 teaspoon soy sauce
- ⅛ teaspoon salt
- 2 teaspoons sugar
- 2 teaspoons toasted sesame oil
- 3 tablespoons canola, soy, or peanut oil

salad

- 1 pound romaine lettuce (a large head or "hearts")
- 2 cooked chicken breasts (see page 154), sliced, shredded, or cut into bite-sized chunks; or about 2 cups shredded or sliced cooked chicken
- 1½ cups (about 4 ounces) shredded red cabbage
- 1 cup (about 3 ounces) mung bean sprouts
- 2 medium carrots, shredded (about 1 cup, packed)
- 2 scallions (white and tender greens parts), cut into very thin strips about 1-inch long
- ½ cup loosely packed cilantro leaves
- ⅔ cup cashews and/or slivered almonds, lightly toasted

1. To make the dressing, combine all the ingredients in a smallish bowl and whisk until blended. (Or put all the ingredients in a small jar with a tight-fitting lid and shake it emphatically.)

2. Separate the romaine leaves, and then wash them in very cold water and spin them very dry. (If you have purchased hearts of romaine in a sealed pack, you can skip the washing; just cut off the stems and separate the leaves.) Tear the leaves into bite-sized pieces.

3. Combine the romaine, chicken, cabbage, bean sprouts, carrots, scallions, and cilantro in a large bowl, and toss to mix well. Just before serving, whisk the dressing—or shake it, if it's in a jar—to recombine, and add about half. Toss to coat, and give it a taste. You might want to add the rest of the dressing now, or just let people add their own at the table. Top with nuts and serve immediately.

GET CREATIVE

- Toss in some sliced water chestnuts (an 8-ounce can, rinsed and drained).

- If you like a little heat, add a few dashes of Chinese chile oil to the dressing (start slow and taste as you go).

- Whisk a teaspoon of wasabi paste or a pinch of powdered wasabi into the dressing for extra zing.

- Toss in some mandarin orange segments (fresh seedless ones, or the drained contents of an 11-ounce can).

- Sprinkle some chow mein noodles (the crunchy kind that come in a can) over the top.

- Substitute chopped roasted peanuts for some or all of the cashews and/or almonds.

- Sprinkle in 1 to 2 teaspoons white or black sesame seeds as you toss the salad. (They add a terrific little crunch.)

- Toss in a handful of fresh snow peas, cut lengthwise into thin strips.

- *Make this vegan by replacing the chicken with strips of firm tofu.*

wilted spinach salad with hazelnuts, goat cheese, and golden raisins

Makes 4 servings

ilting fresh spinach leaves just slightly is a really nice alternative to serving them utterly raw. Here, the wilting is done by dressing the leaves with heated oil, which cooks them slightly upon contact, tenderizing them perfectly. The oil is spiked with garlic and hazelnuts for flavor and texture, beautifully balanced by creamy-tangy goat cheese and the subtle sweetness of golden raisins. As you can see, this is a salad with no separate dressing, per se. Instead, the dressed salad comes together as you go, right in the bowl. Once assembled, this salad doesn't keep well, so aim for putting it together just before serving. You can peel the garlic and chop the nuts well ahead of time, making the final preparations very quick.

About ¾ pound baby spinach leaves (two 6-ounce bags), washed and well dried

4 to 5 tablespoons olive oil

1 cup coarsely chopped hazelnuts (also known as filberts)

1 teaspoon minced garlic (about 1 good-sized clove)

⅛ teaspoon salt

3 tablespoons golden raisins

⅓ cup crumbled goat cheese (a 5-ounce package)

3 tablespoons balsamic vinegar or red wine vinegar

Freshly ground black pepper

1. Place the spinach leaves in a large bowl. Break them into bite-sized pieces, if necessary, and remove the stems (or not, depending on your preference).

2. Pour the olive oil into a medium-small skillet and place it over low heat. Add the hazelnuts and cook, stirring intermittently, for 5 to 8 minutes, or until they begin to turn golden. Add the garlic during the last minute or so, cooking it slightly but not "frying" it. (Browning the garlic causes it to taste unpleasantly bitter.)

3. Drizzle this hot mixture directly over the spinach, scraping in as much of the oil as you can. (You can also toss some of the spinach back into the hot pan, stirring it around to swab up any extra oil left behind.) Use tongs to toss the spinach until it is completely coated with the oil, and the nuts and garlic are well distributed. Sprinkle with the salt as you toss. Add the raisins and goat cheese, and mix well.

4. At the very end, sprinkle in the vinegar and toss until it is thoroughly distributed. Serve immediately, passing a pepper mill.

GET CREATIVE

- Use a high-quality olive oil for more flavor.

- Use a good wine vinegar (such as sherry vinegar or Spanish Moscatel vinegar), one that is infused with fruit (such as raspberry vinegar), or cider vinegar.

- Add a thinly sliced medium-sized tart green apple along with the raisins and cheese.

- Slice 2 strips of bacon or pancetta into ¼-inch-wide strips. Brown these in a small skillet over medium-high heat until they are crisp and nicely browned. Drain them on a paper towel and add them to the oil along with the garlic.

- Chop a hard-boiled egg (see page 34) and sprinkle some over each serving—especially good if you're adding bacon.

- Top each serving with a still-warm, freshly poached egg—also fabulous with the addition of bacon.

- Slice a small, perfectly ripe avocado and lay slices over each serving as a garnish.

- Use 3 tablespoons dried cherries or cranberries instead of, or in addition to, the raisins.

- Substitute pumpkin seeds or coarsely chopped almonds or walnuts—all lightly toasted—for the hazelnuts.

- *Make this vegan by omitting the goat cheese.*

taco salad with cumin-lime-cilantro dressing

Makes 2 to 3 large dinner-sized salads,
or 4 to 6 smaller side salads

When you're in the mood for a Mexican meal but want to keep it light, this is a nice way to go—crunchy and brimming with bright flavors. For a dinner party, taco salad is a perfect accompaniment to Steak Fajitas (page 176). The dressing keeps for weeks in a tightly lidded jar in the refrigerator.

cumin-lime-cilantro dressing

¼ cup fresh lime juice

¼ teaspoon minced garlic (half a small clove)

½ teaspoon ground cumin

Heaping ¼ teaspoon salt

2 teaspoons sugar

1 tablespoon minced cilantro leaves

6 tablespoons olive oil

salad

One 15-ounce can pinto beans or black beans (about 1½ cups cooked beans)

1 pound romaine lettuce (a large head or "hearts")

1 small red bell pepper, cut into thin strips (or bite-sized pieces of any shape)

⅓ cup very thinly sliced red onion (about half a medium onion)

1 cup (packed) crumbled Mexican cheese (such as queso fresco or Cotija); or grated Cheddar, jack, or a combination of the two

6 ounces tortilla chips (any flavor or color you like), broken into bite-sized pieces

1 medium-sized perfectly ripe tomato, sliced

Freshly ground black pepper

1. To make the dressing, combine the lime juice, garlic, cumin, salt, sugar, and cilantro in a small-ish bowl. Whisk until thoroughly combined, then continue whisking as you drizzle in the olive oil. When all the olive oil is incorporated, set the dressing aside. (Or you can put all the ingredients in a small jar with a tight-fitting lid and just shake it emphatically.)

GET CREATIVE

• Top with shredded leftover Grandma Betty's Brisket (page 173), sliced Pan-Grilled Boneless Chicken Breasts (page 154), or strips of Steak Fajitas (page 176)—warm or at room temperature.

• Brown ½ pound ground beef or soy crumbles in a skillet with ¼ cup finely minced onion, 1 teaspoon minced garlic, and ½ teaspoon chili powder. Sprinkle with 1 tablespoon fresh lime juice, and divide evenly over the salads.

• Top each serving with a few avocado slices or a spoonful of guacamole (store-bought or homemade—see page 224).

• Garnish each serving with a dollop of sour cream.

• Top each serving with a spoonful or two of your favorite salsa.

• For a spicy kick, add a pinch of red pepper flakes, a few dashes of hot sauce, or 1 to 2 teaspoons thin jalapeño slices to the dressing. (If using jalapeños, wash the knife, cutting board, and your hands with warm water and soap after handling.)

• Serve in store-bought crisp tortilla bowls.   (Continued)

2. Set a colander in the sink and pour in the beans. Give them a quick rinse and allow them to drain.

3. Separate the romaine leaves, and then wash them in very cold water and spin them very dry. (If you have purchased hearts of romaine in a sealed pack, you can skip the washing; just cut off the stems and separate the leaves.) Tear the leaves into bite-sized pieces.

4. Combine the lettuce, bell pepper, and onion in a large bowl, and toss to mix well, sprinkling in the beans and cheese as you go.

5. Just before serving, toss in the tortilla chips. Whisk the dressing—or shake it, if it's in a jar—to recombine, and add about half of it to the salad. Toss to coat, and give it a taste. You might want to add the rest of the dressing right now, or bring it to the table (along with the pepper mill) for people to add more to their own portions. Top with the tomato slices and a few grinds of black pepper, and serve immediately.

- Toss a handful of strips of peeled jicama (see below) into the vegetables.

- Garnish with a generous sprinkling of toasted pumpkin seeds or Peppy Pepitas (page 228).

- *Make this vegan by omitting the cheese.*

JICAMA

Jicama (HEE-ka-ma), that large, brown potato-like thing you may have pondered in the produce section, is a great addition to pretty much any salad. It has the crunchy texture of a radish with the mild, somewhat sweet, starchy flavor of a water chestnut. Look for one on the small side, which will have more flavor. Use a sharp paring knife to cut off a chunk as large as you think you'll need, and then peel that piece with the knife. Discard the peel, and cut the flesh into slices or sticks for snacking on, dipping into guacamole or salsa, and tossing into salads. Or serve jicama sticks as a party nibble, drizzled with lime juice and dusted with chili powder.

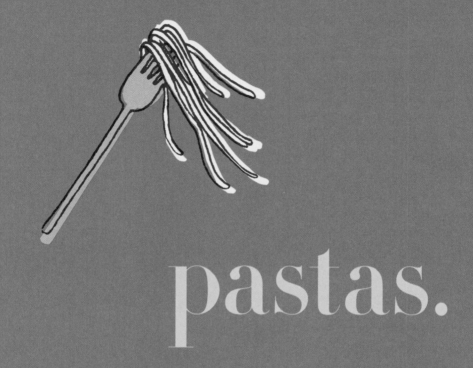

pastas.

Pasta: Limitless Possibilities

In terms of dinnertime readiness, pasta is your culinary insurance policy. Keep a few kinds in the cupboard, and you're always pretty much covered. In this chapter, you'll find a number of good, dependable pasta dishes to look forward to eating at the end of a full day. Most of them can be ready in the time it takes the water to boil and the pasta to cook. But there's an even simpler recipe you can always follow: Just about any pasta, plus just about any ingredients, plus olive oil, garlic, black pepper, red pepper flakes, and Parmesan cheese, and you've got yourself a meal.

Often, a pasta meal can be accomplished simply by combining a few flavorful things (like some leftover chicken or vegetables) in a bowl with a little olive oil, then tossing in some hot pasta and letting the pasta warm everything upon contact. You can save a bit of the pasta cooking water before you drain the pasta and stir a few tablespoons into the dish. In addition to helping to heat the ingredients and moisten things up, the pasta cooking water has a bit of salt and starch in it that will help bring the flavors together.

Or put some olive oil in a skillet that has been warmed over medium heat, add whatever ingredients you think might work—mushrooms, that same leftover chicken, that one last zucchini (sliced) and Roma tomato (diced)—along with a bit of minced garlic. When the pasta is cooked, drain it and toss it into the skillet, adding a bit more olive oil and some pasta water till it all looks saucy.

A "designer" sausage or two (like chicken-apple or basil–dried tomato) will go a long way toward turning a little pasta and a handful of leftovers into a tasty, substantial dinner. Brown the sausages in a little oil in a skillet, then slice them and toss them with the pasta.

Then there are the endless possibilities of pasta and red sauce. I've provided a basic recipe for making it from scratch—either vegetarian (marinara) or with ground meat (Bolognese). If you'd prefer to just use some out of a jar, that's fine (and there are some really good ones available). Find brands of marinara or other tomato-based pasta sauces you like. The variety and quality is improving all the time, so explore and expand your horizons. Heat and toss with cooked pasta, or doctor with anything from vegetables to canned tuna or leftover cooked chicken, meat, or fish.

And finally, you can take Italian-style pasta in an Asian direction just by adding a few well-chosen ingredients, like soy sauce, oyster sauce, toasted sesame oil, fresh ginger, garlic, scallions, and cilantro. Or, even easier, buy a prepared Asian sauce (such as curry or sweet and sour), or use the super-versatile peanut sauce on page 92 as a base to create your own homemade Asian-style noodle bowls.

Finally, when you haven't shopped in a week and there appears to be nothing edible anywhere in your kitchen, toss any kind of pasta with a little butter or olive oil and some Parmesan. For more flavor, add parsley, garlic, Roasted Garlic Paste (page 5), and/or red pepper flakes. It's comforting, warm, cheap, fast, and tasty. Think of it as moving beyond ramen noodles.

And those are the basics of your pasta insurance policy. Keep a bunch of packages around. They'll last for a year or more, and they'll always be there when you need them.

PASTA SHAPES

Pasta shapes are endless, and in cultures where pasta rules (like Italy and much of Asia), there are all kinds of sacred creeds about which shape best holds and complements which sauce. That's all good, but in your kitchen, here's a rule you can use: Any pasta will really go with any sauce (just don't repeat this to an Italian). Tradition pairs pesto with a long pasta like linguine, chunky meat sauces with tubular pastas like rigatoni, and so on. If you'd like to learn more about this, by all means buy a good Italian cookbook. But guess what: Rigatoni with pesto and linguine with meat sauce are fabulous, too, so stock up on the shapes and types you like, and experiment. If you cook any kind of pasta well and add the right amount of something tasty to it, you can't go wrong.

QUANTITIES

Four ounces (¼ pound) of dry pasta per person is a basic formula to remember, and the recipes in this chapter are based on that amount. If you and whomever you're cooking for have smallish appetites—or if you're making a dish with a lot of other ingredients— you may find that those 4 ounces are more than you need per person. But with pasta, it's better to err on the side of too much, rather than too little—you won't add much expense, and you'll end up with tasty leftovers. You don't need to actually weigh the pasta; just eyeball based on the weight of the full package. For spaghetti, a bundle about the size of a quarter (as in the coin) is about 4 ounces.

When it comes to quantities of sauce and other ingredients, remember, pasta is forgiving. A little more, a little less . . . it all tends to work out in the end. In other words, if a recipe calls for a 24-ounce jar of sauce and you've got a 26-ounce jar, go ahead and use it all.

OLIVE OIL

Buy two kinds: one that's relatively inexpensive, which you can use for sautéing things and for dressing pasta in general, and one high-quality extra-virgin oil that has a lot of flavor (and usually a higher price tag), which you can use in combination with the cheaper oil. Here's the rub: The less you cook the oil, the more you'll be able to tell the difference a good extra-virgin will make. So use it sparingly, in pastas (and other dishes) in which it's added toward the end of cooking, or drizzled on as a garnish.

GET THIS **PASTA SHAPES**

Familiar favorites

- Spaghetti

- Linguine

- Fettuccine

- Rigatoni

- Macaroni

- Penne

- Angel hair

- Lasagna noodles

And a few less common ones to check out

- Orecchiette ("little ears"—great with chunky sauces)

- Gemelli ("twins"—double-helix spirals with great texture)

- Orzo (looks like grains of rice; add to soups or toss with feta)

- Campanelle (aka trombette: ruffle-edged trumpets—fun shape, lots of texture, great with roasted vegetables)

GET THIS **PASTA STAPLES TO STOCK**

- Jarred tomato sauce (marinara, roasted vegetable, mushroom, etc.)

- Canned tomatoes (sauté with garlic and onion to make a quick sauce)

- Tomato paste in a tube (stores almost indefinitely in the refrigerator; unlike a can, the tube lets you use as much as you like and reseal the rest)

- Parmesan cheese (buy a chunk and grate as needed for best flavor)

- Really good olive oil (extra-virgin is usually the best bet), for drizzling as a finishing touch

- Capers (toss into all kinds of pastas for a salty, tangy hit of flavor)

- Olives (buy pitted ones, or smash them with the heel of your hand to extract the pit; use as you would capers)

- Anchovies or anchovy paste. (Don't be squeamish—a hint adds lots of flavor and most people who "hate anchovies" turn out not to when they don't know they're there. Case in point: Caesar salad. And, of course, strict vegetarians can just read on.)

- Red pepper flakes (use both in cooking and for sprinkling at the table)

- Garlic (if you're not into mincing, invest in a garlic press)

- Frozen peas (surprisingly good in all kinds of pastas)

TIMING AND COOKING

If you're planning to have pasta for dinner, it's usually a good idea to put the pot of water on the stove to heat before you do anything else, because it takes a while to come to a boil. And since a watched pot never boils, once it's on the stove, you can get busy preparing the sauce or ingredients you'll be using to dress the pasta.

Traditional methods call for using plenty of water—a few quarts for a half-pound of pasta to allow the noodles to swim around freely. (Current discussion in the food world, based on experiments by noted food expert Harold McGee, notes that there are benefits to cooking pasta in a much smaller quantity of water. However, that requires more monitoring by the cook, and I want to keep this as easy for you as possible. So, let's stay traditional for now.) Add a tablespoon of salt to the pasta water. The pasta will absorb some of it and take on more flavor. There's no need to add olive oil (or any kind of oil) to pasta water.

When it's time to add the pasta, toss it into the water and give it a good stir so the pieces don't settle and stick together. Once the water returns to a full, rolling boil, there's no need to keep stirring it as long as you have plenty of water in the pot.

When is pasta ready? The best advice for determining this is "read the package." Virtually all packaged pastas give suggested cooking times. The second-best advice is "don't believe everything you read." No two stoves or pots or quantities of cooking water are alike, so use the suggested cooking time as a guide, but start pulling pieces of pasta from the boiling water and tasting them a few minutes before that time is up, until you like the texture. It should be firm, not mushy. Some people call that *al dente*. You'll know it when you taste it.

GO FOR A GARNISH

A garnish is more than just a fancy finishing touch for restaurant food. Especially if you're cooking for friends, adding a little something to the presentation can make a big difference in the overall effect and the flavor. What makes a good garnish? One handy rule of thumb is to use an ingredient that went into the making of the dish. If you use a fresh herb, for example, save a few sprigs to top each finished serving. Most pastas made with oil benefit from the addition of a final drizzle of a flavorful olive oil. Breadcrumbs, toasted in a skillet with a small amount of olive oil, add an appealingly crunchy finish. You can always throw on a perfect leaf of Italian parsley, or chop a few sprigs roughly and scatter them over the pasta.

GO-WITHS **ROUNDING OUT A PASTA MEAL**

- **SALAD** Think green with red, red with green: a green salad with a red-sauced pasta, a tomato salad with pesto. (The salad chapter, beginning on page 29, offers many options and ideas.)

- Good crusty bread, warmed in the oven

- That same bread, toasted, rubbed with garlic, and sprinkled with olive oil, salt, and pepper (congratulations, you just made bruschetta). (By the way, pronounce it "brus-ketta.")

- Breadsticks from a package or a bakery

- A plate of Italian sliced meats, like prosciutto, mortadella, and salami, and an assortment of olives

- Marinated vegetables from a jar (roasted red peppers, artichoke hearts, eggplant relishes, etc.)

- An assortment of tasty cheeses with some sliced apples or pears

LOVE YOUR LEFTOVERS

The next time you cook pasta, make extra on purpose. Most pasta dishes reheat well and last a few days in the refrigerator, sealed in an airtight container. Take them to lunch, or reheat them for dinner, warming them in the microwave or on the stovetop (gently, so you don't actually cook them more). Most pastas also taste great at room temperature—a great way to re-enjoy last night's pasta as tonight's side dish or pasta salad.

Those quarter-full boxes and bags that pile up in the cupboard are good for all kinds of things. Throw the pasta into a soup or stew to thicken it and give it more substance. Combine a few types of similar sizes and shapes to make a pasta salad. Break up spaghetti, brown it in a little oil in a skillet, and add it to raw rice before you cook it. Or cook orzo, macaroni, or other small pasta and stir it into tuna salad or cooked vegetables like spinach or broccoli.

But enough from the General Pasta Information Desk. Let's start using those noodles.

homemade italian tomato sauce

Makes 3 to 4 cups

There are many very good commercially prepared tomato sauces available, and it's fine to use them (especially if you have found one or two that you really like). But there's nothing like simmering a batch of your own. It isn't difficult, and it will make you feel as though you've been temporarily transported to an Italian hillside, even if just for the day. Canned crushed tomatoes work best, but canned diced ones will work, too; they just make a chunkier sauce. This will keep, in a tightly covered jar or container in the refrigerator, for a week. It can also be frozen—just be sure to leave space in the jar or container, as the sauce will expand a bit as it freezes.

This recipe is followed by two variations; one adding vegetables, the other adding meat. For each of these, the yield will be increased to about 6 servings.

This recipe is vegan.

2 tablespoons olive oil

1 medium onion, finely diced
    (about 1 cup)

1 medium green bell pepper, finely diced

1 tablespoon minced garlic
    (about 3 good-sized cloves)

1 teaspoon dried basil

½ teaspoon dried oregano

½ teaspoon dried thyme

¾ teaspoon salt

One 28-ounce can crushed tomatoes

½ cup water

3 tablespoons tomato paste

⅛ teaspoon freshly ground black pepper

A generous handful or two of chopped
    flat-leaf parsley

1. Place a large pot or a Dutch oven over medium-high heat. After about a minute, add the olive oil and swirl to coat the pan. Add the onion, bell pepper, garlic, herbs, and salt, and cook, stirring occasionally, until the onion is very tender, 10 to 15 minutes.

2. Add the tomatoes, water, tomato paste, and black pepper. Use a spoon to break up the tomatoes if they are in rather large chunks. Bring to a boil, reduce the heat to medium-low, and simmer, partially covered, stirring occasionally, for 30 minutes.

3. Add the parsley, stir, and serve.

marinara

Makes about 5 cups

This recipe is vegan.

1 medium stalk celery, finely diced
    (about ⅓ cup)

½ pound mushrooms, finely diced

1 medium zucchini (about 6 inches long),
    finely diced

2 medium tomatoes, finely diced

¼ cup minced fresh basil

Add the celery, mushrooms, and zucchini to
the pan when you add the onion and bell pepper. Add the diced tomatoes when you add the
crushed tomatoes. Stir in the basil when you
add the parsley.

bolognese

Makes 5 to 6 cups

To make a Bolognese-style meat sauce, cook
the meat ahead of time. Here's what to do.

1 tablespoon olive oil

½ pound ground beef or turkey

1. Place a large pot or a Dutch oven over
medium-high heat. After about a minute,
add the olive oil and swirl to coat the pan.

2. Add the meat and cook, stirring occasionally, for 5 to 7 minutes, or until it is no longer
pink and the outside edges are starting to
brown. While it is cooking, use a thin-bladed
metal spatula to break up the meat into bite-
sized pieces. Then transfer it to a bowl (use a
slotted spoon), and set aside. Use paper towels to wipe out any fat left in the pan.

3. Proceed with the recipe for plain or marinara sauce, stirring the cooked meat back
into the pot when you add the tomatoes.

spaghetti and meatballs

Serves 4 to 6

Here's a basic standby you can fall back on for years to come. This is really a recipe for meatballs, which aren't at all hard to make, and a method for simmering them quickly in store-bought sauce (to keep things simple for now), piling it all onto freshly cooked pasta, topping with cheese and pepper, and sitting down to a perfect meal. Start making the meatballs about an hour before you want to eat, to allow time for shaping and browning them and then simmering them in the sauce while the pasta cooks. Or, even better, make the meatballs and cook them in the sauce a day or two ahead and then reheat them (slowly, over low heat, stirring gently from time to time) while the pasta cooks. The flavors will become deeper this way.

One 24-ounce jar prepared tomato
    sauce, or about 3 cups
    Homemade Italian Tomato Sauce
    (page 67)

Meatballs (recipe follows)

Salt for the pasta water

1 pound spaghetti

3 tablespoons olive oil

Grated Parmesan cheese

Freshly ground black pepper

Red pepper flakes

A handful or two of chopped
    flat-leaf parsley

1. Pour the tomato sauce over the meatballs in the pot they cooked in. Turn the heat to low, and simmer gently while you cook the pasta.

2. Put a large pot of cold water to boil over high heat, and add a tablespoon of salt. Place a large colander in the sink. When the water boils, add the spaghetti, keeping the heat high. Cook for the amount of time recommended on the package, tasting a strand toward the end of the suggested time to be sure it is not getting overcooked. When it is *just* tender enough to bite into comfortably but not yet mushy, dump the water-plus-pasta into the colander. Shake to mostly drain (it's okay to leave some water clinging), then transfer the spaghetti to a large bowl and immediately drizzle with the olive oil. Toss to coat.

3. You can serve this in one of two ways: Dump all the sauce-plus-meatballs into the bowlful of pasta, shake and toss to mix, top with Parmesan, black pepper, red pepper flakes, and parsley, and serve right away. Or make individual servings, using tongs to place some spaghetti onto each plate and then ladling on a generous amount of the meatballs and sauce. Serve hot, passing around the Parmesan, black pepper, red pepper flakes, and parsley so people can customize their spaghetti-and-meatball experience.

GET CREATIVE

- Don't forget the joys of a meatball sandwich. Just split a sandwich roll (toast it under the broiler or, buttered, in a skillet, if you like), ladle on meatballs and sauce, and sprinkle some grated Parmesan on top.

- You can also add these meatballs to a soup, or make them smaller and serve them, sauceless, on toothpicks for a great party snack.

- Add a teaspoon of dried oregano (or 2 teaspoons minced fresh oregano) to the meatball mixture.

meatballs

Makes about 24 medium-sized meatballs

Of course meatballs go superbly with spaghetti, but they're also great as a main dish on their own, with or without the tomato sauce. If you're going the classic spaghetti-and-meatballs route, brown the meatballs in a soup pot or a Dutch oven so you can add the sauce to the same pot. If your meatballs have a different destiny that does not involve a sauce, you can cook them in a skillet instead.

⅓ cup toasted whole wheat breadcrumbs
   (see page 81)

⅓ cup milk

1 large egg

¼ cup grated Parmesan cheese

A handful of chopped flat-leaf parsley

½ cup very finely minced yellow onion

¾ teaspoon salt

Freshly ground black pepper

1 pound ground chuck

1 to 2 tablespoons olive oil

1. In a medium-large bowl, stir together the breadcrumbs and milk. Let sit for a minute or two.

2. Lightly beat the egg in a small bowl. Add the egg, cheese, parsley, onion, salt, and about 5 grinds of black pepper to the breadcrumb mixture, mixing well with your fingers.

3. Crumble in the ground beef, and use your hands to mix everything gently until it's just combined.

4. Set out a tray or a couple of dinner plates to hold the formed meatballs. Wet your hands with cold water and gently roll the meat mix-ture into 1½-inch balls, placing them on the tray or plate as you go. You should end up with about 24 meatballs. Wash your hands thor-oughly after handling the raw meat.

5. Place a soup pot, Dutch oven, or large (10- to 12-inch) heavy skillet over medium heat. After about a minute, add 1 tablespoon of the olive oil and swirl to coat the pot. Add just enough meatballs to fit comfortably, and cook undisturbed for about 2 minutes, or until the surface touching the pot is deeply browned.

6. Turn the meatballs carefully with tongs to brown them all over. They are done when no longer pink in the middle (you can peek with the tip of a sharp knife). Total cooking time should be 10 to 12 minutes. If you have more raw meatballs to cook, take the cooked ones out of the pot, set them on a clean plate, and cover them loosely with foil. Brown the re-maining ones, adding more olive oil to the pot for each batch.

7. Once all the meatballs are fully cooked, return them to the pot to reheat briefly. They're now ready to be eaten as is, or simmered gently in your favorite tomato sauce and tossed with pasta.

quick and easy spinach lasagna

Makes 8 to 10 servings

Nothing (not even the noodles!) needs to be precooked in this easy vegetarian lasagna (unless you make your own sauce, which you can do a week or more ahead of time). So it's more like a DIY project, quickly assembled by stacking uncooked lasagna noodles, store-bought sauce, ricotta, mozzarella, and fresh baby spinach. Magically, all this raw stuff bakes itself into a good, honest lasagna. And by the way, there's no need to buy official "no boil" noodles. The liquid in the spinach and the sauce, plus a little water, will perfectly cook regular lasagna noodles (the kind with the curly edges that you usually have to preboil).

2 jars (about 6 cups) prepared tomato sauce, or 1 recipe Homemade Italian Tomato Sauce (page 67)

¾ pound lasagna noodles (about 12 noodles)

1 pound ricotta cheese

6 ounces (a few good-sized handfuls) fresh baby spinach

1 pound mozzarella cheese, grated (about 4 cups)

½ cup grated Parmesan cheese

1. Adjust the oven rack to the center position and preheat the oven to 375°F (350°F if you'll be using a glass pan). Have ready a 9- by 13-inch baking pan or its equivalent.

2. Spoon a generous cup of the tomato sauce into the baking pan and spread it around. It won't completely cover the bottom, but that's okay. Cover the sauce with a single layer of noodles, edges touching (you can break some,

if necessary, to make a single layer that covers the whole pan).

3. Drop spoonfuls of the ricotta cheese here and there over the noodles, using half the ricotta. You don't need to cover the noodles completely with the cheese. Spoon, and lightly spread, another cup or so of the tomato sauce over the ricotta. Don't worry if there are chunks in the sauce and it spreads somewhat unevenly. Layer on half of the spinach leaves, pressing them into the sauce. (Don't be alarmed if this looks like a lot of spinach. It cooks down during baking.) Then sprinkle the spinach with about half of the mozzarella.

4. Place another single layer of noodles on top of the mozzarella, and drop spoonfuls of the remaining ricotta on top, using up all the ricotta.

5. Spoon on half of the remaining sauce, spreading it around. Layer on the rest of the

spinach, pressing it down, and sprinkle the remaining mozzarella over the spinach.

6. Make a final layer of noodles on top of the spinach, and spoon the remaining sauce on top of the noodles.

7. Cover the pan very tightly with aluminum foil and bake, undisturbed, for 1 hour.

8. Remove and save the foil, sprinkle the top of the lasagna with the Parmesan, and return the pan to the oven. Bake, uncovered, for 15 to 20 minutes, or until the top is golden.

9. Remove the pan from the oven and cover it with the foil again. Let the lasagna rest for 15 minutes before cutting and serving. (This step helps ensure that the noodles are completely cooked and that the lasagna has solidified, so it will come out in neat squares or rectangles.)

GET CREATIVE

- If you use store-bought sauce instead of making your own, your selection will greatly influence the final flavor of your lasagna. So experiment with various brands and flavors (mushroom, basil, roasted garlic, etc.) to find your favorite.

- Stir 1 tablespoon minced garlic and/or ¼ cup (packed) minced basil into the ricotta.

- Use fresh ricotta—the kind sold in bulk at the cheese counter of some markets. It's a splurge, but it tastes extra-creamy and rich.

- Add up to 2 cups of chopped cooked vegetables, such as mushrooms, broccoli, or cauliflower, to the sauce.

genuine homemade mac & cheese

Makes 4 to 5 servings

Yes, the stuff in the blue box is cheap and fast. But it is no match for this real MacCoy—with its crunchy, chewy crust on top and the soft, creamy pasta underneath. This version is made with a classic cheese sauce that comes together in about the time it takes to cook the pasta. The rest happens in the oven, so it's really not that much trouble for a huge payoff. You can use packaged grated Cheddar or your own mix of good-quality cheeses. The tastier the cheese, of course, the better the dish will be.

Vegetable oil spray for the pan

Salt for the pasta water

½ pound elbow macaroni

2 tablespoons butter

1½ tablespoons unbleached all-purpose flour

Heaping ¼ teaspoon salt

1 tablespoon dry mustard

A big dash of cayenne pepper (up to ⅛ teaspoon)

2 cups milk

1 cup (packed) grated sharp Cheddar cheese

½ cup grated Parmesan cheese

2 slices whole wheat bread, toasted and crumbled (see "Toasted Breadcrumbs," page 81)

1. Spray a 1-quart gratin dish or an 8-inch square baking pan with vegetable oil spray, and set aside.

2. Set the oven rack on the highest rung that will fit your baking pan (this will help the top brown nicely) and preheat the oven to 350°F.

3. Put a medium-sized pot of cold water to boil over high heat, and add a tablespoon of salt. Place a large colander in the sink. When the water boils, add the macaroni, keeping the heat high. Cook for the amount of time recommended on the package, tasting the macaroni toward the end of the suggested time to be sure it is not getting overcooked. When it is *just* tender enough to bite into comfortably but not yet mushy, dump the pasta-and-water into the colander. Run cold water over the pasta to bring it to room temperature so that it stops cooking. Shake to mostly drain (it's okay to leave some water clinging). Leave it in place—you'll need it in just a few minutes.

4. To make the cheese sauce, melt the butter over low heat, in the same pot you used to cook the macaroni. When the butter is melted, use a whisk to beat in the flour, salt, mustard, and cayenne. Keep whisking for a few seconds, until the mixture forms a thick paste. Then slowly drizzle in the milk, still vigorously whisking, so the sauce becomes smooth as the milk is incorporated. Keep cooking and stirring (switching from the whisk to a wooden spoon) for 2 to 3 minutes, or until the mixture is velvety, thick, and smooth. Sprinkle in about two-thirds each of the Cheddar and the Parmesan, and stir until the cheeses are fully blended in. Remove the pot from the heat.

5. Add the cooked macaroni and the remaining Cheddar to the cheese sauce. Stir until all the pasta is well coated. Transfer the mixture to the prepared baking pan, and top with the breadcrumbs and the remaining Parmesan. Set the pan on a foil-lined baking tray to catch any drips, and bake, uncovered, for about 20 minutes, or until bubbly around the edges and crisp and golden on top. Serve hot.

GET CREATIVE

- Use whole wheat macaroni instead of white.

- Mince a medium-sized clove of garlic and add it when melting the butter.

- Stir up to 2 teaspoons prepared horseradish and/or prepared mustard (in addition to the dry mustard) into the cheese sauce before adding the pasta.

- If you have cooked broccoli or cauliflower on hand, add up to 2 cups (chopped) when mixing the pasta with the sauce; or add up to 2 cups chopped raw broccoli or cauliflower to the macaroni during the last minute of cooking.

- Mix a handful of chopped walnuts with the breadcrumbs before sprinkling them over the mac and cheese.

- You might want to make this cheese sauce separately, to serve on top of cooked vegetables or potatoes. It's multipurpose!

linguine with clam sauce

Makes 2 to 3 servings

Fresh clams, cooked with a little white wine, garlic, and onion, create a classic pasta sauce that will wow you with its complex flavor. Don't be put off by the idea of buying and cooking fresh clams. It's really quite foolproof and actually kind of fun. A note on timing: Ideally, you want the hot pasta and just-opened clams to be done at about the same time, so check the pasta package for its suggested cooking time and calculate accordingly. It's fine if the pasta is done a few minutes before the clams, because you can reheat it a bit when you add it to the clams and sauce.

Salt for the pasta water

½ pound linguine or spaghetti

3 tablespoons olive oil
(plus a little extra for the
hot pasta)

½ cup minced onion

¼ teaspoon salt

2 teaspoons minced garlic
(about 2 good-sized cloves)

Big pinch of red pepper flakes
(plus extra to pass at the table)

¾ cup dry white wine

2 pounds fresh littleneck or Manila
clams (in the shell)

1 tablespoon butter

A handful of chopped flat-leaf parsley

Freshly ground black pepper

1. Put a large pot of cold water to boil over high heat, and add a tablespoon of salt. Place a large colander in the sink. When the water boils, add the linguine, keeping the heat high. Cook for the amount of time recommended on the package, tasting the pasta toward the end of the suggested time to be sure it is not getting overcooked. When it is *just* tender enough to bite into comfortably but not yet mushy, dump the water-plus-pasta into the colander. Shake to mostly drain (it's okay to leave some water clinging), and drizzle lightly with olive oil. Leave it in place—you'll need it in just a few minutes.

2. While the pasta is cooking, place a soup pot or a Dutch oven (something large and deep with a lid at the ready) over medium heat. Let this pot heat for a minute, then add the 3 tablespoons oil and swirl to coat the bottom of the pot. Add the onion and salt, and cook over medium heat, stirring often, for about 5 minutes, or until the onion softens.

3. Stir in the garlic and red pepper flakes, then pour in the white wine, and cook, uncovered, over medium heat for about 3 minutes, or until the wine cooks down to about half of its original volume. (This allows some of the wine, plus some of its alcohol, to evaporate, concentrating the flavors.)

KEEPING CLAMS

Buy your clams (or any shellfish) from a store with a high turnover so you can be sure they're as fresh as possible. Don't leave them in a closed plastic bag once you get them home. Instead, pour them into a bowl, cover them with a damp cloth, and put them in the refrigerator, where they'll keep for a day or two. Just before cooking, rinse the clams and scrub them with a vegetable brush under cold running water to clean them.

GET CREATIVE

• Drizzle each serving with a bit of high-quality olive oil at the table.

• Add about a dozen cherry tomatoes along with the onion. They'll burst during cooking, creating a light tomato-clam sauce. Or add a few squirts from a tube of tomato paste along with the onion.

• Add a tablespoon of minced fresh oregano or thyme (or a teaspoon of dried oregano or thyme) along with the onion.

• Sauté some breadcrumbs in a skillet with a little olive oil, minced garlic, and minced parsley; sprinkle over each serving as a garnish.

4. Add the clams, cover, and cook, shaking the pot occasionally, for 3 minutes without opening the lid. After this amount of time, take a look to see if the clams have opened. If some are still unopened, give the pot a shake, cover the pot again, and cook for another minute or so, until all of the clams open. (Discard any that fail to open.) With the pot still over the heat, add the cooked linguine and toss for about 30 seconds to mix well.

5. Remove the pot from the heat. Add the butter, sprinkle in the parsley, grind in some black pepper, and toss again.

6. Serve right away, using tongs to put some linguine in each bowl, and then topping with some of the clams. Be sure to include some of the liquid at the bottom of the pot in each serving. Pass the pepper mill and a shaker of red pepper flakes.

spaghetti alla carbonara

Makes 3 to 4 servings

Kind of like having bacon and eggs for dinner. And spaghetti. What could be bad? This classic Italian pasta will make a great addition to your cooking repertoire. Once you master it, as long as you've got bacon (keep some in the freezer), eggs, Parmesan, and spaghetti, you can turn out a luxury dish for yourself and your friends on very short notice. The heat of the pasta cooks the eggs just enough to turn them into a creamy sauce. Just how creamy depends on how quickly you work and how much reserved pasta water you add. It sounds tricky, but you'll discover you really can't go wrong, and you'll see how simple the whole process really is. This is definitely a "make just before serving" kind of dish. Leftovers can be reheated in a microwave or skillet, but the egg will go from silky to scrambled. Still tasty, just less texturally amazing.

3 large eggs

½ cup grated Parmesan cheese
(plus extra to pass at the table)

¼ teaspoon minced garlic
(about half a small clove)

A handful of chopped flat-leaf parsley

⅛ teaspoon freshly ground black pepper

6 ounces (about 6 strips) bacon

Salt for the pasta water

¾ pound spaghetti

2 tablespoons olive oil

1. Crack the eggs into a large bowl and beat them lightly with a whisk until you no longer see bits of egg white. Add the Parmesan, garlic, parsley, and black pepper, and continue whisking to combine everything. Set aside.

2. Cook the bacon in a skillet or in the microwave (see page 233) until it is crisp; then let it cool and break it into ¼-inch pieces.

3. While the bacon is browning, put a large pot of cold water to boil over high heat, and add a tablespoon of salt. Place a large colander in the sink. When the water boils, add the spaghetti, keeping the heat high. Cook for the amount of time recommended on the package, tasting a strand toward the end of the suggested time to be sure it is not getting overcooked. When the pasta is *just* tender enough to bite into comfortably but not yet mushy, ladle out and save a generous cup of the pasta water, then dump the remaining water-and-

pasta into the colander. Shake to mostly drain (it's okay to leave some water clinging).

4. Working quickly, add the hot pasta to the bowl containing the egg mixture and stir it immediately with tongs or a fork to coat the pasta thoroughly. Add the olive oil, the bacon, and 2 tablespoons of the reserved pasta water and stir to combine. The sauce should have a thick, creamy consistency. If the pasta looks dry or sticky, add another tablespoon or two of the pasta water. Serve right away, passing around additional Parmesan, plus a pepper mill.

GET CREATIVE

- Use a good, thick-cut bacon or Italian-style pancetta, which is not smoked and has a sweeter, more delicate flavor than bacon.

- You can also make this with turkey bacon or "veggie" bacon.

- Pass a shaker of red pepper flakes at the table.

- Sauté some sliced mushrooms in olive oil, and add them to the pasta along with the bacon.

- Stir a few tablespoons of heavy cream into the pasta just before serving (and add a little less reserved pasta water).

rigatoni al forno with roasted asparagus and onions

Makes 3 to 4 servings

Baked pasta dishes are great for bringing to someone else's place. This one is especially suited for that purpose because it tastes as good warm or at room temperature as it does hot. This recipe uses a single pan to first roast the vegetables in olive oil (which gives them amazingly deep, sweet, complex flavor) and then to bake the pasta. The other big flavor secret here is a generous amount of balsamic vinegar, which reduces and intensifies in the oven. If you like, cut one of the onions into smaller chunks (½-inch or smaller) and the other into larger (¾-inch) pieces. The smaller ones will become part of the sauce, and the larger ones will add a slightly (and delightfully) crunchy texture.

Salt for the pasta water

4 tablespoons olive oil

2 medium onions,
    cut into 1-inch chunks

1 pound asparagus (about ½-inch
    diameter), trimmed and cut
    diagonally into 2-inch pieces
    (see page 197)

½ pound rigatoni or penne pasta
    (or any kind of tube shape)

1 teaspoon minced garlic
    (1 good-sized clove)

½ cup grated Parmesan cheese

½ cup balsamic vinegar

½ teaspoon salt

2 slices whole wheat bread,
    toasted and crumbled
    (see "Toasted Breadcrumbs,"
    opposite)

Freshly ground black pepper

1. Adjust the oven rack to the center position, and preheat the oven to 425°F (375°F if you'll be using a glass pan). Put a large pot of cold water to boil over high heat, and add a tablespoon of salt. Place a large colander in the sink.

2. Pour 3 tablespoons of the olive oil into a 9- by 13-inch baking pan, and add the onions and asparagus. Shake and tilt the pan to get all the vegetables coated with the oil. Roast in the oven for 15 to 20 minutes, or until the vegetables are fork-tender and the onion edges are beginning to brown. Remove from the oven and set aside. Turn the oven down to 300°F.

3. When the pasta water boils, add the rigatoni, keeping the heat high. Cook for the amount of time recommended on the package, tasting the pasta toward the end of the suggested time to be sure it is not getting overcooked. When it is *just* tender enough to bite into comfortably but not

yet mushy, ladle out and save 1 cup of the pasta water, then dump the rest of the water-plus-pasta into the colander. Shake to mostly drain (it's okay to leave some water clinging). Then transfer the pasta to the pan containing the roasted onions and asparagus.

4. Toss in the remaining 1 tablespoon olive oil, plus the garlic and a heaping ¼ cup (a little more than half) of the Parmesan. Pour in the vinegar and the reserved cup of pasta cooking water, sprinkle in the salt, and stir to combine.

5. Sprinkle the breadcrumbs and the remaining Parmesan over the top, put the pan in the oven, and bake, uncovered, for 15 to 20 minutes, or until lightly golden on top. Serve hot, warm, or at room temperature, topped with a good amount of freshly ground black pepper.

TOASTED BREADCRUMBS

These work just about anywhere, and you'll find them suggested as a finishing touch in recipes throughout this book. To make them, toast some really good whole wheat or rustic artisan-style bread until it is crisp but not too dark. Let the toast cool completely, so it's quite hard. Then put it in a bowl and crumble it with your fingers, or put it in a plastic bag and roll with a bottle or a rolling pin. For more flavor, toss the crumbs in a skillet over medium heat with just enough good-quality olive oil to moisten them, stirring frequently, until the crumbs are golden and crisp. Toasted without oil, breadcrumbs keep for a long time and are multipurpose; toasted with oil, they are best used quickly and are incomparably delicious.

GET CREATIVE

- Sprinkle some chopped toasted walnuts on top just before serving.

- Add up to 1 cup of extra cheese when stirring in the Parmesan. You can use diced fresh mozzarella or other soft white cheeses, including jack or fontina. You could also add some crumbled Gorgonzola, but use a light hand (say, about ½ cup) to accommodate its very strong flavor.

- *Make this vegan by using eggless pasta and omitting the cheese.*

linguine with spinach and peas

Makes 3 to 4 servings

Culinary secret: A great dish, even a great pasta, doesn't have to involve a lot of actual *cooking*. In this one, the heat of the pasta does most of the work, wilting the spinach, melting the cheese, warming the peas, and bringing all the flavors together beautifully. It's an easy weeknight supper that could also double as an elegant little dish to serve to friends. Use the baby spinach that comes prewashed in bags or boxes—no stemming necessary.

Of all the *get creative* suggestions in the list that follows, I strongly recommend throwing on a few toasted pine nuts. (Put them in a dry skillet over low heat and shake them often until they are lightly browned, watching them like a hawk so they don't burn.) Very worthwhile.

Salt for the pasta water

About ½ bag (about 5 ounces) fresh baby spinach leaves

5 tablespoons olive oil

2 teaspoons minced garlic (2 good-sized cloves)

½ teaspoon salt

⅛ teaspoon red pepper flakes (plus extra to pass at the table)

¾ pound linguine

⅔ cup grated Parmesan cheese (plus extra to pass at the table)

One 10-ounce package frozen peas, defrosted and at room temperature

1. Put a large pot of cold water to boil over high heat, and add a tablespoon of salt. Place a large colander in the sink.

2. While the water is coming to a boil, tear the spinach into large bite-sized pieces (this pretty much means just tearing the leaves in half, since they're already small) and drop them into a large bowl. Pour the olive oil over the spinach, then sprinkle in the garlic, salt, and red pepper flakes. Use tongs or a long-handled fork to mix, and set aside.

3. When the water boils, add the linguine, keeping the heat high. Cook for the amount of time recommended on the package, tasting the pasta toward the end of the suggested time to be sure it is not getting overcooked. When the linguine is *just* tender enough to bite into comfortably but not yet mushy, dump the water-plus-pasta into the colander. Shake to mostly drain (it's okay to

GET CREATIVE

- Use a high-quality olive oil for more flavor.

- Sprinkle the finished pasta with a few lightly toasted pine nuts.

- Increase the garlic to 1 tablespoon for more intense flavor.

- Add a few teaspoons of Roasted Garlic Paste (page 5) along with the fresh garlic, mashing it into the olive oil.

- Use arugula in place of some or all of the spinach to add a more peppery flavor.

- Add ¼ cup crumbled feta or goat cheese when you add the peas.

- Stir a teaspoon or two of freshly grated lemon zest into the finished pasta.

- *Make this vegan by using eggless pasta and omitting the cheese.*

DEFROSTING PEAS

To defrost frozen peas, remove them from the box or bag, put them in a microwave-safe dish, and microwave them until they are thawed. You can also simply put them in a strainer and run cool water over them. Or even easier, just put the box or bag in a bowl and thaw in the refrigerator overnight.

leave some water clinging). Then transfer the pasta to the bowl containing the spinach mixture, mixing it in with the tongs or the fork until all the pasta is coated with olive oil. The spinach will wilt on contact with the hot pasta.

4. Immediately sprinkle in the Parmesan and toss well, so the cheese gets evenly distrib-

uted and melts nicely. Add the peas, mixing them in very gently so you don't break them. (Just shake the bowl a few times, and they'll mix themselves in.)

5. Serve hot, warm, or at room temperature, passing extra Parmesan and red pepper flakes for people to add at the table.

penne with broccoli and pesto

Makes 3 to 4 servings

Convenience squared: You toss chopped broccoli into the pot right along with the pasta, and then drain and sauce everything with pesto (which, if it's store-bought, makes things even easier). If you do go with purchased pesto, you'll have better results with the fresh kind (sold in plastic tubs in the refrigerator case), rather than the kind that comes in a jar (which is cooked in the packaging process and has much less flavor). Or even better (and much cheaper), make your own (see page 220). The pesto needs to be at room temperature, so take it out of the refrigerator shortly before you need it. Leftovers? Chill. You'll have a perfect cold pasta salad for tomorrow's lunch.

¼ cup olive oil

¾ cup pesto, store-bought or homemade (page 220)

Salt for the pasta water

¾ pound penne

1 large head of broccoli (1½ pounds), tough stem ends discarded, and the rest cut on the diagonal into 2-inch spears

⅓ cup grated Parmesan cheese

¾ teaspoon salt

Freshly ground black pepper

1. Pour the olive oil into a large bowl. Add the pesto and whisk until uniformly blended. Set aside.

2. Put a large pot of cold water to boil over high heat, and add a tablespoon of salt. Place a large colander in the sink. When the water boils, add the penne, keeping the heat high. Cook for close to the amount of time recommended on the package. Taste the pasta, and when it looks like the penne have about a minute or so to go, add the broccoli directly to the boiling water. (The broccoli will cook in seconds.) When the pasta and broccoli are *just* tender enough to bite into comfortably but not yet mushy, ladle out and save about 1 cup of the pasta water, then dump the remaining water-plus-pasta-plus-broccoli into the colander. Shake to mostly drain (it's okay to leave some water clinging), and then transfer the pasta-plus-broccoli to the pesto mixture.

3. Mix well, so all of the pasta and broccoli is evenly coated with pesto and olive oil. Toss in the Parmesan as you mix (it will melt, coating everything nicely), and then stir in the salt plus about 6 grinds of black pepper (or to taste). If the pasta looks dry, stir in some of the reserved pasta water, a few tablespoons at a time. Serve the pasta hot, warm, at room temperature, or even cold.

WARMING PASTA INGREDIENTS

When working with ingredients (such as pesto) that need to be at room temperature, but not cooked, an easy way to warm them just enough is to spread them across the bottom of the large serving bowl in which you'll be mixing them with the pasta and, while the pasta is cooking, set the bowl over the boiling pasta water for a few seconds. Stir just until the bowl gets a bit warm. Make sure your bowl is not ice-cold and is made of something heatproof, like metal or heavy earthenware.

GET CREATIVE

- Use a high-quality olive oil for more flavor.

- Mix in up to 1 cup of fresh ricotta for extra creaminess (let it come to room temperature and give it a stir before adding).

- Toss in a handful or two of lightly toasted pine nuts or chopped toasted walnuts.

- Stir in about ½ cup halved cherry tomatoes when you add the hot pasta.

pasta shells with chickpeas and arugula

Makes 3 to 4 servings

There's a luxury ingredient in this quick pasta, and it's one that makes a major difference: fresh mozzarella—the soft white kind that comes in a tub of liquid, not the rubbery kind that's sold shrink-wrapped. You can cut a few pieces into chunks or, even easier, use *bocconcini,* those bite-sized fresh mozzarella balls, whole or cut in halves or quarters if they're on the large side. Don't make the pieces too small, though, because it's nice to bite into a serious chunk of fresh mozzarella in this texturally fun dish. Young, small (and thus not-so-bitter) arugula is best here. If you have older, larger arugula, remove and discard the stems. Not an arugula fan? Substitute baby spinach leaves, torn or cut into bite-sized pieces.

One 15-ounce can chickpeas (about 1½ cups cooked chickpeas)

¼ cup balsamic vinegar

1 teaspoon minced garlic (about 1 good-sized clove)

¾ teaspoon salt (plus more for the pasta water)

½ teaspoon dried thyme

½ teaspoon dried oregano

¼ cup olive oil

½ pound fresh mozzarella cheese, cut into large dice

Freshly ground black pepper

½ pound small or medium-sized (up to 1-inch) pasta shells

¼ cup grated Parmesan cheese

2 cups (packed) coarsely chopped arugula

1. Set a colander in the sink and pour in the chickpeas; give them a quick rinse and allow them to drain.

2. In a large bowl, combine the vinegar, garlic, salt, thyme, oregano, and olive oil; whisk to blend. Stir in the chickpeas and mozzarella, and grind in a generous amount of black pepper. Cover the bowl with plastic wrap, foil, or just a plate, and let it stand at room temperature for at least 30 minutes or up to an hour. (You can do this step up to 2 days ahead—in which case, refrigerate the mixture and bring it back to room temperature before proceeding.)

3. When you are ready to assemble the dish, put a large pot of cold water to boil over high heat, and add a tablespoon of salt. Place a large colander in the sink. When the water boils, add the pasta, keeping the heat high. Cook for the amount of time recommended on the package,

tasting the pasta toward the end of the suggested time to be sure it is not getting overcooked. When it is *just* tender enough to bite into comfortably but not yet mushy, dump the water-plus-pasta into the colander. Shake to mostly drain (it's okay to leave some water clinging), and then add the pasta to the chickpea mixture in the bowl.

4. Toss well from the bottom of the bowl, sprinkling in the Parmesan and arugula as you go. Serve hot, warm, or at room temperature, as is or garnished with any of the extras listed at right.

GET CREATIVE

- Use a high-quality olive oil for more flavor.

- Garnish with a few sun-dried tomatoes—either dry or marinated in oil—cut into thin strips.

- Toss in a handful of chopped toasted walnuts along with the Parmesan and arugula.

- Add a few handfuls of halved tiny, sweet cherry tomatoes along with the Parmesan and arugula.

- Turning this dish into a pasta salad is as simple as combining all the ingredients as directed and then covering and chilling in the refrigerator. Toss to recombine just before serving, and if you like, throw in a few handfuls of halved cherry tomatoes.

- Use fresh thyme and oregano in place of dried; increase the amount to 1½ teaspoons of each, since fresh herbs have a more delicate flavor than dried.

- *Make this vegan by using eggless pasta, omitting the Parmesan cheese, and replacing the mozzarella with tofu.*

farfalle with roasted garlic, nuts, and raisins

Makes 3 to 4 servings

Here's another no-cook way to dress pasta for success. The garlic, raisins, and nuts make for a nice mix of sweet, salty, chewy, and crunchy. You can also try making this with cashews and pistachios, which add a sensational richness. (For detailed nut-toasting instructions, see page 53.)

Plump sweet golden raisins are best in this dish, but if you don't have them on hand, black ones work fine. You'll need to make the Roasted Garlic Paste ahead of time. It's good to keep some on hand, anyway, so you can throw this (and many other delicious items) together on short notice.

½ cup olive oil

2 tablespoons Roasted Garlic Paste
(page 5)

Salt for the pasta water

¾ pound farfalle (bowtie pasta)

½ to ¾ cup minced flat-leaf parsley

½ cup raisins (preferably golden ones)

½ cup chopped walnuts, lightly toasted

½ cup chopped almonds, lightly toasted

3 scallions (white and tender green parts),
finely minced

¾ teaspoon salt

Freshly ground black pepper

Red pepper flakes

1. Place the olive oil in a large bowl. Add the Roasted Garlic Paste, mashing it into the oil with the back of a fork. Set aside.

2. Put a large pot of cold water to boil over high heat, and add a tablespoon of salt. Place a large colander in the sink. When the water boils, add the farfalle, keeping the heat high. Cook for the amount of time recommended on the package, tasting the pasta toward the end of the suggested time to be sure it is not getting overcooked. When it is *just* tender enough to bite into comfortably but not yet mushy, dump the water-plus-pasta into the colander. Shake to mostly drain (it's okay to leave some water clinging), and then transfer the pasta to the bowl containing the oil and garlic paste.

3. Use a fork or a wooden spoon to toss and turn the pasta until it becomes coated with the oil. Keep tossing as you add the parsley, raisins, nuts, scallions, and salt. Grind in a generous amount of black pepper, and sprinkle in a big pinch of red pepper flakes (according to your heat preference). Toss quickly and thoroughly. (Shaking the bowl helps.) Serve right away, making sure you dig down to the bottom of the bowl to scoop up all the tasty morsels that might have landed beneath the pasta.

pasta with tuna, white beans, and artichoke hearts

Makes 3 to 4 servings

Want to never be stuck with nothing for dinner? I've got two words for you: cans and jars. Stock up on decent tuna, canned white beans, and jars of marinated artichoke hearts, and you've got a great start. Any kind of tuna is fine for this recipe (white or light, water- or oil-packed), and it's great with all kinds of pasta beyond the more traditional fettuccine—orecchiette (little ears), gemelli (twists), or whatever looks like fun to you. It's light yet substantial, and great on a warm evening. And it's definitely not your grandmother's tuna noodle casserole.

One 15-ounce can cannellini or
    navy beans (about 1½ cups
    cooked beans)

⅓ cup olive oil

1 teaspoon minced garlic
    (1 good-sized clove)

3 tablespoons fresh lemon juice

¼ teaspoon salt (plus more for
    the pasta water)

Freshly ground black pepper

One 12-ounce can tuna, drained

One or two 6-ounce jars
    marinated artichoke hearts

3 or 4 scallions (white and
    tender green parts), minced

A handful of chopped flat-leaf
    parsley

¾ pound fettuccine
    (or any pasta)

1. Set a colander in the sink and pour in the beans; give them a quick rinse and allow them to drain.

2. Pour the olive oil into a large bowl. Add the garlic, lemon juice, and salt, and stir to combine. Add the beans and 5 to 6 grinds of black pepper. Stir gently to coat all the beans, and let sit for at least 30 minutes to marinate. (You can do this step up to 2 days ahead—in which case, cover and refrigerate the mixture and then bring it back to room temperature before proceeding.)

3. Add the tuna to the beans, flaking it with a fork and then mixing it in gently, so as not to break the beans. Stir in the artichokes (including all of their marinade), along with the scallions and parsley.

4. Put a large pot of cold water to boil over high heat, and add a tablespoon of salt. Place a large colander in the sink. When the water boils, add the fettuccine, keeping the heat high. Cook for the amount of time recommended on the package, tasting the pasta toward the end of the suggested time to be sure it is not getting overcooked. When it is *just* tender enough to bite into comfortably but not yet mushy, dump the water-plus-pasta into the colander. Shake to mostly drain (it's okay to leave some water clinging), and then add the pasta to the bowl with the bean mixture.

5. Gently stir the pasta and sauce until well combined. (The best utensil for stirring will depend on the shape of the pasta: tongs for longer shapes like fettuccine, a large spoon for shorter ones.) Serve right away.

GET CREATIVE

- Use a high-quality olive oil for more flavor.

- Add a handful of assorted olives (the variously shaped multicolored ones from the olive bar) to the mix when you add the tuna.

- Add a tablespoon of capers along with the tuna.

- If you want to extend the sauce and make it a little more Mediterranean, add a drained 15-ounce can of diced tomatoes.

- Add a few chopped anchovies or a bit of anchovy paste along with the tuna. If you do, use less salt.

- Try some tuna packed in olive oil. Expensive, but worth it. You can use the oil in the jar to make up part of the ⅓ cup of oil called for in the recipe.

chinese-style peanut noodles

Makes 4 to 6 servings

Y ou'll be surprised at how Chinese-restaurant-y (in a good way!) this easy peanut sauce tastes. Make the sauce ahead of time, if you like, and keep it in the refrigerator. That way you can enjoy this pasta on a busy weeknight just by reheating a bit of the sauce and spooning it over individual servings of cooked pasta—not to mention chicken, vegetables, tofu, or beef. "Natural" peanut butter (the kind made just from peanuts, and perhaps also salt, but nothing else) is the best kind to use for this.

1½ cups peanut butter

1 teaspoon minced garlic
   (1 good-sized clove)

4 cups boiling water

¼ cup cider vinegar

½ cup (packed) brown sugar
   (light or dark)

3 to 4 tablespoons soy sauce

Up to 1 teaspoon salt
   (plus more for the
   pasta water)

1 pound angel hair pasta

Red pepper flakes

1. Put the peanut butter and garlic in a large bowl. Add about 2 cups of the boiling water, and mash with the back of a large spoon to help the peanut butter start softening. As it softens, switch from the spoon to a whisk, and gently whisk as you slowly pour in the remaining 2 cups of boiling water. When the peanut butter and the water have become uniformly mixed, stir in the vinegar, brown sugar, and 3 tablespoons of the soy sauce. Taste the mixture to see if it needs more soy sauce (different brands have varying salt contents), and add more if you like. Also add some salt to taste, beginning with ¼ teaspoon and possibly adding up to a full teaspoon if it seems to need it. Set the sauce aside. (You can make this sauce up to a week ahead of time and store it, covered, in the refrigerator. If you do, warm it in the microwave, or in a saucepan over low heat, before using.)

2. Put a large pot of cold water to boil over high heat, and add a tablespoon of salt. Place a large colander in the sink. When the water boils, add the pasta, keeping the heat high. Cook for the amount of time recommended on the package, tasting the pasta toward the end of the suggested time to be sure it is not

getting overcooked. When it is *just* tender enough to bite into comfortably but not yet mushy, dump the water-plus-pasta into the colander. Shake to mostly drain (it's okay to leave some water clinging), and transfer the pasta to the bowl of sauce.

3. Use a fork or tongs to gently mix the noodles into the sauce, using a lifting motion as you turn the bowl. Serve right away, topped with a scattering of red pepper flakes.

GET CREATIVE

- If you like a little heat, add some chile oil to the sauce (a few drops at a time, tasting after each addition) after you add the soy sauce.

- For a little more complex flavor, add a teaspoon of toasted sesame oil to the sauce.

- Add some minced cilantro to the sauce and/or a few whole cilantro leaves to decorate the top. (Use as much as you like. I tend to throw in a ton!)

- Stir in some thinly sliced scallion greens, or sprinkle them on top as a garnish.

- Garnish with some chopped peanuts.

- Toss in a cup of warm chopped cooked broccoli, carrots, cabbage, summer squash, mushrooms, or cauliflower along with the pasta.

- Mix in (or sprinkle on) a cup of shredded or sliced cooked chicken (pages 154 and 156), diced firm tofu, or scrambled eggs.

- *Make this vegan by using eggless pasta.*

vegetarian entrées.

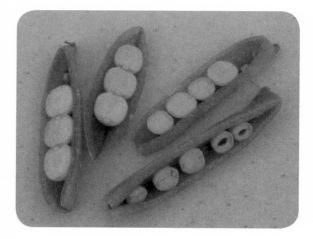

The Greening of Dinner

I've spent an entire career creating and writing vegetarian recipes, and my "off-duty" cooking is very heavily (and happily) skewed this way as well. I do eat bits of meat from time to time, but I pretty much always *think* like a vegetarian, and "plant cuisine" is my Forever culinary home base. This is the food that I love and that makes me feel best, not only in body and soul, but creatively, in the garden and kitchen. And because I want to share this kind of cooking with everyone, and not further the misperception (to people who might love their burgers as well as their broccoli) that vegetarian cuisine is some kind of exclusive club, I prefer to call it "garden-and-orchard-based eating," and thus (hopefully) fling the door to this paradise wide open. "Garden-and-orchard-based eating" is a mouthful, I know, and it doesn't exactly roll off the tongue (which is why it's not the title of this chapter). But with high hopes that this approach to food will become a *literal* mouthful—and a positive factor in your lives—here are the recipes I have created just for you, to get you launched into the universe of green-leafy-delicious.

This chapter, therefore, is not just for you official "Big V" vegetarians. It's also for meat lovers who might want some really tasty, easy options to try out a few nights a week as a break from burgers and chicken. I think you'll discover that eating a little less meat, loving it when you do eat it, and doing good for the planet (since plant-based choices are far less damaging to the environment) is a win-win-win.

These recipes are designed to give you a basic repertoire of meatless entrées, based on favorite ideas from my decades of loving to cook this way. Along with some of the pastas in the pasta chapter (or the suggested meatless versions of them), you'll have quite a few good options to choose from.

Most of these dishes are complete meals with the addition of a green salad or, in the case of the stir-fry and the curries, a bowl of rice to serve them over. And most of them are, or can be, vegan-friendly, with the exception of the quiche, cornbread, calzones, and Popover Pie. Where cheese is called for—other than in the recipes just mentioned—you can simply leave it out.

One of the things I like best about mostly-plant-based eating is that it defies all the old rules about what goes on a plate. Who says you can't serve any of these vegetarian entrées with any of the recipes in the Sides chapter? As far as I'm concerned, the more garden food we all eat, the better. Mashed potatoes with quiche? Sounds like a plan!

acorn squash stuffed with apple-almond-cherry basmati pilaf

Makes 4 servings

A corn squash is a natural edible bowl that was born to be stuffed. Here, it's filled with a fragrant pilaf of basmati rice, sweet onions, garlic, almonds, apples, and dried cranberries. Use plain raw almonds (not roasted, salted, or otherwise processed), chopped with a sharp heavy knife on a cutting board, or buzzed very briefly in a food processor. They don't need to be too fine—just coarsely chopped. Some people like the skin of cooked acorn squash. If that's you, eat this with a fork and a sharp knife, such as a steak knife, to make cutting through the skin easier.

You can cook the rice and bake the squash at the same time. I've provided a simple rice method here. You could also use a rice cooker (follow the manufacturer's instructions) or the slightly unconventional method on page 181, but for this smallish amount, I recommend just doing it as described below.

1 cup brown basmati rice

1½ cups water (possibly more)

1½ tablespoons olive oil

2 medium acorn squash (about 2 pounds each), halved and seeded (see page 99)

1 teaspoon butter

½ medium red or yellow onion, minced

⅓ cup chopped almonds

¼ teaspoon minced garlic (about half a small clove)

Heaping ¼ teaspoon salt

1 medium apple, chopped (unpeeled)

¼ cup dried cherries (halved or quartered, if large)

1. Combine the rice and water in a medium-sized saucepan and bring to a boil. Then turn down the heat to the lowest possible setting (insert a waffle heat absorber under the pot, if you have one), cover the pot, and let the rice simmer undisturbed for 40 minutes.

2. Meanwhile, adjust the oven rack to the center position and preheat the oven to 400°F. Line a baking tray with foil, and pour 1 tablespoon of the olive oil on it. Use your fingers to distribute the oil so that it coats the area where you'll put the squash. Place the squash, cut side down, on the olive oil. Roast for 35 to 40 minutes, or until you can easily insert a fork or a sharp knife into the squash from the skin side.

3. While the squash is roasting and the rice is cooking, place a small skillet over medium heat. After about a minute, add the remaining ½ tablespoon (that's 1½ teaspoons) olive oil, and swirl to coat the pan. Add the butter and swirl until it melts into the oil. Add the onion, and cook, stirring often, for 10 minutes, or until it becomes very soft and is beginning to turn golden. (If it appears to be browning too quickly, turn the heat to medium-low.) Add the almonds and cook them with the onions, stirring frequently, for 5 to 8 minutes, or until the almonds begin to toast and give off a lovely aroma. Stir in the garlic and salt, and cook for 5 minutes longer. Remove the pan from the heat.

4. When the squash is done, remove the tray from the oven, and set it aside. Turn the oven down to 300°F.

5. After 40 minutes of undisturbed cooking, you may now disturb the rice by fluffing it with a fork. Give it a taste. If it is a little too crunchy, add another 3 tablespoons water, and without fluffing or stirring it further, put the top back on and let it sit for another 10 minutes with the heat turned off. It will steam itself a little further and become more tender.

6. When the rice is done to your liking, transfer it to a medium-large bowl. Add the onion-almond mixture (using a rubber spatula to scrape in all the delicious essence that might otherwise be left in the pan) and toss until well combined. Add the apple and cherries, and mix until thoroughly combined.

7. Turn the squash halves over, so their cavities are facing up. Divide the rice mixture among the squash, using a soup spoon to fill the cavities; pack down the filling and then mound the top. (There will be a generous amount of filling. If it's too much, you can snack on it or serve it as a side-dish-refill component of the meal. I assure you no one will complain.)

8. Cover the filled squash loosely with a tent of foil, and return the tray to the oven. Bake for about 10 minutes, or just long enough to heat everything through. (If you like, you can skip this step and just serve the squash halves as soon as you stuff them.)

SPLITTING AND SEEDING ACORN SQUASH

Cutting an acorn squash, especially when you want to end up with two matching halves, is a process requiring both an appropriate knife and a few minutes of utter focus. Make sure the knife is very sharp (always, but especially here). Watch your squash-holding hand carefully as you steady the squash and insert the point of the knife about ½-inch deep into the side of the squash, directly into a groove between the ridges. After this initial cut, patiently rock the knife to coax the squash open, continuing to follow the groove. Keep at it, and at a certain moment the squash will split itself in half. Use scissors to loosen the stringy flesh holding the seeds, then scrape out the cavity with a spoon. (If you'd like to toast the seeds, see page 28). The squash is now ready to roast.

GET CREATIVE

- *Make this vegan by omitting* *the butter.*

- Drizzle with some high-quality olive oil just before serving.

- Substitute dried cranberries, golden raisins, and/or dried currants for the dried cherries.

- Try other nuts, such as pecans, walnuts, or pine nuts.

- The filling makes a great pilaf on its own to serve as a side dish or to top with a cooked vegetable like Deeply Roasted Cauliflower (page 200) or Delightfully Spiced Carrots (page 204).

- This is always a great way to prepare acorn squash without stuffing. Simply roast the squash halves, cut side down, as directed. When they're cooked, you can eat them "as is," or sprinkle a little brown sugar and melted butter over the cut sides, return them to the oven (turned down to 300°F), and bake for 10 minutes, until the sugar is melted and lightly caramelized.

- Toast the squash seeds (see page 28) and sprinkle a few on top just before serving.

- Serve with a green salad with Creamy Balsamic-Honey Dressing (page 36).

vegetarian chili with homemade cornbread

Makes about 6 servings

This chili is very straightforward. There's a bit of vegetable prep, and the rest is about as challenging as opening a few cans. But it tastes thoroughly, comfortingly homemade, especially if you serve it with scratch-baked cornbread. (Make the cornbread first, and then start the chili once the bread is in the oven.) As long as you stir it occasionally, you can't really overcook this chili. It gets richer and deeper the longer it simmers, and it's even better when you reheat it. So make a big batch, and refrigerate or freeze the extra in a tightly covered container. (Freezing it in individual serving-size containers or resealable freezer bags can be very convenient for future spontaneous dinners.)

This chili recipe is vegan.
(But not the cornbread.)

2 tablespoons olive oil

1 medium red or yellow onion, minced

2 tablespoons chili powder

2 teaspoons ground cumin

¾ teaspoon salt

1 medium carrot, diced

1 medium stalk celery, diced

1 tablespoon cider vinegar

1 tablespoon minced garlic
(about 3 good-sized cloves)

1 small bell pepper (any color), diced

Three 15-ounce cans red kidney beans
(about 5 cups cooked beans)

One 28-ounce can crushed tomatoes

One 15-ounce can diced tomatoes

Up to ¼ teaspoon freshly ground black pepper

Cornbread (recipe follows)

1. Place a soup pot or a Dutch oven over medium heat. After about a minute, add the olive oil and swirl to coat the pan. Add the onion, chili powder, cumin, and ¼ teaspoon of the salt. Cook, stirring occasionally, for about 5 minutes, or until the onion softens.

2. Stir in the carrot, celery, and remaining ½ teaspoon salt, and reduce the heat to medium-low. Cook, stirring occasionally, for about 15 minutes, or until the vegetables are very soft.

3. Add the vinegar, garlic, and bell pepper. Cook for another 5 minutes, stirring often. Meanwhile, set a colander in the sink and pour in the beans; give them a quick rinse and allow them to drain.

4. Add the beans and the crushed and diced tomatoes (with all their liquid) to the pot. Bring to a boil, then turn the heat all the way down to the lowest possible setting. Cover the pot with the lid slightly askew and simmer gently, stirring occasionally, for 15 minutes.

5. Grind in some black pepper to taste, and serve hot, with the cornbread alongside.

GET CREATIVE

- For four-alarm chili, add a big pinch or two of red pepper flakes along with the onion. You can also pass a shaker of red pepper flakes at the table so people can add their own.

- Top each serving with a dollop of sour cream or yogurt; some grated Cheddar, jack, or pepper jack cheese; a spoonful of salsa; finely diced red onion; and/or some minced cilantro and/or parsley.

- Garnish with Peppy Pepitas (page 228).

- Add up to a cup of pitted black olives along with the beans.

- Substitute 1 can of corn, drained (or 2 cups frozen or fresh corn kernels) for one of the cans of beans.

- Stir in a tablespoon of Dijon mustard along with the vinegar for extra-tangy flavor.

cornbread

Makes 6 servings

Use regular fine-milled cornmeal for this, not the coarser polenta. If you don't have any vegetable oil spray on hand, use a little softened butter to grease the pan instead.

Also, you could swap 1 cup buttermilk for the milk-plus-vinegar.   (Continued)

Vegetable oil spray for the pan

1 cup cornmeal

1 cup unbleached all-purpose flour

2 teaspoons baking powder

½ teaspoon baking soda

½ teaspoon salt

¼ cup sugar

3 tablespoons butter

1 cup milk

2 teaspoons vinegar (any kind)

1 large egg, lightly beaten

1. Adjust the oven rack to the center position, and preheat the oven to 350°F. Lightly coat an 8-inch square baking pan (or its equivalent, such as a 6- by 9-inch pan) with vegetable oil spray.

2. Combine the cornmeal, flour, baking powder, baking soda, salt, and sugar in a medium-sized bowl, and whisk together to completely blend.

3. Melt the butter in a small saucepan over low heat, or in a microwave-safe bowl in the microwave (about 30 seconds on high power).

4. Measure the milk into a 2-cup-capacity measuring cup with a spout (so you'll have room to mix and it will be easy to pour). Add the vinegar, egg, and melted butter, and whisk until uniform.

5. Pour the milk mixture into the cornmeal mixture, and use a wooden spoon to mix just enough to blend. (Don't try to beat it or over-mix. Just stir.) Transfer the batter to the prepared baking pan, scraping in every last bit with a rubber spatula.

6. Bake for 20 minutes, or until the center feels firm when lightly touched and a toothpick or sharp knife inserted all the way into the center comes out clean. Remove the pan from the oven and let the cornbread cool in the pan for at least 10 minutes before slicing and serving. Serve warm or at room temperature.

GET CREATIVE

- Add up to ½ cup canned, frozen, or fresh sweet corn kernels to the batter.

- Add one 4-ounce can diced roasted green chiles (spicy or mild, depending on your taste) to the batter.

- Add ½ cup (packed) grated Cheddar cheese to the batter.

mushroom-zucchini ragout over creamy polenta

Makes 4 servings

I can think of few things more comforting than a hearty, aromatic vegetable stew served over a hot portion of creamy, soft polenta. Good any time of year, and downright great in the winter, this tastes best when made with a combination of domestic (white or cremini) mushrooms, shiitakes, and portobellos. If all three are available, buy equal amounts to make a combined total of ½ pound. If you can only get regular domestic mushrooms, increase the quantity to ¾ pound to compensate for the fact that these mushrooms shrink more during cooking and have a milder flavor than the other two kinds. Before starting, see "Mushroom Prep Tips" (page 113). Make the ragout first, and then while it simmers (the final step) make the polenta, so they'll be ready at the same time.

This recipe is vegan.

2 tablespoons olive oil

1 large red or yellow onion, chopped

½ teaspoon salt

½ to ¾ pound mixed fresh mushrooms (stemmed if using shiitakes), sliced or diced

2 small zucchini, cut into ¼-inch-thick slices

2 small yellow crookneck or summer squash, cut into ¼-inch-thick slices

1 teaspoon minced garlic (about 1 good-sized clove)

½ teaspoon Italian seasoning (or a combination of oregano, basil, thyme, and rosemary)

⅛ teaspoon freshly ground black pepper

One 15-ounce can diced tomatoes

About ⅓ cup water

Creamy Polenta (recipe follows)

1. Place a large (10- to 12-inch) heavy skillet or a Dutch oven over medium heat. After about a minute, pour in the olive oil and swirl to coat the pan. Add the onion and ¼ teaspoon of the salt, and cook, stirring occasionally, for 8 to 10 minutes, or until the onion becomes translucent. Add the mushrooms and the remaining ¼ teaspoon salt, and cook, stirring occasionally, until the mushrooms begin to soften and any liquid they have given off has evaporated, about 5 minutes.

2. Add the zucchini and yellow squash, plus the garlic, Italian seasoning, and black pepper. Cook for just 2 minutes, stirring often. Reduce the heat to medium-low and add the tomatoes with all their liquid, plus the water. Cover the pot with the lid slightly askew and simmer gently, stirring occasionally, for 15 minutes. (While the ragout is simmering, make the polenta.)

3. Serve the polenta in soup bowls or pasta plates, topped with the ragout.

GET CREATIVE

- Garnish with crunchy coarse salt.

- Pass grated Parmesan cheese at the table for sprinkling over the ragout.

- Drizzle a high-quality olive oil over each serving.

- For a richer flavor, you can substitute butter for half of the olive oil.

- You could serve the ragout with penne pasta instead of polenta. Boil 6 ounces penne, drain, and toss with the warm ragout.

creamy polenta

Makes 4 servings

Polenta, the dish, is Italian-style cornmeal mush. Polenta, the ingredient, is coarsely ground corn-meal, often found in the bulk bins in supermar-kets and also commonly available packaged. Rich, creamy polenta isn't difficult to make. As long as you keep it warm and keep stirring, it will stay nice and soft. You can add a little water if it starts to get too thick. It will firm up the more you let it cool.

4 cups cold water

1 teaspoon salt

1 cup polenta

1. Pour the water into a medium heavy-bottomed saucepan, add the salt, and bring to a boil over high heat. Then very gradually sprinkle in the polenta while whisking continuously.

2. Reduce the heat to low and cook, whisking or stirring very frequently, for 15 minutes, or until the grains are no longer crunchy and the texture is smooth and creamy. Serve immediately.

GET CREATIVE

- To make this polenta richer, stir in 2 tablespoons butter and ¼ cup grated Parmesan or other flavorful grating cheese (such as pecorino or Asiago). You can also add a spoonful of Gorgonzola.

- You can pour fully cooked polenta into a loaf pan (rinse the pan first with cold water but don't dry it) and refrigerate it. Once it's chilled, unmold it, cut it into thick slices, and fry them in butter or olive oil in a nonstick skillet until golden brown. Serve with your favorite toppings or just a sprinkling of Parmesan cheese and black pepper.

artichoke, goat cheese, tomato, and red onion focaccia

Makes 2 or 3 servings

Focaccia, that soft, irresistible bread that's so popular in restaurants and sandwich shops, is basically just pizza dough baked in a pan with sides, so it rises a bit higher than pizza and takes on a squared-off shape. It's easy to bake your own using store-bought pizza dough, which is sold both fresh (in the refrigerator case) and frozen (often near the pie dough) in many supermarkets. Topping it with a few vegetables and some goat cheese is all it takes to turn focaccia into a great main dish. Look for whole wheat dough, which is particularly nice in this recipe. The topping amounts suggested below are on the modest side, because that's the balance I like, but feel free to increase them a bit—just be sure to leave some dough showing through here and there so it browns nicely. You can cut this into large pieces for dinner, or into smaller ones to serve warm or at room temperature for lunch or as a party snack. It wouldn't be a bad breakfast-grab, either.

1 tablespoon cornmeal or unbleached all-purpose flour

1 pound store-bought pizza dough (thawed according to package directions, if purchased frozen)

One 6.5-ounce jar marinated artichoke hearts, drained and sliced in half, if large

6 large cherry tomatoes (about 1-inch diameter), cut into 3 slices each

1 medium red onion, cut into ¼-inch-thick slices

½ teaspoon dried rosemary, crumbled

½ cup crumbled goat cheese (plain or herbed)

Freshly ground black pepper

1. Adjust the oven rack to the center position and preheat the oven to 450°F.

2. Sprinkle the cornmeal or flour onto a baking tray, and spread it into a thin layer. Place the dough on top of the cornmeal, and gently stretch and press it into a 9- by 13-inch rectangle (see "Working with Pizza Dough," below). Let the dough rest for 20 to 30 minutes to rise and puff up slightly.

3. Arrange the artichokes, tomato slices, onion slices (separated into individual rings), and rosemary over the surface of the dough, and then scatter the goat cheese evenly on top.

4. Bake for about 10 minutes, or until the dough is golden brown on the bottom and the cheese is turning brown around the edges. Allow to cool at room temperature for a minute or two before slicing.

5. Serve hot, topped with a few grinds of black pepper.

WORKING WITH PIZZA DOUGH

Before using frozen pizza dough, let it defrost completely in the refrigerator. If it's too sticky to handle, flour your hands and the work surface very lightly, or spray both your palms and the work surface with vegetable oil spray. Most kinds of dough tighten up the more they are handled. For this recipe, since you want the dough to be supple enough to stretch out, don't knead it or work it very much. Just stretch it into the desired shape and leave it alone. If it seizes up and won't stretch, let it rest for about 10 minutes, and then resume.

broccoli–cheddar cheese calzones

Makes 4 servings

Store-bought pizza dough to the rescue again! It's what makes these impressive calzones completely doable and fun to assemble. For pointers on handling the dough, see "Working with Pizza Dough" (page 107). And if it's frozen, let it thaw completely before you begin (check the package instructions). If you have any leftover filling, it makes a great baked potato topping or omelet filling.

1 tablespoon cornmeal or unbleached all-purpose flour

Vegetable oil spray or a drizzle of oil for the work surface

1 pound store-bought pizza dough, cut into quarters

1½ tablespoons olive oil

½ cup minced red or yellow onion

2 heaping cups chopped broccoli

¼ teaspoon salt

⅛ teaspoon freshly ground black pepper

¾ cup (packed) grated sharp Cheddar cheese

1. Adjust the oven rack to the center position and preheat the oven to 450°F. Sprinkle the cornmeal or flour onto a baking tray, and spread it into a thin layer.

2. Lightly spray a work surface (a clean countertop, a second baking tray, or a large wooden cutting board) with vegetable oil spray, or coat it with a slick of oil (about a teaspoon, spread around with a pastry brush or your hands). One at a time, place each of the 4 pieces of dough on the prepared surface and use your fingers to press and stretch them into 7-inch rounds that are about ¼-inch thick. If the dough wants to shrink back on you, let it rest for about 10 minutes and try again. Once you have stretched out all 4 dough rounds, let them rest while you proceed with the filling.

3. Place a large (10- to 12-inch) skillet over medium heat. After about a minute, add the olive oil and swirl to coat the pan. Add the onion and cook, stirring occasionally, for about 3 minutes, or until it begins to soften.

4. Stir in the broccoli and salt, and cook, stirring occasionally, for about 8 minutes, or until the onion is golden and the broccoli is tender but not mushy. Remove the pan from the heat and let the vegetables cool for about 5 minutes. Then add the pepper and cheese, and stir until well combined.

5. Divide the filling into 4 equal portions (about ½ cup apiece). Place a portion of the filling on each of the dough rounds, keeping the filling to one side of the round and leaving a 1-inch edge. Use your fingers or a pastry brush to lightly moisten the edge of the round with a little water.

6. Carefully fold the unfilled half of the dough over the filling, and then press the edges tightly closed all around with a fork. (The fork will make a nice-looking edge.)

7. Transfer the filled calzones to the prepared baking tray. Put the tray in the oven and bake for 15 to 20 minutes, or until the calzones are golden brown all over. Serve them hot out of the oven.

GET CREATIVE

- *Make this vegan by omitting the cheese.*
  (You could slightly increase the broccoli.)

- Add up to 2 teaspoons yellow mustard or 1 teaspoon prepared horseradish to the filling. Or just use prepared mustard (any kind) as a condiment at the table, for spreading on the calzones or using as a dip.

- Warm about a cup of Homemade Italian Tomato Sauce (page 67) or a good commercial pasta sauce and ladle some over each calzone when serving. Sprinkle with grated Parmesan.

- Sauté a cup of sliced mushrooms along with the broccoli.

- Beat an egg with 1 tablespoon water and brush the mixture lightly over the calzones before putting them in the oven. This egg wash will give them a beautifully shiny golden brown appearance.

green pea and feta quiche

Makes 4 to 6 servings

Quiche isn't at all difficult or time-consuming to make, and using a frozen pie crust makes it even easier. Look for the "deep-dish" kind of crust. There's no need to defrost it first; just fill it, still frozen, and put it right in the oven to bake. The fresh mint in (and on) this quiche—a classic complement to the flavors of both peas and feta—really makes it special. The best kind of peas to use here are the small ones called "petit pois" or "tender tiny peas." You'll find them in the frozen foods section of most supermarkets. Buy them in bags rather than boxes, so you can use just what you need.

1½ cups frozen green peas (about half a 1-pound bag)

1 small bunch fresh mint

¾ cup (packed) crumbled feta cheese

One unbaked 9-inch deep-dish pie crust

6 large eggs

¾ cup milk

1 tablespoon unbleached all-purpose flour

⅛ teaspoon salt

Freshly ground black pepper

2 scallions (white and tender green parts), finely minced

1. Adjust the oven rack to the center position and preheat the oven to 375°F.

2. Put the peas in a colander and run them under room-temperature water for about 30 seconds to defrost. Turn the water off, give the colander a shake, and then leave it in the sink for a few minutes to drain.

3. Pull about 10 mint leaves from the bunch, and cut them into thin strips with a sharp knife. Set aside the rest of the bunch for garnishing.

4. Scatter the crumbled feta into the pie crust. Shake the peas in the colander a couple more times, then dump them into the crust on top of the cheese. Tilt and gently shake the pie pan a few times to evenly distribute the peas.

5. In a medium bowl, whisk together the eggs, milk, flour, salt, and a few grinds of black pepper. Stir in the scallions and the mint strips.

6. Pour the egg mixture carefully over the feta and peas, filling the crust right up to the top. (If there's any extra, you can save it to add to your scrambled eggs for tomorrow's breakfast.)

7. Carefully transfer the pie to a foil-lined baking tray (which will catch any filling that might overflow during baking, saving you possible oven cleanup), and slide the tray into the oven. Bake for about 1 hour, or until the crust is golden, the filling is puffed up, and the surface feels tender but solid when you (carefully) touch it with a fingertip. If the edges of the crust become too dark before the hour is up, cover the quiche very loosely with foil to protect it.

8. Remove the tray from the oven and let the quiche rest for 10 minutes before serving. During this time, cut the remaining mint leaves into thin strips to sprinkle over each serving. Serve hot, warm, or at room temperature.

GET CREATIVE

- Drain and chop a few marinated roasted peppers or sun-dried tomatoes and add these along with the scallions.

- Accompany this with sliced tomatoes drizzled with olive oil and sprinkled with coarse salt and oregano. Or serve it with a big salad; Greek Salad (page 46) is a particularly good match.

mushroom popover pie

Makes 2 to 3 servings

Popovers you know. Ditto pie. So what's a popover pie? It's what I call this large, dramatically puffed, Yorkshire pudding–like, custardy-centered pancake (that's the popover part), baked with mushrooms and served in wedges (that's the pie part). And if you're a mushroom lover, you'll call it addictive. The recipe calls for both white mushrooms and fresh shiitakes for lots of deep mushroom flavor. If you can't find shiitakes, it's okay to substitute cremini (brown) mushrooms or just use all white ones. Room-temperature eggs take on much more volume when beaten than cold ones, and for recipes like this that are all about puff, that's important. The best way to bring eggs to room temperature is to break them into a bowl while they are still cold, and then cover the bowl with plastic wrap or a plate and leave it out for about an hour before you begin.

2 tablespoons butter

½ cup finely minced red or yellow
  onion

½ pound fresh white mushrooms,
  stemmed and chopped into
  ¼-inch pieces

¼ pound fresh shiitake mushrooms,
  stemmed and chopped into
  ¼-inch pieces

1 teaspoon minced garlic
  (about 1 good-sized clove)

1¼ teaspoons salt

½ teaspoon dried thyme

¼ teaspoon dried rosemary,
  crumbled

3 large eggs, at room temperature

1 cup milk

1 cup unbleached all-purpose flour

⅛ teaspoon freshly ground black
  pepper

1. Adjust the oven rack to the center position and preheat the oven to 375°F.

2. Melt 1 tablespoon of the butter in a 10-inch cast-iron pan or a heavy stainless steel skillet with an ovenproof handle. Add the onion and sauté over medium heat for 5 minutes.

3. Stir in the white and shiitake mushrooms, garlic, ¾ teaspoon of the salt, and the herbs. Cook, stirring often, for about 15 minutes, or until the liquid the mushrooms have given off evaporates and the mushrooms are becoming golden brown around the edges.

4. While the mushrooms are cooking, place the eggs, milk, flour, remaining ½ teaspoon salt, and black pepper in a blender, and blend on high speed for a few seconds, until everything is just combined to make a smooth batter. (If you don't have a blender, whisk all of this together in a medium-sized bowl. It's okay if the mixture has a few lumps.) Set this aside until the mushrooms are done cooking.

5. When the mushrooms are ready, transfer them to a plate or bowl and set aside. Thoroughly wash and dry the pan, and return it to the stove. Add the remaining 1 tablespoon butter, turn on the heat to low, and heat just until the butter melts and begins to foam. Immediately remove the pan from the heat and swirl until the melted butter completely coats the bottom and sides of the pan. Add the mushrooms, spreading them out in a fairly even layer, and then pour in the batter.

6. Put the pan in the oven and bake for 25 to 30 minutes, until the mixture has become puffed and golden, the top feels solid when touched lightly with a fingertip, and the edges have shrunk from the sides of the pan and become quite brown. Remove the pan from the oven. Serve hot or warm, cut into wedges.

MUSHROOM PREP TIPS

It's best to store mushrooms in the refrigerator in a brown paper bag, not in the plastic bag you might have brought them home in. This helps them stay dry and fresh. To clean them, wipe the caps with a lightly damp cloth or paper towel. (Don't immerse them in water, or they will soak it up and get soggy.) With domestic mushrooms, if the stem is tight, leave it on and simply trim and discard its tough, brown, dry tip. If the stem is loose or in any way funky, just pull it out and throw it away. With shiitakes, always trim off the entire stem using scissors or a sharp paring knife.

GET CREATIVE

- Sprinkle some snipped chives or minced flat-leaf parsley over the top as a garnish.

- Pass some grated Parmesan cheese at the table for sprinkling on top.

- This recipe, minus the entire mushroom part, works wonderfully as a giant sweet pancake you can serve for brunch or dessert. Just make the batter, heat 1 tablespoon butter in the skillet, and bake as directed. As soon as the pancake comes out of the oven, squeeze a little fresh lemon juice over the top and sprinkle on some powdered sugar (using a kitchen strainer to sift the sugar). Serve with warm maple syrup.

baked stuffed potatoes

Makes 1 or 2 servings

B ar munchie becomes dinner entrée with just a few deft strokes of your increasingly skilled hands! You simply bake a potato, scoop out the insides, mix them with a few choice ingredients, stuff this back in, and stick it under the broiler for a few minutes. Throw together a salad while the potato bakes, and you've got dinner. This compact little recipe works really well in a toaster oven, and can easily be multiplied to serve more people (in which case, use a regular oven).

1 medium-large russet potato
  (¾ pound)

1 tablespoon olive oil

½ cup minced red or yellow
  onion

¼ teaspoon minced garlic
  (half a small clove)

1 ounce (about 1 cup, lightly
  packed) fresh baby spinach,
  finely chopped

¼ cup sour cream

2 tablespoons minced scallion
  (green tops only)

½ teaspoon salt

⅛ teaspoon freshly ground black
  pepper

2 tablespoons grated sharp
  Cheddar cheese

1. Adjust the oven rack to the center position and preheat the oven to 400°F. Scrub the potato under running water and pat it dry with paper towels or a clean dish towel.

2. Place the potato directly on the oven rack. Let it bake for 50 minutes to an hour, or until the outside becomes crisp and the inside is tender when you pierce it with a sharp knife. (For this recipe it's better to overcook it a bit than to have it be underdone.)

3. While the potato is baking, place a small (6-inch or so) skillet over medium heat. After about a minute, add the olive oil and swirl to coat the pan. Add the onion, turn the heat down, and cook over low heat, stirring occasionally, for about 15 minutes, or until the onion becomes deep golden brown and very soft. Stir in the garlic, remove the pan from the heat, and set it aside until the potato is ready.

4. Remove the potato from the oven and when it's just cool enough to handle, slit it in half lengthwise. Use a soup spoon to scoop the flesh into a medium bowl, being careful to leave the potato skin intact and boat-like. Mash and lightly fluff the potato flesh with a fork. Place the empty skins on a baking tray lined with foil. Heat the broiler to high.

5. Add the onion mixture to the mashed potato, being sure to scrape in every last bit of the olive oil and delicious tidbits from the pan. Add the spinach, sour cream, scallion, salt, and pepper, mixing lightly with the fork until everything is thoroughly combined.

6. Divide the mixture evenly between the two empty potato skins, mounding it slightly. Sprinkle the cheese over the tops, patting it gently into place so it won't fall off. Broil a few inches from the heat source for 2 to 3 minutes, or until the cheese melts and is lightly golden. Serve right away.

GET CREATIVE

- Cook 1 or 2 slices of bacon (see page 233) or "veggie" bacon. Let it cool, crumble it, and sprinkle it over the potatoes before adding the cheese.

- Try various cheeses to find your favorite. Cheddar and Gruyère both work very well with spinach, and so do feta, Gouda, and many others. This is a fun way to experiment, and to make this slightly different each time.

- If you love things extra-cheesy, you can also stir a few tablespoons of grated cheese into the stuffing mixture and/or sprinkle a little more on top.

greek-style stuffed eggplant

Makes 4 main-dish servings, or 8 side dishes if you cut them in half

This a real crowd-pleaser—the kind of dish your friends will be flattered that you went to the trouble to prepare. But your secret will be that it's really not that much trouble. The flavor is complex, the texture is a combination of smooth, chewy, and crunchy in all the right ways, and the overall effect is one of celebration. This would be a great choice for someone's birthday dinner. Much of the preparation can be done in advance. You can even make and bake the eggplant 2 to 3 days ahead and store them, tightly wrapped in foil, in the refrigerator. They will reheat well, still wrapped in the foil, in a 300°F oven for 20 to 25 minutes.

2 medium eggplants (1 pound each)

2 tablespoons olive oil

1 medium red or yellow onion, diced

1 teaspoon dried basil

½ teaspoon dried oregano

½ teaspoon dried thyme

1 tablespoon minced garlic
(about 3 good-sized cloves)

1 medium bell pepper (any color),
chopped

½ teaspoon salt

One 15-ounce can diced tomatoes,
drained

One 12-ounce jar marinated
artichoke hearts, drained and
coarsely chopped

Heaping ½ cup crumbled feta
cheese

2 cups toasted breadcrumbs
(see page 81)

¼ teaspoon freshly ground black
pepper

⅓ cup pine nuts or chopped walnuts

1. Adjust the oven rack to the center position and preheat the oven to 350°F.

2. Carefully cut the eggplants in half lengthwise with a large, sharp knife. Try to get equal halves with clean edges.

3. Use a soup spoon or teaspoon to dig into the flesh of each eggplant half and scrape it out. You

will find that it comes out fairly easily, mostly in longish strips, once you get it started. Pull and scrape out the flesh, leaving a shell about ¼-inch thick. Set the eggplant shells aside.

4. Transfer the eggplant flesh to a cutting board, and chop it into roughly ½-inch pieces. Transfer the chopped eggplant to a bowl, and set aside.

5. Place a large (10- to 12-inch) heavy skillet over medium heat. After about a minute, add the olive oil and swirl to coat the pan. Add the onion and herbs, and cook over medium heat, stirring often, for about 5 minutes, or until the onion begins to soften. Stir in the garlic and cook for another minute. Then add the chopped eggplant, bell pepper, and salt. Stir until well combined, turning up the heat to medium-high. Continue to cook, stirring frequently, for 5 to 8 minutes, or until the eggplant is soft. Add the drained tomatoes and artichoke hearts, keeping the heat at medium-high. Stir and cook for 5 minutes longer. Don't cover the pan—you want the juices from all the vegetables to evaporate as much as possible.

6. Turn off the heat, and stir in the feta, breadcrumbs, and black pepper. Stir until thoroughly combined, then set aside until cool enough to handle comfortably.

7. Arrange the eggplant shells in a 9- by 13-inch baking pan, facing up as squarely as possible. (Ideally they will just fit, with the sides touching to prop one another up. It's okay if it

seems crowded—they will shrink a little while baking.) Divide the filling evenly among the 4 shells, pushing it gently into the cavities and mounding it with the back of a spoon. Cover the pan tightly with aluminum foil, and bake it in the oven for 45 minutes.

8. Remove the pan from the oven, and carefully (so as to avoid a steam burn) lift off the foil. Sprinkle the pine nuts or walnuts over the tops of the filled eggplant halves, and gently (and carefully) press them into place. Return the uncovered pan to the oven for another 15 minutes of baking. Serve hot or warm.

GET CREATIVE

- *Make this vegan by omitting the cheese.*

- A few handfuls of minced parsley added to the filling will add color and some flavor.

- Instead of breadcrumbs, you can use the same amount of cooked bulgur (see page 183), rice (see page 181), or orzo (rice-shaped pasta) for a heartier dish.

- Add ½ cup lightly toasted sunflower seeds to the filling, or sprinkle a few untoasted sunflower seeds on top instead of, or in addition to, the nuts.

- Red pepper flakes (a big pinch or two) will add some zing to the filling or just on top.

- Sprinkle with fresh basil and/or mint leaves, cut into strips, just before serving.

- Use crumbled goat cheese instead of feta for a slightly milder flavor.

chickpea and mango curry

Makes 4 servings

This is an impressively simple recipe with fabulous flavor. The first step is finding an excellent curry powder. Since curry is a blend of spices (usually turmeric, cumin, cardamom, mustard seed, and others) and no two are alike, the only way to know what one will taste like is to try it. When you find The One, stock up—even if it's just for this recipe. I predict you'll make it often. While fresh mango is wonderful, it's unpredictable in texture and yield, and the peeling and pitting makes for a fair amount of messy work. For a cooked recipe like this, I recommend using frozen mango chunks, one of my favorite convenience foods. They're not expensive, and they keep for months in your freezer. Just take whatever quantity you need out of the bag, close it up again, and put the bag back in the freezer. You don't even need to defrost the mango before adding it to this dish. In fact, if you let it defrost into the curry as it cooks, the resulting sauce will be that much better. This curry goes perfectly with basmati rice, so put some on to cook before you begin (see page 181).

1 tablespoon canola, soy,
  or peanut oil

1 teaspoon butter

1 medium red or yellow onion,
  diced

1 heaping tablespoon
  curry powder

½ teaspoon salt

Two 15-ounce cans chickpeas
  (about 3 cups cooked
  chickpeas)

2 heaping cups (about 12
  ounces) frozen mango chunks

A few dashes cayenne pepper

1. Place a large (10- to 12-inch) heavy skillet over medium heat. After about a minute, add the oil and swirl to coat the pan. Toss in the butter, and swirl until it melts into the oil. Add the onion, curry powder, and salt. Cook, stirring occasionally, for about 5 minutes, or until the onion begins to soften.

2. Meanwhile, set a colander in the sink and pour in the chickpeas; give them a quick rinse and allow them to drain.

3. Add the chickpeas to the skillet, stirring until they get completely coated with the onion and spices. Turn the heat to medium-low, and cook, stirring occasionally, for 5 minutes.

4. Stir in the mango and cover the pan. Let it cook on its own for another 5 minutes, then give it a stir. If it looks like it needs more "sauce," you can add up to ½ cup water. If you do, let it come to a boil, then turn the heat back down to low, cover the pan again, and cook slowly for an additional 10 minutes. (At this point, the curry benefits greatly from being allowed to just sit, covered, off the heat for 5 to 10 minutes. Not absolutely necessary, but this helps develop the flavor.)

5. Serve hot, over rice, topped with a fine dusting of cayenne.

GET CREATIVE

- *Make this vegan by replacing the butter with an extra tablespoon of oil.*

- If you can't find mangoes, you can substitute fresh or frozen peaches.

- Serve lime wedges on the side for squeezing on top.

- Garnish with a small amount of finely minced red onion or shallot.

- Add some chopped cilantro, mixing it in at the end of cooking and/or sprinkling it over each serving.

- Throw in a handful or two of fresh baby spinach leaves when you add the mango. It will cook in.

- Stir a large spoonful of yogurt into the sauce just before serving, or just top each serving with a small dollop.

- Add up to ½ cup canned coconut milk (light or regular) when you add the mango to make a rich, creamy sauce.

- Top each serving with whole or chopped toasted cashews or roasted peanuts.

vegetarian entrées. 119

thai green curry with coconut milk, vegetables, and tofu

Makes 4 servings

As ethnic food products become more readily available in supermarkets, it's easier than ever to make quite credible simulations of our favorite restaurant dishes at home for a fraction of the price. In the Thai arena, Thai Kitchen is among the best-known supermarket brands. I love their curry pastes that come in little jars; you can use just a bit (and be advised, "just a bit" packs quite a punch) and then simply screw the top back on and stick the jar in the refrigerator for next time. This recipe uses green curry paste, which is complex, authentic-tasting, and surprisingly fiery. All you do is whisk it into a blend of coconut milk and vegetable broth, add a few other touches of seasoning, and simmer vegetables directly in the sauce, so it's a one-pot wonder. (Actually two pots. You'll need to cook some basmati or jasmine rice ahead of time—see page 181.) Thai Kitchen also makes a fermented fish sauce, called *nam pla*. It's pungent and salty—a thin, clear, amber liquid made from fermented salted fish (usually anchovies) that adds another layer of complexity to the flavor. It keeps forever in your cupboard. If you don't have fish sauce, or you want to keep this totally vegan-vegetarian, you can substitute soy sauce.

This recipe is vegan if made with soy sauce instead of fish sauce.

2 teaspoons Thai green curry paste

One 14-ounce can coconut milk, light or regular (about 1¾ cups)

1½ cups vegetable broth or reconstituted bouillon

1 small slice lemon

2 to 3 tablespoons Thai fish sauce or soy sauce

½ medium red or yellow onion, diced

1 small yellow crookneck or summer squash, cut into ½-inch-thick slices

1 small zucchini, cut into ½-inch-thick slices

2 heaping cups cauliflower florets

2 heaping cups chopped broccoli

1 medium carrot, diced

½ pound small white mushrooms, cleaned, stem ends trimmed, mushrooms halved or left whole, depending on the size

Half a medium red bell pepper, diced

½ pound firm tofu, cut into ½-inch cubes

⅓ cup minced fresh cilantro

GET CREATIVE

- Add 1 tablespoon minced fresh ginger to the sauce along with the curry paste. Or add two slices of ginger (about ¼-inch-thick; no need to peel it) along with the curry paste; remove and discard the ginger slices just before serving.

- Add a handful of fresh basil leaves (regular or Thai basil), roughly chopped or sliced into strips, instead of, or in addition to, the cilantro.

- Top each serving with whole or chopped toasted cashews or roasted peanuts.

- Add other vegetables—for example, unpeeled slices of a long, thin eggplant, or some small chunks of peeled butternut squash or sweet potato.

1. Put the curry paste in a medium-large saucepan, add the coconut milk and broth or bouillon, and whisk until smooth. Add the lemon slice.

2. Set the pan over high heat and bring the mixture to a boil. Then turn the heat all the way down to the lowest possible setting and simmer gently, stirring occasionally, for 15 minutes. Between stirrings, keep the pan partially covered. About 10 minutes into the simmering, remove and discard the lemon slice.

3. Stir in the fish sauce or soy sauce, along with all the vegetables and the tofu. Bring it back to a boil. Then once again turn the heat all the way down to the lowest possible setting. Simmer, partially covered, for about 10 minutes, or until the vegetables are just tender. Stir in the cilantro at the very last minute, and serve hot, over rice.

vegetable-tofu stir-fry with orange-ginger glaze

Makes 4 servings

Stir-fry is about very high heat and cooking things quickly in a specific order so that every component ends up at just the right degree of doneness at the same time. There are two keys to this. First, have all of your ingredients prepped and close at hand. Second, read the recipe carefully and get a thorough sense of it before you start. The idea is that once you start cooking, it's continuous—you should never have to stop to search for something or read about what to do next. This beautiful, colorful, and gratifying dish was designed to give you the hang of stir-fry, and it will make you feel like an accomplished cook. There's a fair amount of preparation—mostly cutting vegetables, which is fun and quick if your knife is good and sharp. But you can do this prep a good hour ahead of time, and you can make the glaze up to several days in advance (store it in a tightly lidded jar in the refrigerator). Once all that's

done, the actual cooking time is just a matter of minutes.

A nice large wok and a metal wok spatula (the kind that looks like a shovel) are best for stir-frying, but a large deep skillet and a serving spoon will work well, too. The first step of this recipe, simmering the tofu for 10 minutes, is optional. I always do it because I like how it firms up the tofu, making it sturdier for stir-frying and a bit more satisfying to bite into. If you like softer tofu and/or want to save a step, just cut it into cubes, skip the simmering, and add it in as directed. Start some rice (see page 181) before you begin, so it will be ready to eat when the stir-fry is done.

the glaze

This recipe is vegan.

½ cup orange juice
   (from 1 medium orange)

2 tablespoons cider vinegar

1 tablespoon soy sauce

1 tablespoon light brown sugar or honey

1 tablespoon minced fresh ginger

2 teaspoons minced garlic
   (2 good-sized cloves)

1 teaspoon toasted sesame oil

½ teaspoon red pepper flakes

1 tablespoon cornstarch

the stir-fry

1 pound firm tofu, cut into ¾-inch cubes

2 tablespoons canola, soy, or peanut oil

1 medium red or yellow onion,
   cut into large (1½-inch) square pieces

¾ teaspoon salt

2 medium carrots,
   sliced ¼-inch thick on the diagonal

3 heaping cups cauliflower florets

3 heaping cups chopped broccoli

About 15 mushrooms,
   stems trimmed if necessary, quartered

2 small zucchini
   (preferably 1 yellow, 1 green),
   chopped or diced

1 medium red bell pepper,
   cut into 1-inch squares

1. Combine all the glaze ingredients except the cornstarch in a liquid measuring cup with a spout, and whisk until blended. Place the cornstarch in a small bowl and drizzle in about ¼ cup of the glaze, whisking constantly until the cornstarch is dissolved. (The mixture will be cloudy.) Pour this solution back into the measuring cup, whisking it in. Set aside, leaving the whisk in the cup.

2. Put a large pot of cold water to boil over high heat, and place a colander in the sink. When the water boils, add the tofu and reduce the heat to medium-low. Simmer the tofu for 10 minutes, then gently pour it into the colander and let it drain. Set aside.

3. Have all the cut-up vegetables and the simmered tofu in bowls or containers near the stove. Place a wok or a large, deep skillet over medium heat. After about a minute, add 1 tablespoon of the oil and swirl to coat the pan (or just push the oil around with a wok spatula or serving spoon). Turn the heat to high, add the onion and ¼ teaspoon of the salt, and stir-fry for 1 minute. Add the remaining 1 tablespoon oil, the carrots, cauliflower, and broccoli, and another ¼ teaspoon of the salt. Keeping the heat high and the vegetables moving, stir-fry for approximately 2 minutes, or until the broccoli turns bright green and shiny.

4. Add the mushrooms and tofu, and the remaining ¼ teaspoon salt. Keeping the heat high, continue to stir-fry for another minute, stirring all the vegetables up from the bottom of the pan. Add the zucchini and bell pepper, and cook for 1 minute more.

5. Whisk the glaze to reincorporate the cornstarch (it will have settled to the bottom), and then quickly pour the whole cupful into the wok or skillet. Cook, stirring, over high heat for just about 1 minute. The glaze will coat everything and thicken a little. Serve immediately, over rice.

GET CREATIVE

- Garnish with whole or chopped toasted cashews or roasted peanuts.

- Scatter some scallion greens, thinly sliced on the diagonal, over the finished dish.

- Throw in a handful of snow peas or sugar snap peas along with the bell pepper.

- Add up to ½ cup fresh or drained canned pineapple chunks along with the bell pepper.

- Add up to 1 tablespoon grated orange zest to the glaze (zest the orange before juicing it).

- You can fry the tofu until crisp after it's simmered: Pat it dry with towels. Heat a large nonstick skillet over medium-high heat for about a minute, then add 1 tablespoon canola, soy, or peanut oil and swirl to coat the pan. Fry the tofu, turning it occasionally, for about 5 minutes, or until it's brown on all sides. Sprinkle ¼ teaspoon garlic powder and 1 tablespoon soy sauce over the tofu, stir to coat evenly, and cook for another minute.

- Pass shaker bottles of soy sauce, chile oil, and toasted sesame oil at the table.

burgers.

How to Build a Burger

It's no accident that burgers have become the great American default meal. They're tasty, fast, portable, satisfying, inexpensive, and these days, whether you're eating out or grocery shopping, you can find a burger form and flavor for every style of eating, from ground beef to turkey to a wider range of meatless options than you might have imagined. If you love burgers and eat them often, over time, you'll save lots of money by making your own at home.

For the purposes of this chapter, I'm defining burgers as patties or cutlets that are cooked in a skillet and are perfect on a bun with the classic condiments—ketchup, mustard, mayo, pickles, relish, and the like. All of these recipes work well without the bun, too, simply served as an entrée with or without any of the suggested toppings.

TWO TOOLS FOR BURGER SUCCESS

A good heavy skillet is essential for making burgers. Avoid thin, lightweight frying pans, as they're likely to char the outside of the burger well before the inside is cooked. The perfect choice? A cast-iron skillet: heavy-bottomed, indestructible, and affordable.

A thin-bladed metal spatula will also make life easier (and your burgers better). Whether you go with a long curved-tip one (with a blade about the shape of a large tongue depressor) or a fish spatula (which has slots running up and down the blade), *thin* is the operative word. The narrower the blade, the easier it will be to maneuver the spatula around and under the burgers for checking doneness and flipping, as well as for scraping up the good stuff that sticks to the pan.

THE FIRE DRILL

Think of the heat at which you cook burgers—or any food—as part of the seasoning. It really does affect flavor and texture. So pay close attention to the heat level called for in these recipes, just as you would the amount of any ingredient. Keep an eye on the burgers and the burner, and adjust the heat if it looks like the browning is happening too quickly or too slowly.

For most burgers, it's a good idea to turn on the fan over the stove if you have one, and/or to open the nearest window, so you don't set off the smoke alarm.

If you have a gas or charcoal grill, by all means use it to cook the Excellent Homemade Hamburgers, the Turkey Burgers, and the Portobello Faux Burgers. Preheat the grill on high (or build a hot charcoal fire—meaning you can hold your hand a few inches above the grill grate for only 2 or 3 seconds, max), and cook the burgers or mushrooms for 4 to 5 minutes on each side. The rest of the burgers in this chapter are best made in a skillet as directed.

The beauty of burgers is that they're straightforward, simple, and self-contained. Experiment with seasonings, condiments, and different kinds of buns. You really can't go wrong. So, with that in mind, let's get flipping.

excellent homemade hamburgers

Makes 4 burgers

These are generous, juicy burgers. Dress them up right with a good roll and condiments, and you'll eat way better than you would at most burger joints. Keep some uncooked patties, well wrapped, in the freezer so you'll always have a fall-back plan for dinner. Look for chuck labeled 80/20 or 20% fat. It makes the juiciest, tastiest burgers. Any leaner and you'll be compromising the flavor. The onion is added for flavor more than texture and should be minced quite fine so it cooks at the same speed as the meat. Ground beef should be cooked all the way through until no longer pink inside. You can check by cutting into a patty with a sharp knife, or if you want to be absolutely sure, use an instant-read thermometer, slid several inches into the burger from the side (not the top). For beef burgers, it should register 160°F.

1 pound ground beef chuck

⅓ cup very finely minced red or
    yellow onion

½ teaspoon salt
    (plus extra for the pan)

Freshly ground black pepper

4 burger buns (optional)

Your favorite condiments
    (any combination of mayonnaise,
    mustard, ketchup, lettuce, onion,
    tomato, pickles)

1. Preheat the oven to 350°F or preheat the broiler (this is for the buns).

2. In a large bowl, combine the beef, onion, salt, and about ⅛ teaspoon black pepper. Use your hands to mix gently—just enough to combine. (Don't squeeze the mixture through your fingers. It will toughen the burgers.) Rinse your hands, wet your hands with cold water, and gently form 4 patties, each about ½-inch thick.

3. Place a large (10- to 12-inch) heavy skillet over medium heat. After about a minute, turn the heat to medium-high, sprinkle a little salt into the pan to make a light, even layer, and add the patties directly on top of the salt. Cook for 2 to 3 minutes on the first side, until deeply browned on the bottom (use a metal spatula to peek, disturbing the burgers as little as possible). If the burgers appear to be browning too quickly, reduce the heat to medium.

4. Use the metal spatula to carefully loosen each burger and flip it over. Cook on the second side for 2 to 3 minutes, or until the meat is no longer pink in the middle and the bottom surfaces are nicely browned.

5. Meanwhile, split the buns, put them on a baking sheet, cut side up, and heat them in the oven or slide them under the broiler to toast the cut sides. Watch carefully so they don't burn.

6. Spread the cut sides of the buns with some of your chosen condiments (the spreadable ones), put a burger patty on each bun bottom, and top with your other selected condiments (the sliced items) and a bun top. Serve right away.

- Add 2 tablespoons Worcestershire sauce to the mixture for a tangier, "steakier" taste.

- If you're craving Asian flavor, add 2 tablespoons bottled teriyaki sauce to the meat and replace the onion with finely minced scallions.

- For cheeseburgers, lay a slice of cheese over each patty as soon as you flip it. You can cover the skillet with a lid for a minute toward the end of cooking to help the cheese melt.

- Top with any of the classic restaurant add-ons, like bacon, crumbled bleu cheese, sautéed mushrooms, thinly sliced red onions (raw or sautéed), avocado, guacamole (store-bought or homemade—see page 224), salsa, or pesto (store-bought or homemade—see page 220).

BURGER BASICS

When making burgers, curb your enthusiasm. Handle the meat as little as possible, mixing it just until everything is combined. The more you work it, the tougher it will be. Shape burgers by forming flat disks, rather than making balls and smashing them down.

Resist the temptation to fiddle with burgers as they cook. They'll form a beautiful crust when simply left alone, so avoid moving them around in the pan. Peek at the undersides as un-invasively and infrequently as possible. And despite what you see short-order cooks doing, never press patties down with a spatula in the pan. That's a technique used to speed up cooking, but it toughens and compacts the meat, and squeezes out moisture you don't want to lose.

turkey burgers

Makes 4 burgers

G round turkey (white meat alone, or a combination of white and dark) is easy to find and very reasonably priced. You can keep it in the freezer until ready to use, so stock up, and you'll have this great dinner option on hand for when you need something simple and quick. (Defrost the meat thoroughly in the refrigerator, beginning a day ahead of time, before making the burgers.) Ground turkey cooks to a softer, more delicate texture than red meat, so egg is often added to help firm the patties up. Turkey burgers should be cooked all the way through until no longer pink inside. Check for doneness by cutting into a patty with a sharp knife, or if you want to be absolutely sure, use an instant-read thermometer, slid several inches into the burger from the side (not the top). For turkey burgers, it should register 170°F.

These patties freeze and reheat well *after* they've been cooked. Once you've cooked them, let them cool and then freeze them in a heavyweight resealable plastic bag. Reheat them in the micro-wave or in a small skillet over low heat.

1 large egg

½ cup very finely minced red
    or yellow onion

½ teaspoon salt

Freshly ground black pepper

1 pound ground turkey

1 to 2 tablespoons olive oil

4 burger buns (optional)

Your favorite condiments
    (any combination of
    mayonnaise, mustard,
    ketchup, lettuce, onion,
    tomato, pickles)

1. Preheat the oven to 350°F or preheat the broiler (this is for the buns).

2. Break the egg into a medium-large bowl and beat lightly with a fork. Add the onion, salt, and about ⅛ teaspoon pepper, and mix well. Add the turkey and mix lightly but thoroughly, using your hands. Rinse your hands, wet them with cold water, and gently form 4 patties, each about ½-inch thick.

3. Place a large (10- to 12-inch) heavy skillet over medium heat. After about a minute, add 1 tablespoon of the olive oil and swirl to coat the pan. Place the turkey burgers in the pan and cook, undisturbed, for 4 minutes, or until golden brown on the bottom.

4. Use a metal spatula to carefully loosen each burger and flip it over, adding a little more oil if the pan seems dry. Cook on the second side for about 4 minutes, or until the undersides are nicely browned.

5. Meanwhile, split the buns, put them on a baking sheet, cut side up, and heat them in the oven or slide them under the broiler to toast the cut sides. Watch carefully so they don't burn.

6. Spread the cut sides of the buns with some of your chosen condiments (the spreadable ones), put a burger patty on each bun bottom, and top with your other selected condiments (the sliced items) and a bun top. Serve right away.

GET CREATIVE

- You can add up to ⅓ cup toasted breadcrumbs (see page 81) to give the burgers more a bit heft.

- Add a few tablespoons of chopped fresh parsley or chives to give the burgers more color and flavor.

- Add ½ teaspoon dried oregano and ½ teaspoon dried mint to make a Mediterranean-style burger. Serve in pita breads spread with hummus (store-bought or homemade—see page 226) or yogurt.

- For a change of pace, these can be formed into 1½-inch-diameter meatballs. (For meatball cooking directions, see page 71.) Serve in pita breads spread with hummus (store-bought or homemade—see page 226) or yogurt, or spear with toothpicks and serve as a party snack.

- Top with pickled peppers and fresh avocado slices, plus a dab of mayo and/or salsa.

- Serve with cranberry sauce and chopped toasted pecans.

- Top with any of the classic restaurant add-ons, like bacon, crumbled bleu cheese, sautéed mushrooms, thinly sliced red onions (raw or sautéed), avocado, guacamole (store-bought or homemade—see page 224), salsa, or pesto (store-bought or homemade—see page 220).

salmon burgers

Makes 4 burgers

Here's a tasty way to enjoy your salmon without breaking the bank. You might be surprised to discover that most canned salmon is made from high-quality wild salmon, and if you are concerned about over-fishing, this is a great way to extend a modest quantity of fish into a great entrée. When you open a can of salmon, you'll see that most of it looks attractive, but some parts may look a bit, well, sketchy. This would be bits of skin, bones, and fat. No worries. It's all nutritious, and the canning process makes it all edible, so you can just mix these parts in and they won't be noticeable in the finished burgers.

These patties freeze and reheat well *after* they've been cooked. Once you've cooked them, let them cool and then freeze them in a heavyweight resealable plastic bag. Reheat them in the microwave or in a small skillet over low heat.

Two 7.5-ounce cans salmon

½ cup toasted breadcrumbs (see page 81)

2 large eggs, well beaten

3 tablespoons very finely minced red
    or yellow onion

¼ teaspoon salt

¼ teaspoon freshly ground black pepper

1 to 2 tablespoons olive oil

Lemon wedges

1. Open each can of salmon and use the lid to press the salmon down in the can as you tilt it over the sink until most of the liquid has drained out. Put the salmon in a medium-large bowl. Using a fork or your clean fingers, flake the salmon into small pieces. Add the breadcrumbs, eggs, onion, salt, and pepper, and mix until thoroughly combined.

2. Divide the mixture into 4 equal portions and shape them into patties, each a generous ½-inch thick.

3. Place a large (10- to 12-inch) heavy skillet over medium heat. After about a minute, add 1 tablespoon of the olive oil and swirl to coat the pan. Place the salmon patties in the pan and cook, undisturbed, for 3 to 4 minutes, or until golden brown on the bottom.

4. Use a metal spatula to carefully loosen each burger and flip it over, adding more oil if the pan seems dry. Cook on the second side for about 3 minutes, or until the undersides are nicely browned. Serve each burger with a wedge of lemon.

GET CREATIVE

- Add up to ½ teaspoon dried dill or tarragon (or 2 teaspoons minced fresh) to the mix.

- These are great on their own as an entrée, or you can give them the burger treatment and serve them on a toasted soft bun with mayo or tartar sauce, lettuce, tomato, and thinly sliced cucumbers.

- Serve on a plate, topped with a generous dollop of Shortcut "Hollandaise" (page 161).

- Top with avocado slices, bacon, and crumbled bleu cheese and serve on warm ciabatta bread or a burger bun.

- Serve topped with marinated artichoke hearts (drained, direct from the jar).

tuna burgers

Makes 4 burgers

This recipe is very similar to the one for salmon burgers, with just a few changes to accommodate the different flavor of the fish. Look for light tuna canned in olive oil—it's tastier and moister (and usually less expensive) than white tuna packed in water, although either kind will work.

These patties freeze and reheat well *after* they've been cooked. Once you've cooked them, let them cool and then freeze them in a heavyweight resealable plastic bag. Reheat them in the microwave or in a small skillet over low heat.

Two 6-ounce cans tuna

⅓ cup toasted breadcrumbs
   (see page 81)

¼ cup very finely minced red or
   yellow onion

2 large eggs, well beaten

A small handful of finely minced parsley

¼ teaspoon (a few squirts)
   fresh lemon juice

⅛ teaspoon freshly ground black pepper

1 to 2 tablespoons olive oil

Lemon wedges

1. Open each can of tuna and use the lid to press the tuna down in the can as you tilt it over the sink until most of the liquid has drained out. Put the tuna in a medium-large bowl. Using a fork or your clean fingers, flake the tuna into small pieces. Add the breadcrumbs, onion, eggs, parsley, lemon juice, and pepper, and mix until thoroughly combined.

2. Divide the mixture into 4 equal portions and shape them into patties, each a generous ½-inch thick.

3. Place a large (10- to 12-inch) heavy skillet over medium heat. After about a minute, add 1 tablespoon of the olive oil and swirl to coat the pan. Place the tuna patties in the pan and cook, undisturbed, for 3 to 4 minutes, or until golden brown on the bottom.

4. Use a metal spatula to carefully loosen each burger and flip it over, adding a little more oil if the pan seems dry. Cook on the second side for about 3 minutes, or until the undersides are nicely browned. Serve immediately, accompanied by a wedge of lemon.

- You can serve these "as is" with lemon wedges and tartar sauce on the side, or turn them into burgers by serving them on toasted soft rolls or English muffins, with mayo, lettuce, tomato, and thinly sliced cucumbers.

- To make tuna melts, top each burger with a slice of Swiss or jack cheese while the second side is cooking.

- To take these in a Japanese direction, add a teaspoon of teriyaki sauce to the patty mixture. Spread some mayonnaise and wasabi (Japanese green horseradish) on a toasted sesame roll, then add a tuna burger and top with pickled ginger (the kind served with sushi, sold in Asian groceries).

very crisp panko-coated
eggplant cutlets

Makes 4 to 6 servings

Thick rounds of eggplant with a crisp coating and meltingly tender insides make really good cutlets that you can eat burger-style on a bun or just serve on a plate. Look for a big, round eggplant with a shape that will yield the most uniform round slices. The skin should be tight and shiny with no wrinkles, soft spots, or blemishes, because you won't be peeling the eggplant. You'll need to cook these in batches, so I've included directions for keeping the first batch warm in the oven. If you have two good heavy skillets, you can get them both going at the same time to speed things up. Just be sure to keep an eye on the undersides of all the cutlets as they cook, and adjust the heat accordingly.

1 large eggplant (about 1¾ pounds)

2 large eggs

1 teaspoon water

1 cup panko (Japanese-style
   breadcrumbs—see page 163)

1 teaspoon salt

⅛ teaspoon freshly ground black pepper

3 to 4 tablespoons olive oil

1. Preheat the oven to 250°F. Set up a rack in a baking tray on which you can put the cooked cutlets.

2. Slice off and discard the eggplant top and bottom. Use a sharp knife to cut the eggplant crosswise into ½-inch-thick slices. You should end up with 12 to 14 rounds.

3. Break the eggs into a pie pan, then beat with a fork or a small whisk, adding the teaspoon of water as you go. When the eggs become smooth, stop beating and set aside.

4. Combine the panko, salt, and pepper on a dinner plate. Have a second dinner plate (or two) ready to hold the coated eggplant slices. Have some damp paper towels ready, as well, to wipe your hands as needed.

5. One at a time, dip the eggplant slices into the egg and then let any excess egg drip off back into the pie pan. Put the moistened slice into the panko mixture, pressing it down firmly so the crumbs will adhere. Then turn it over, and press the second side into the crumbs until it becomes completely coated all over. Shake off any extra panko mixture, and transfer the coated slice to the clean plate.

6. Place a large (10- to 12-inch) heavy skillet over medium heat. After about a minute, add about a tablespoon of the olive oil and swirl to coat the pan.

7. Carefully transfer the coated eggplant slices (as many as will fit in a single layer) to the hot pan. Cook, undisturbed, for 4 to 5 minutes, or until golden brown on the bottom.

8. Use a metal spatula to carefully loosen each piece, keeping its coating intact (you don't want to lose any of it to the pan). Flip it over, and cook on the second side for 4 to 5 min-

utes, until the coating is evenly golden all over and the eggplant is fork-tender. (You might need to drizzle in additional olive oil as you go, if the pan seems dry or the coating starts sticking to the pan.)

9. Transfer the cooked slices to the rack in the baking tray, and put the tray in the oven to keep them warm while you repeat the cooking process with the remaining slices. Serve as soon as possible.

GET CREATIVE

- *Make this vegan by using ½ cup plain soy milk in place of the eggs and water.*

- Add up to 1½ teaspoons Italian seasoning (or a combination of dried thyme, basil, and oregano) to the panko for extra flavor.

- Add up to ¼ cup grated Parmesan cheese to the panko to make the crust crisper and more flavorful.

- Scatter some grated mozzarella and Parmesan cheese over the cooked cutlets, and melt briefly under the broiler (or in the toaster oven, on the broil setting). Serve with marinara sauce for an easy eggplant Parmesan effect.

- Serve on a plate or a toasted soft roll with pesto (store-bought or homemade—see page 220) or mayo mixed with a bit of pesto. You can also add a dollop of tomato sauce for color and flavor contrast.

black bean burgers

Makes 4 burgers

No, not the Texas-style bean burger, which is a beef burger smothered in refried beans, tortilla chips, and Cheez Whiz. This is a literal bean burger made from actual beans. Far from tasting like bland hippie food from the '70s, these are full of assertive flavor, creamy on the inside and wonderfully crisp on the outside. The batter is quite soft, so you'll need to form the patties directly in the pan, using a spoon to keep things neat and intact. To save on cleanup, use the same skillet for sautéing the onions and cooking the burgers.

These patties freeze and reheat well *after* they've been cooked. Once you've cooked them, let them cool and then freeze them in a heavyweight resealable plastic bag. Reheat them in the microwave or in a small skillet over low heat.

2 to 3 tablespoons olive oil

½ cup finely minced red or yellow onion

Two 15-ounce cans black beans (about 3 cups cooked beans)

1 large egg, well beaten

1 cup toasted breadcrumbs (see page 81)

2 teaspoons ground cumin

2 teaspoons minced garlic (about 2 good-sized cloves)

Scant ½ teaspoon salt

⅛ teaspoon freshly ground black pepper (or more, to taste)

1. Place a large (10- to 12-inch) heavy skillet over medium heat. After about a minute, add 1 tablespoon of the olive oil and swirl to coat the pan. Add the onion, and cook in the center of the pan, stirring often, for 3 to 4 minutes, or until the onion softens. Set aside to cool slightly.

2. Set a colander in the sink and pour in the beans; give them a quick rinse and allow them to drain thoroughly. Transfer the drained beans to a medium-large bowl, and use a potato masher or fork to mash them as smooth as possible. Stir in the beaten egg, breadcrumbs, cumin, garlic, salt, and pepper. Scrape in the cooled onion, and mix until thoroughly combined.

3. Wipe out the skillet with a paper towel, and then return the skillet to medium heat. After about a minute, add 1 tablespoon of the olive oil

- *Make this vegan by omitting the egg. It will not hold together too well, but it will still taste good.*

- Add ½ cup minced walnuts to the batter for flavor, texture, and a little extra protein.

- One teaspoon of chili powder added to the batter will give these burgers a nice hit of heat.

- Add a teaspoon of soy sauce to the batter for a meatier flavor.

- A handful of minced cilantro mixed into the batter will freshen up the flavor.

- Top with shredded jack or Cheddar cheese while the second side is cooking.

- Serve on a toasted soft roll with mayonnaise, minced cilantro, salsa, lettuce, and tomato.

- Serve open-face on a warmed corn or flour tortilla, topped with guacamole (store-bought or homemade— see page 224) or avocado slices, sour cream, salsa, and a scattering of cilantro leaves, with tortilla chips on the side. You can also crumble on some queso fresco (a crumbly white Mexican cheese) or goat cheese.

and swirl to coat the pan. Use a large spoon to scoop 4 equal mounds of the bean mixture into the hot pan, and then, with the back of the spoon, flatten and push each one into a patty about ½-inch thick and 3½ inches in diameter. Cook, undisturbed, for about 3 minutes, or until golden brown on the bottom.

4. Use a metal spatula to carefully loosen each burger and flip it over, adding a little more oil if the pan seems dry. (If the burger falls apart as you turn it, don't worry. Just push it back into shape and keep cooking.) Cook on the second side for about 3 minutes, or until the undersides are nicely browned. Serve immediately.

portobello faux burgers

Makes 4 "burgers"

Portobello mushrooms are about as meaty as the vegetable kingdom gets, and their shape, size, texture, and flavor make them a perfect natural burger alternative. These are cooked under the broiler, making them super-easy. Just keep an eye on them as they broil, so the tops don't burn. The secret of their greatness is all in the marinade—a bold mixture of balsamic vinegar, garlic, and olive oil. You might think that, like a sponge, the mushrooms would plump up as they absorb it, but surprisingly, the salt drains out some of their moisture, causing them to shrink and firm up a bit as they take on more and more flavor. An hour of marinating is a must, but the longer the better. I once let them soak for an entire week, and they were amazingly flavorful. So if you like, you can marinate a batch and cook one or two mushrooms at a time over the course of a few meals, leaving the uncooked ones to bathe in the marinade.

This recipe is vegan.

⅓ cup balsamic vinegar

½ cup olive oil

1½ teaspoons minced garlic
(about 2 medium-sized cloves)

½ teaspoon dried rosemary,
or 2 teaspoons chopped fresh
rosemary

½ teaspoon dried thyme,
or 2 teaspoons minced fresh thyme

1 teaspoon salt

⅛ teaspoon freshly ground black pepper

4 portobello mushrooms
(4 to 5 inches in diameter)

1. In a small bowl, or in a jar with a tight-fitting lid, combine the vinegar, oil, garlic, rosemary, thyme, salt, and pepper; whisk or shake to combine.

2. Carefully (so as not to tear the mushroom caps) pull off and discard the mushroom stems. Place the mushroom caps in a large flat dish (a medium-sized baking pan will work well) with their tops facing up. Pour about a table-spoon of the marinade over each top to cover them. Turn the mushrooms over and divide the rest of the marinade evenly among them. Let the mushrooms sit at room temperature for at least an hour, or cover the dish tightly with plastic wrap and refrigerate overnight.

3. Shortly before serving time, preheat the boiler.

4. Lift the mushrooms out of their marinating dish (leave the marinade behind) and without turning them over, transfer them to a foil-lined ovenproof dish or rimmed baking tray. Broil for 5 to 8 minutes, or until the mushrooms are heated through and the tops are nicely browned. (You don't need to flip them.) Serve right away.

GET CREATIVE

- About halfway through the broiling process, sprinkle the tops with a little grated mozzarella and/or Parmesan cheese, and then continue broiling until the cheese melts and turns a light golden brown.

- Instead of broiling, you can cook the mushrooms in the microwave. This will take only about 1 minute. The flavor will be less toasty and intense, and the texture will be moist, but they'll still be very good.

- You can serve these just like burgers—on toasted buns or soft rolls with lettuce, tomato, and the classic toppings.

- Leftover broiled mushrooms make a great room-temperature sandwich for tomorrow's bag lunch.

- Top with a thick slice of red onion, also broiled or seared quickly on both sides in a little olive oil in a skillet over very high heat.

spice-crusted tofu cutlets

Makes 4 cutlets

Unlike packaged tofu burgers, which are often a mysterious mélange of beige ingredients, these cutlets are slabs of pure tofu, coated heavily with spice and cooked in the Cajun "blackened" way by searing them in a hot pan with no oil. The result is a terrific contrast between a smoky, crisp flavorful outer surface and a creamy pure interior. (Note that they won't actually turn black, but more of a deep, dark golden brown.) I like to make this with a spice mix called *za'atar*, which is a Middle Eastern blend. You can make your own or buy it ready-made at some specialty foods stores and supermarkets. You can also use a store-bought Cajun spice blend, or work up your own secret mix, using the *za-atar* recipe below as a starting point.

I always simmer firm tofu before cooking with it. This firms up its proteins and cooks out excess water (similar to pressing it under weights overnight, as many recipes suggest, but quicker—and I like the texture better this way).

This recipe is vegan.

1 pound very firm tofu,
    cut into 4 slices, each about
    ¾-inch thick

za-atar spice mix

3 tablespoons sesame seeds

1 teaspoon dried thyme

1 teaspoon dried marjoram or
    oregano

¼ teaspoon garlic powder

¼ teaspoon freshly ground black
    pepper

¾ teaspoon salt

⅛ teaspoon red pepper flakes

1. Put a medium-large pot of water to boil over high heat, and place a colander in the sink. When the water boils, turn the heat to low and add the 4 slices of tofu. Simmer for 10 minutes. Then gently slip the tofu into the colander to drain, being careful not to break the slices.

2. Meanwhile, combine the spice mix ingredients in a small bowl. Pour the mix into a pie pan and spread it out.

3. Turn on the stove fan and/or open the kitchen window (this process can create a fair amount of smoke). Place a large (10- to 12-inch) heavy skillet over medium heat and wait for about a minute.

4. While the pan is heating, carefully place one of the tofu slices in the spice mix, patting it down

GET CREATIVE

- There will be a lot of flavor left in the pan. You can retrieve it (this is called deglazing) by pouring in 1 to 2 tablespoons olive oil (be very careful pouring it in—it will sizzle) and stirring it so the oil picks up all the leftover spice mix. Spoon this over the tops of the cutlets for a delightful finish.

- You can serve these on toasted burger buns or soft rolls with lettuce, tomato, and mayonnaise.

- They're also wonderful on toasted split baguettes with a thick layer of hummus (store-bought or homemade—see page 226). Garnish with parsley, sliced cucumbers, and cherry tomatoes. (NOTE: The reddish spread under the cutlet in the photo is hummus blended with tomatoes.)

- Use the cutlets just as you would use a grilled chicken breast—sliced into strips to top a Caesar Salad (page 44) or a green salad, rolled in a tortilla with rice and beans to make a wrap, or in a bag-lunch sandwich.

to coat one side; then sprinkle the mix on top and pat it on with your fingers to coat the surface evenly. Transfer the slice to a plate and repeat with the other 3 slices. Some of the coating may fall off; try to sprinkle as much of it as you can back onto the tofu, using up all of the mixture.

5. Gently transfer the tofu slices to the hot pan, and let them cook, undisturbed, for about 2 minutes, or until they are golden underneath.

6. Use a thin-bladed metal spatula to carefully loosen each cutlet and gently flip it over. Cook on the second side for 2 minutes, or until the undersides are nicely browned. (If some of the spice mix falls off, scoop it up with the spatula and put it back on. Most of it will stick. You can also push some of the fallen spice mix onto the sides of the tofu slices.)

7. Transfer the cooked cutlets to serving plates, and serve right away.

chicken, fish, and meat.

Chicken, Fish, Meat, and You

When it comes to pure protein, we've all got our favorite sources. This chapter is for those of you who enjoy chicken, fish, shrimp, and red meat.

Now, most of you who love animal-based proteins, I'm guessing, also love this planet and want to live in a way that respects the environment. And no doubt you've heard about the links between livestock raising and global warming. Well, there are two things you can do about this without giving up meat altogether. You can eat it less often (and eat smaller servings of it when you do), and you can also do your best to purchase meat that has been responsibly, sustainably, and, if possible, locally raised.

Find a good meat, poultry, and seafood market with a knowledgeable staff whom you can trust for recommendations. The prices may be a bit higher than what you'd find at the supermarket, but for good reason. You're getting what you pay for, and this will help you make a new pledge to yourself: "Self, from now on, quality will always trump quantity when it comes to meat (and all food choices, for that matter)." And that said, small butchers tend to feature great specials on whatever they're trying to sell quickly, so keep your eyes peeled.

HERE'S THE (GRASS-FED) BEEF

If you secretly love a few bites of a good steak but avoid it for fear that it is bad for you (or that you will be stigmatized for this weakness of character), here is some good news. Grass-fed beef can be a very clean and healthy choice, and assuming you are willing to shop carefully and spend a little more on the meat that comes from pasture-raised, grass-fed cattle, you are in for a treat. It tastes really good, and when eaten in modest amounts it can provide you with a much lower dose of both overall fat and saturated fat compared with other beef, and—surprise!—it also delivers a significant amount of healthy omega-3 fatty acids (the terrific-for-you kind found in wild salmon and flax seed) and a nice hit of vitamins A and E as well. Why does this kind of beef stack up so well? Because unlike the starchy, low-fiber corn and soybeans that are the mainstay of feedlot cattle (and are accompanied by frightening doses of antibiotics that help Bossie assimilate this otherwise indigestible-to-her stuff), grass provides a low-starch, high-protein, high-fiber diet that translates into healthier cows. They are also likely to be happier, because they get to wander around outside, rather than being cooped up for months in a tightly packed, unclean confinement. And they tend not to become afflicted with E. coli and other toxicity, because they are eating their original pre-industrial-age diet, and they stay healthier and in better balance (and better immunity) this way.

BUYING MEAT

Shop at a busy market to get the freshest product. Raw meat should be moist but not wet or sticky, and should have no off-putting odor. Avoid anything with extra liquid in the package. The meat should be bright red, with white fat on the edge and running though the meat. (Some fat running around the edge of a steak is a good thing; it helps hold the meat together and flavors it. If you don't want to eat it, cut it off with a sharp paring knife *after* the meat is cooked. Marbling, the fat that runs across the interior of a cut of meat in thin lines, is also a good thing, adding juiciness, tenderness, and flavor.)

For your basic pan-cooked, broiled, or grilled steak, you want cuts that are tender and have good flavor, the best of which come from the rib and the loin. The New York strip and rib-eye are good one-person steaks. Tenderloin steaks (filet mignons) are pricy and very tender but don't have as much flavor as a strip or rib-eye. The T-bone and porterhouse are big luxury cuts with a T-shaped bone that separates what are actually two steaks: on one side of the bone is a New York strip, on the other, a tenderloin (the porterhouse has a bigger tenderloin piece). The bone gives T-bones (and any bone-in steak or chop) more flavor during cooking.

On the somewhat tougher but very flavorful side, flank steak and skirt steak (both best when marinated) are good choices, as is the large, thick London broil, which is very lean and should be cooked rare and sliced very thin.

"Prime" is the top USDA grade for meat, then "Choice," then "Select." The lower the grade, the less marbling the meat will have, and thus the less flavor and tenderness. "Select" is typical supermarket meat-case fare, but it can be delicious, especially if you marinate it.

BUYING FISH AND SEAFOOD

Buy fish from a reputable store where they can tell you its source and how it was caught. Check out seafoodwatch.org for guidelines on buying sustainable seafood—there's even an iPhone application, so you can get a read on what you're buying while you're at the store.

Really fresh fish will never smell fishy. Rather, it should smell like the ocean. The flesh should be glossy and firm with no dark spots, mushiness, or separation. Your best bet is always simply to start by asking, "What's fresh?"

BUYING POULTRY

Here again, go with a trusted source—a good market committed to offering sustainable/organic local options. Try to get poultry that has been pasture-raised, which means the chickens get to walk—or whatever they do—around outside, pecking their food. And ideally, that food they're pecking at is healthy, organic, and hormone-free. Your purveyor will tell you, so always ask. Or, if you shop in a supermarket, check out specialty brands that are sustainably produced. Look for poultry that is plump, with creamy-yellow skin and no strong odors.

STORING

There's a reason your refrigerator has a meat compartment: It's generally colder in there, and that's where meat, seafood, and poultry fare best. If you don't have one, go with the coldest part of refrigerator, which is usually toward the bottom. Keep meat and poultry in the refrigerator for no more than 3 to 4 days, seafood for only a day or two. Or wrap meat or poultry very well, put it in a resealable freezer bag, mark the date on the outside, and freeze it for up to 3 months.

HANDLING

When handling raw meat, seafood, and poultry, you want to keep things cold and clean to avoid any possibility of bacterial contamination. It's a good idea to designate a separate cutting board (preferably not made from wood) just for meat, poultry, and seafood (you can even mark one side for just seafood and poultry and the other for meat). Wash the board well in hot soapy water (or, even better, in the dishwasher if the cutting board is dishwasher-safe), and be careful to clean up well after you finish your prep. That means washing your hands thoroughly, as well as the countertop, your knives, and any other implements you've used.

MENU PLANNING

Menu planning around a main dish of meat, poultry, or fish generally means giving some thought to side dishes—a potato, rice, or grain dish, plus a vegetable or two and maybe a salad—so check out the recipes in those chapters and plan accordingly. You may need to get potatoes or rice cooked ahead of time, and you want to factor in your vegetable preparation as well in putting together the meal. Don't stress about the timing, though. Most things that are good hot are also good

mostly hot or even warm, so do your best to coordinate (sit down and think it through first)—but beyond that, just do what works and enjoy.

EASY MEETS TASTY AND AFFORDABLE

My choice of recipes for this chapter was based first and foremost on their high simplicity-to-deliciousness ratio, with an eye toward keeping things affordable. We're working with reasonably priced cuts of meat and types of fish here, not the high-end stuff. But the good news is, some of the best flavor lives at that low end of the price spectrum. "Give me a brisket over a filet mignon any day," say my meat-appreciating friends, and I know they're talking about the meat itself and not just the price.

Many of these recipes work well as tonight's dinner plus leftovers to be chilled and turned into other meals, and you'll find lots of suggestions along those lines. So even if you're cooking for one, prepare the full recipe and you can "bank" a second or third meal while you're at it. Leftover meat and chicken are great added to other things, like salads (lay thin strips or chunks on top), soups, rice and grains (cut the meat into small pieces and stir it in toward the end of cooking), tacos, omelets, and quesadillas.

COOKING IT RIGHT

Most of the meat and fish included here is cooked in a skillet on the stovetop. Find and adopt a favorite "meat skillet"—a big, wide frying pan made out of heavy material. I vote for cast iron, which is indestructible and remarkably inexpensive, especially when purchased at a garage sale or a thrift store. Some people insist that a cast-iron pan needs to be seasoned—a process involving heating it with oil. Others, including me, believe that all you need to do is dry it very thoroughly after each use, so it doesn't rust. A good way to do this is to heat the clean, well-rinsed, wiped-dry pan for a few minutes over low heat on the stove. Just don't walk away and forget to take it off the heat.

Avoid thin-bottomed pans for cooking meat. You'll end up browning the outside long before the inside is done. Heavier pans, on the other hand, distribute the heat more evenly and gradually.

You'll sometimes need a lid for your meat skillet, but it doesn't have to actually match. Any lid that's a reasonably snug fit is fine.

CHECKING DONENESS

These recipes all include ways to check for doneness. The most reliable of these is using an instant-read thermometer. If you're new to meat cooking, do yourself a favor and buy one. You can find an inexpensive version in the cooking supplies section of any supermarket. Just make sure what you're buying is an *instant-read* thermometer—a needle-like probe with a point at one end and a dial or digital readout at the other. Most measure temperatures from 0° to 220°F. (What you're *not* looking for here is a candy/deep-frying

thermometer, which will have a bigger probe and measures higher temperatures, typically up to 400°F; a meat thermometer, which gets inserted in the raw meat and stays in throughout the cooking process; or an oven thermometer, which is a dial with no probe that sits or hangs in your oven.)

The concept with an instant-read thermometer, as the name suggests, is that you use it to take the temperature of cooked meat simply by inserting it, waiting a few seconds, reading the dial, and then removing it. Always insert the probe lengthwise so you get as much of it into the meat as you can; aim for the center of the thickest part of the meat and avoid any bones, which can give you a false reading. If, after you read the temperature, you find that whatever you're preparing needs more cooking time (see "When Is It Done?" on the following page), take the thermometer out and reinsert it when you're ready to check for doneness again.

GIVE IT A REST

When you cook meat, there's an important step that happens after it comes out of the pan or off the grill. It's called "resting," and it simply means letting the meat sit (on a plate with a rim to catch any juices) for 5 to 10 minutes before you serve it. During cooking, the outer surface of the meat dries out and tightens up, and the juices migrate toward the center. Cut the meat open the minute it's cooked, and it'll gush juices from the center—not a good thing. Let it rest, and the outer surfaces will "relax" and reabsorb their juices, making the meat juicier and more tender throughout. Note that during resting, even at room temperature, the meat will continue to cook a bit and the internal temperature is likely to rise by around 5°F, so factor that in when you first check the temperature for doneness.

Okay, omnivores, carnivores, piscivores, and "poultrivores." Let's get meating!

WHEN IS IT DONE?

STEAK	**120°–125°F** = rare
	130°–135°F = medium-rare
	140°F = medium
	150°F = medium-well or well-done
GROUND MEAT	Cook to **160°F**
CHICKEN AND TURKEY	Cook to **165°F** for white meat **170°F** for dark meat
PORK	Cook to at least **140°F**
FISH	Cook to **140°F**

Note that for food-safety reasons, most sources recommend cooking meat to at least 145°F.

baked cut-up chicken with fruit

Makes 4 to 5 servings

I recommend this recipe for absolute beginners. Very little cutting or fussing is required, and the fruit, onion, garlic, and chicken juices come together on their own to create a sweet, succulent dish. It takes some time to bake, so plan accordingly. But there's no work involved during that time, except occasionally basting the chicken. Try to get an organic orange for this—a particularly good idea when a recipe includes the peel. A blood orange, which is dark sangria-red on the inside, looks especially lovely. The various dried fruits are negotiable. If you can't find (or don't love) any of them, you can swap in more of the ones you prefer. That said, I have to tell you that the combination as written is delicious, and worth trying once. You'll be surprised at how everything gets transformed as it all bakes together. And if you adore fruit and want to add more, don't hold back. You can really pack it into the pan!

One 3- to 4-pound cut-up chicken

½ teaspoon salt

¼ teaspoon freshly ground black pepper

1 teaspoon mild paprika

1 medium red or yellow onion

8 to 10 good-sized cloves garlic, peeled (left whole)

Approximately 20 of each:

- Dried apricots

- Pitted dried plums (prunes)

- Dried figs (stems trimmed off and discarded)

1 blood orange or navel orange

1. Adjust the oven rack to the center position and preheat the oven to 375°F.

2. Rinse the chicken pieces under cold running water, then pat dry with paper towels. If there is any extraneous fat here or there, you can trim it off with scissors and throw it away. Arrange the chicken pieces, skin side up, in a 9- by 13-inch baking pan.

3. Combine the salt, pepper, and paprika in a small bowl, and then sprinkle this mixture over the chicken. Use your fingers to rub it into the skin on as much surface area as possible.

4. Cut the ends off the onion, peel it, and cut it in half lengthwise (from root end to stem end). Lay each half, cut side down, on a cutting board, and cut it lengthwise into ¼-inch-thick slices. Scatter the onion and the garlic cloves over the chicken, and then scatter the dried fruit over the chicken, packing it into the spaces between the pieces and letting some of it land on top.

5. Leaving the peel on, cut the orange in half lengthwise (from top to bottom). Lay each half on the cutting board and cut it crosswise into ¼-inch-thick half-moons. Scatter the orange slices over the chicken, and cover the pan tightly with aluminum foil. Bake, undisturbed, for 1 hour.

6. Remove the pan from the oven, and very carefully lift the foil (the accumulated steam can be hot enough to burn you). Flip the chicken pieces over, using tongs or a fork. Using a mitt or a pot holder, tilt the pan slightly with one hand, and using a baster or a large spoon, baste the juices over both chicken and fruit with the other hand. This distributes and mingles the flavors as well as the moisture, yielding delicious results. If any of the fruit looks dry at this point, or at subsequent bastings, just push it down into the juices.

7. Cover the pan tightly with the foil again, and return it to the oven for another 20 minutes of undisturbed baking.

8. Repeat the basting procedure, and then flip the chicken pieces back to skin-side-up position. Return the pan to the oven (without covering it this time) and bake for another 10 to 15 minutes, or until the chicken is golden on top.

9. Remove the pan from the oven, baste the chicken and fruit a few more times, and then tent it loosely with foil. Let it rest for about 10 minutes.

10. Serve hot or warm, being sure to include a generous portion of fruit with each serving.

A CUT-UP CHICKEN

Buying chicken already cut into individual pieces saves time and makes cooking easier. Look for cut-up chickens in the poultry case of the supermarket, or better yet, go to a butcher shop or a market with working butchers, where you can buy a whole chicken and get it cut up to order. If you go this route, ask the butcher to cut each breast half into two pieces, which makes for easier serving and eating.

HOW ABOUT THOSE GIBLETS?

Whole chickens are often sold with the giblets (the liver, heart, and gizzards) and neck stuffed inside the bird in a little plastic bag. You can cook the liver in a hot skillet with a little olive oil, sprinkle it with salt and pepper, and enjoy it as a snack. As for the rest, you can make a simple broth by simmering them in a small pot in water to cover. This broth can then be combined with the pan juices after cooking to make a light sauce. Or simply toss the giblets and neck in the roasting pan and let them cook along with the chicken so they add some flavor to the pan juices. Then discard them when you collect and skim the juices.

GET CREATIVE

• For a more exotic Middle Eastern flavor, you can add either a tablespoon of *za'atar* spice mix (see page 142), or 2 teaspoons ground cumin plus ½ teaspoon cinnamon.

• Serve with additional fresh orange slices, plus a few lemon wedges so you can squeeze fresh lemon juice on each portion.

• If you like things spicy, serve with a bit of *harissa,* a delicious Middle Eastern chili sauce sold in jars in Middle Eastern groceries and in the ethnic foods section of some supermarkets.

• This dish goes well with couscous (see page 183) and Absolutely the Best Broccoli (page 198). You can cook them both while the chicken is in the oven.

pan-grilled boneless chicken breasts

Makes 2 main-dish servings or
enough to top 4 main-dish salads

The boneless, skinless chicken breast fillet (which is actually one half of a whole chicken breast) has become the go-to protein for home cooks for a reason. It's quick to cook and super-versatile because its flavor goes with just about anything. So if you love chicken, this simple preparation is an essential building block for cooking. If you have a grill pan (with raised ridges), by all means use it here. It will give the chicken a bit more charred flavor and attractive grill marks. You can eat these chicken breasts right away as an entrée or salad topping, or refrigerate them for up to 4 days in a resealable plastic bag or airtight container and use them later in salads, sandwiches, stir-fries, and countless other wonderful ways. You can reheat the cooked fillets briefly in the microwave (don't overdo it, or they'll turn rubbery), or warm them in a covered skillet over low heat with a little water to keep them moist.

2 boneless, skinless chicken breast fillets
(about 8 ounces each)

¼ teaspoon garlic powder

⅛ teaspoon salt

Freshly ground black pepper

1 tablespoon olive oil (possibly a little more)

1. Pat the fillets dry with paper towels, and season on both sides with the garlic powder, salt, and a few grinds of pepper. Set aside.

2. Place a small heavy-bottomed skillet (just large enough to hold the fillets in a single layer) over medium heat. After about a minute, add the olive oil and swirl to coat the pan. Add the chicken and cook, undisturbed, for 4 to 5 minutes, or until golden brown on the bottom.

3. Use a metal spatula to carefully loosen each fillet and flip it over, adding a little more oil if the pan seems dry. Cook on the second side for 3 minutes or so, or until the bottom surface matches the top. You may need to lower the heat if the chicken begins to burn, or raise it if it is not browning quickly. To check for doneness, insert an instant-read thermometer lengthwise into the thickest part of the breast. It should register 165°F. You can also poke the tip of a sharp knife into the thickest part of the breast; the meat should be opaque white throughout.

4. Transfer the chicken to a plate, and let it rest for about 5 minutes before serving. Serve hot, cold, or at room temperature.

GET CREATIVE

• Make a big green salad and top with warm slices of the chicken.

• Top a Caesar Salad (page 44) with warm slices or cubes of the chicken.

• Serve with any vegetable side dish.

• To make a chicken club, slice warm fillets and layer the slices on a soft roll with mayo, lettuce, tomato, avocado, and a strip of bacon (see page 233).

• Slice the chicken, fan the slices out on plates, squeeze some fresh lime juice over them, and top them with a dollop of guacamole (store-bought or homemade—see page 224) and/or salsa. Serve with sizzling Fajita-Style Peppers and Onions (page 206) and warm tortillas.

• Use the chilled leftovers to make Chinese Chicken Salad (page 54) or a chicken sandwich.

simplest (and best) roast chicken

Makes 3 to 4 servings

This stellar, ultra-easy method of roasting chicken uses an ancient, brilliant seasoning: high heat. That and a large amount of salt produce a bird with crisp skin and very juicy meat. It's a technique simplified from renowned chef Thomas Keller's already simple one (brought to my attention by my son, Sam, who has become quite a master of it). Salt and pepper are the only flavor accents until the very end of roasting, when you can opt to add an herb or two to the juices and baste with them for a final touch. If you have the time and the refrigerator space, season the raw chicken with the salt and pepper, and then let it sit, uncovered, on a deep plate in the refrigerator for up to 24 hours. This will dry the skin out a bit and make for crisper results.

Any reasonably heavy roasting or baking pan (or even a cast-iron skillet) that is large enough to hold the chicken will work. There's no need for a rack. This method does make a fair amount of smoke, so don't forget to turn on your kitchen fan and/or open the window.

1 whole chicken (3 to 4 pounds)

1 tablespoon salt

¼ teaspoon freshly ground black pepper

1. Adjust the oven rack to the center position and preheat the oven to 450°F.

2. Rinse the chicken (inside and out) under cold running water and pat it completely dry (inside and out) with paper towels.

3. Combine the salt and pepper in a small bowl. Place the chicken, breast side up, in a roasting pan. Season both the outside and the

inside of the chicken with the salt and pepper, rubbing the mixture into the skin. (I usually put about a teaspoon of the mixture inside and the rest all over the outside, but it's not an exact science.)

4. Turn on the stovetop fan and/or open the window. Place the pan in the oven, and leave the chicken alone for a good 50 minutes, or until the skin is becoming nicely browned. At that point, start checking for doneness with an instant-read thermometer. To do so, remove the chicken from the oven, insert the thermometer under the leg where it joins the thigh (avoiding the bone), and watch the temperature register. It should stop at 170°F. If you stick the thermometer into the breast meat (again avoiding the bone, and sliding the thermometer in lengthwise along the breast, starting at the top), it should register 160°F. If not, return the chicken to the oven for another 10 minutes and check again. When the chicken has reached 170°F in the leg/thigh area, remove it from the oven.

5. Use a baster or a spoon to suction or scoop up the juices that have gathered in the bottom of the pan (and inside the chicken itself), and gently squirt or dribble them over the entire chicken. Do this about ten times in a row to coat the chicken. When you're finished basting, let the chicken sit in the roasting pan at room temperature for 15 minutes.

6. Hold the chicken upright (drumsticks down) over the pan to drain off any juices that have collected inside it. Transfer the chicken to a cutting board. Skim off and discard as much of the clear yellow fat that has floated to the top of the pan juices as you can, leaving the dark stuff to use as a sauce.

7. Use a knife or poultry shears to cut the chicken into pieces. Serve hot, warm, or at room temperature, with the roasting juices spooned over each serving.

GET CREATIVE

- Add up to 1 tablespoon dried thyme, sage, or rosemary (or a combination) to the pan when you take the chicken out of the oven for basting. The herbs will infuse the basting juices.

- Carve or pull apart some of the warm meat and toss it into a green salad to make a light one-dish meal.

- Prepared mustard (especially Dijon) makes a nice table condiment for this, as does a sauce made from equal parts mustard and mayo.

- Warm a baguette in the oven, cut it into 4-inch lengths, split them open, leaving them hinged, drizzle pan juices on the bread, and pile in some warm sliced or shredded chicken, along with a little mayo and some baby spinach, watercress, or lettuce.

- Serve with a green salad, any cooked vegetable (or several), rice (see page 181), Mashed Potatoes (page 186), and/or some good bread to soak up the delicious juices.

teriyaki chicken thighs

Makes 4 servings (2 thighs apiece)

Chicken teriyaki is about as easy as whisking together a quick no-cook sauce, pouring it over some chicken in a pan, and sliding it in the oven. The chicken comes out juicy and moist, with a beautiful mahogany glaze. Don't worry about overcooking these. You want to err on the side of their being well-done. With all the sauce surrounding them, they'll just get more and more tender, and there's very little danger of their drying out. Once they're baked, the thighs and their sauce can be stored in a tightly covered container or a resealable plastic bag in the refrigerator for up to a week. Reheat them briefly in the microwave, or enjoy them at room temperature.

½ cup soy sauce

½ cup water

1 tablespoon minced garlic
(about 3 good-sized cloves)

1 tablespoon minced fresh
ginger

1 tablespoon dark brown sugar

1 tablespoon honey

8 chicken thighs
(6 to 8 ounces each)

1. Adjust the oven rack to the center position and preheat the oven to 400°F.

2. In a medium bowl or a jar with a tight-fitting lid, combine the soy sauce, water, garlic, ginger, brown sugar, and honey. Whisk or shake to mix well.

3. Rinse the chicken thighs under cold water, pat them dry with paper towels, and arrange them, skin side up, in a single layer in a 9- by 13-inch baking pan. Pour the sauce over the chicken. Bake in the center of the oven for 30 minutes, uncovered and undisturbed.

4. A lot of liquid will have accumulated in the pan. Baste the chicken by spooning this liquid over the tops of the thighs several times, and then bake for 15 minutes longer. Baste again, and cook 15 minutes more.

5. Check the internal temperature of the chicken with an instant-read thermometer inserted parallel to the bone (but not actually touching it) in one of the thighs. If it registers 170°F, the chicken is done. If not, remove the thermometer, baste again, and bake for up to 20 more minutes, checking the temperature and basting every 10 minutes or so until the thermometer reads 170°F.

6. Transfer the chicken to a plate or a platter and let it rest for 5 to 10 minutes. Meanwhile, using a hot pad or an oven mitt, tip the pan and use a large spoon to skim off and discard most of the clear yellow fat that will have accumulated on the surface of the sauce.

7. Serve the chicken hot, warm, or at room temperature, with some of the sauce spooned over it.

GET CREATIVE

• Serve with rice (see page 181) and Absolutely the Best Broccoli (page 198) or Delightfully Spiced Carrots (page 204) on the side; with Vegetable-Tofu Stir-Fry (page 122); or with a green salad with Honey-Mustard Dressing (page 36).

• Garnish with a sprinkling of toasted sesame seeds and/or very thinly sliced scallions (including the green part).

• This recipe also works well with chicken wings, which make a great party snack, appetizer, or potluck contribution. Just substitute 3 to 4 pounds of wings (buy drumettes or cut-up wing sections, rather than whole wings) and follow the recipe as directed.

chicken, fish, and meat. 159

poached salmon

Makes 2 servings

Poaching (that is, cooking something slowly in simmering liquid) is the easiest, most reliable way to cook salmon. You really can't go wrong. Even if you overcook it a bit, it will still be moist and delicate. Best of all, poached salmon is elegant and tasty, and it goes perfectly with a variety of sauces. It's also better cold, as a leftover, than pan-fried or broiled salmon, and once you get the hang of poaching, you can add salmon-topped salads to your list of regular meals. This method works equally well with halibut or other similar firm-fleshed fish. Leftover poached salmon keeps for up to 3 days in a resealable plastic bag or an airtight container in the refrigerator.

1 lemon

Salt for the cooking water

A few thick slices of red or yellow onion

8 whole black peppercorns

1 bay leaf

Two 8-ounce salmon fillets or steaks,
    ¾- to 1-inch thick

1. Cut the lemon in half lengthwise. Cut one of the halves into 4 thick slices and the other half into wedges. Set the wedges aside for serving.

2. Choose a skillet or pot that is large enough to hold the salmon in a single layer and deep enough that you'll be able to cover the fish with water by about an inch. Fill the skillet about two-thirds full with cold water and set it on the stove over high heat. Add 1 teaspoon salt, plus the lemon slices (giving them a squeeze as you drop them in), onion slices, peppercorns, and bay leaf. Bring to a boil.

3. Meanwhile, line a plate with three layers of paper towels and place it near the stove.

4. Gently slide the salmon into the boiling water. Immediately reduce the heat to medium-low, and cook at a gentle simmer for 8 minutes. To check for doneness, remove the salmon with a slotted spoon or slotted metal spatula and gently insert the tip of a small knife into the center. The fish should be opaque pink in the center, not translucent, and it should be firm to the touch. If it's not quite ready, carefully slide it back into the water for another minute or so.

5. Use the slotted spoon or slotted metal spatula to remove the salmon from the water, and drain it briefly on the paper-towel-lined plate. Discard the poaching liquid and serve the salmon hot, at room temperature, or chilled, accompanied with the lemon wedges.

SHORTCUT "HOLLANDAISE"

Real hollandaise is a tricky concoction made by emulsifying butter, lemon juice, and egg yolks over heat. Mayonnaise makes a perfectly wonderful base for a much more practical version. For 4 to 5 servings, just combine ½ cup of your favorite mayo with 1 tablespoon fresh lemon juice and ½ teaspoon dried (or 2 tablespoons minced fresh) tarragon. If you'd like some crunch, stir in a tablespoon of finely minced shallot. Serve this anywhere you've ever heard of serving hollandaise: over asparagus, on top of eggs Benedict (or just poached eggs), as a sauce for poached salmon or other fish, or as a dip for artichokes. It's all good. This keeps in a tightly sealed container in the refrigerator for up to 2 weeks.

GET CREATIVE

- Substitute white wine for up to 1 cup of the water in the poaching liquid to give the fish a little more flavor.

- Serve with Classic Asparagus (page 196), and dress both the fish and the vegetable with Shortcut "Hollandaise" (left).

- Garnish with a sprinkling of capers, a few thin cucumber slices, and/or a sprig or two of fresh tarragon or dill.

- Serve the salmon with a baked potato (page 184) topped with sour cream or yogurt, and/or Braised Brussels Sprouts in Mustard Sauce (page 210).

- Flake the salmon and serve it warm, at room temperature, or cold over a green salad.

- Mash any leftover poached salmon with a bit of mayonnaise and lemon juice to make a salmon salad, which you can use in a sandwich or as a salad topping.

- Pile the warm poached salmon on a toasted French roll, with lettuce, tomato, red onion, cucumber, and dabs of wasabi and mayonnaise.

crispy pan-fried fish fillets

Makes 4 servings

U tter simplicity is the principle behind these classic crunchy-coated fish fillets. The process is surprisingly easy, once you set up the little assembly line of beaten egg and seasoned breadcrumbs. This fish cooks quickly and needs to go directly from the stove to the table without passing Go, so have your side dishes ready ahead of time. This recipe uses both olive oil and butter. Just a tablespoon of butter will infuse the oil with an extra layer of rich flavor, while keeping the coating crisp and light.

1 pound white fish fillets,
    such as sole, snapper,
    or cod (four 4-ounce pieces,
    each ½-inch thick)

1 large egg

1 teaspoon water

½ cup panko (Japanese-style
    breadcrumbs; see page 163)

½ teaspoon salt

⅛ teaspoon freshly ground
    black pepper

2 tablespoons olive oil

1 tablespoon butter

Lemon or lime wedges,
    for serving

1. Rinse the fish under cold running water, then pat it dry with paper towels and set aside.

2. Break the egg into a pie pan, then beat with a fork or a small whisk, adding the teaspoon of water as you go. When no egg white is still visible, stop beating and set aside.

3. Combine the panko, salt, and pepper on a dinner plate. Have a second dinner plate ready to hold the coated fillets.

4. One at a time, dip the fillets into the egg and then let any excess egg drip off back into the pie pan. Put each moistened fillet into the panko mixture, pressing it down firmly so the crumbs will adhere. Then turn it over, and press the second side into the crumbs until it becomes completely coated all over. Shake off any extra panko mixture, and transfer the coated fillet to the clean plate.

5. Place a large (10- to 12-inch—or big enough to hold all 4 fillets) heavy skillet over medium heat. After about a minute, add the olive oil and swirl to coat the pan. Add the butter, and swirl until it melts into the oil.

6. Carefully transfer the coated fillets to the hot pan. Cook, undisturbed, for 2 to 3 minutes, or until deep golden brown on the bottom.

7. Use a metal spatula to carefully loosen each fillet, being careful to keep its coating intact. Flip each fillet over, and cook on the second side for 2 to 3 minutes, or until that side is deep golden brown. A sharp knife should insert easily into the thickest part of the fish, revealing opaque flesh. If necessary, cook a minute or so longer.

8. Serve hot, accompanying each portion with a wedge or two of lemon or lime.

WHY PANKO?

Panko is the name of a kind of very light, coarse-textured Japanese-style breadcrumb, often sold either in the Asian section of supermarkets or with the regular breadcrumbs; it comes packed in a box or a bag. The porous texture and rough oblong shape of panko crumbs make them the absolute best choice when you want to create an extremely-yet-delicately-crisp outer coating on any pan-fried or baked food. If you can't find panko, use ordinary unseasoned breadcrumbs. Their finer, more powdery texture still works for coating, but the result will be less crunchy and light.

GET CREATIVE

- These fillets are great with mayonnaise or with store-bought tartar sauce.

- Serve with Roasted Fingerlings (page 190); be sure to start them far enough in advance so they're ready when the fish is done.

- Mostly Classic Cole Slaw (page 42) also makes a nice accompaniment, and can be made up to a day ahead of time.

pan-seared garlic prawns

Makes 4 servings

Here's a no-fail way to enjoy succulent prawns with just a few minutes of work. I recommend buying frozen large shrimp rather than fresh. ("Prawns" and "shrimp," by the way, are essentially synonyms: "shrimp" tends to be how they're sold, and "prawns" is a nice way to refer to large shrimp when serving them.) Why? Because at most supermarket fish counters the shrimp are previously frozen anyway, and the quality of shrimp deteriorates the longer they sit after thawing. Buying good-quality shrimp from the freezer section means you can have them on hand till you need them, and then thaw them just before you're ready to cook, making for fresher, tastier shrimp. Shrimp are sold by size and classified by the number of them in a pound. In this case, we're using extra-large shrimp (16 to 20 to a pound). Either "easy-peel" or peeled shrimp will work here. "Easy-peel" are deveined but still have the shell and tail on, which preserves their flavor. When you peel them, I suggest leaving the tail on. It'll add flavor and makes the shrimp look much more attractive on the plate.

1 pound frozen extra-large shrimp
("easy-peel" or peeled, deveined)

¼ cup olive oil

1 teaspoon minced garlic
(about 1 good-sized clove)

¼ teaspoon salt

⅛ teaspoon freshly ground black pepper

A big pinch of red pepper flakes
(plus more for passing at the table)

Fresh lime wedges, for garnish

1. Put the shrimp in a colander in the sink and run cold water over them until they are thawed. Drain well, and pat dry with paper towels. If using easy-peel shrimp, remove the shells and, optionally, the tails.

2. In a shallow pie plate or bowl, combine the olive oil, garlic, salt, black pepper, and red pepper flakes; mix well. Add the thawed shrimp and toss to coat well. Cover tightly and refrigerate for at least 20 minutes and up to an hour.

3. Place a large (10- to 12-inch) heavy skillet over medium heat. After about a minute, add the shrimp (leaving the extra marinade behind in the bowl to discard). Cook for 1 to 2 minutes on each side, or until the shrimp turn from glossy to opaque.

4. Transfer to a serving platter and serve immediately, with many fresh lime wedges and additional red pepper flakes if you like.

GET CREATIVE

- Garnish these with a handful of chopped flat-leaf parsley and/or snipped chives.

- Put freshly cooked, still-hot shrimp right on top of a big green salad along with slices of cucumber, red onion, tomato, and avocado.

- Serve the shrimp over rice or couscous (see page 183), with lime wedges on the side for squeezing over everything.

- To turn this into a pasta dish, cook ¾ pound linguine or fettuccine according to the package directions. Meanwhile, sauté the shrimp, using a large skillet that will accommodate the pasta. When the pasta is done, toss it in the skillet with the cooked shrimp to combine. Remove the pan from the heat, drizzle up to 2 tablespoons olive oil over the pasta, and squeeze a few tablespoons of lime juice over it as well, to taste.

peperoni e salsiccia
(italian-style peppers and sausages)

Makes 2 servings

T his traditional home-style Italian dish is a sauté of sweet peppers, onions, slices of browned sausage, and tender potatoes. For this recipe, go with mild or medium-spicy Italian sausage. Meat expert friends of mine say pork sausage is best for this dish, rather than turkey or chicken, but that's their (very educated) taste. If you'd rather go nontraditional, you can use any of those sweeter, fruitier, or spicier "designer" sausages (like chicken-apple or mango-cilantro). Many of these are fully cooked, so if you use them, you just need to brown them, whole, for a few minutes and then slice them and proceed with the recipe as directed.

This dish keeps for up to 5 days in a tightly covered container in the refrigerator. It reheats well, either on the stovetop over medium heat or in a microwave, and you can do all kinds of tasty things with it.

Polenta (see page 105) is a perfect match for Peperoni e Salsiccia. Just spoon the soft polenta into soup bowls and top with the peppers and sausage. Or let the cooked polenta cool slightly, which will cause it to firm up, and then slice or scoop chunks of it onto plates and top with the pepper-sausage mixture.

½ pound small potatoes (Yukon Gold
or Yellow Finn is good), scrubbed and
cut in half

3 tablespoons olive oil

2 sweet or spicy Italian sausages
(about 3 ounces each)

1 large onion, cut into ¼-inch-thick slices

1 large red bell pepper,
cut into ¼-inch-wide strips

1 large yellow bell pepper, cut into
¼-inch-wide strips

1 large green bell pepper, cut into
¼-inch-wide strips

¼ teaspoon salt

1 teaspoon minced garlic
(about 1 good-sized clove)

Freshly ground black pepper

1. Put a medium pot of cold water to boil over high heat, and place a colander in the sink. When the water boils, add the potatoes, and cook for 10 to 15 minutes, or until tender when pierced with a fork. Drain the potatoes in the colander and leave them there until needed.

2. Meanwhile, place a large skillet over medium heat. After about a minute, add 1 tablespoon of the olive oil and swirl to coat the pan. Add the sausages (whole), and cook gently for about 15 minutes, turning them every couple of minutes, until golden brown all over. (The sausages are cooked through when no longer pink in the middle. You can check by cutting in with a small sharp knife to be sure.) Transfer the cooked sausages to a cutting board, let them cool for a few minutes, and then slice them into ¼-inch-thick rounds. Leave them there until needed.

3. Without cleaning it, return the skillet to medium-high heat, and immediately add the remaining 2 tablespoons olive oil. After about 30 seconds, swirl to coat the pan. Add the onion, bell peppers, and salt. Cook, stirring occasionally, for about 10 minutes, or until the vegetables are tender and the onion is golden brown.

4. Reduce the heat to medium, then add the garlic and cook for 1 minute. Add the cooked potatoes and the sausage rounds, and cook, stirring often, for 3 to 5 minutes, or until everything is heated through. If the mixture looks dry, stir in a tablespoon or two of water and heat briefly.

5. Season to taste with freshly ground black pepper (depending on how spicy the sausage is), and serve hot or warm.

GET CREATIVE

- Top this with grated Parmesan cheese and/or chopped flat-leaf parsley.

- Serve with penne pasta: Boil ½ pound of penne pasta, drain, and toss with the warm Peperoni e Salsiccia.

- Serve with a green salad and some crusty bread on the side.

- Make this into an open-face sandwich by piling it onto a split, toasted French roll or a slab of focaccia and topping it with grated Parmesan cheese. You can also top it with sliced mozzarella and melt the cheese briefly in the broiler or toaster oven.

- If you have leftovers, reheat them for breakfast, with or without eggs and toast and maybe a few sliced tomatoes. It also makes a great omelet filling. Add some Skillet Potatoes with Fried Onions (page 192) if you're feeling ambitious and have the time.

stir-fried broccoli beef

Makes 4 servings

Real Chinese restaurant food can be yours at home—from your own pan on your own stove, made by you. The trick, as with all stir-fries worth their salt, is to have all the ingredients ready and lined up near the stove, so you can work ultra-fast (and that means having the rice cooked, too—see page 181). Notice how short the cooking time is in this recipe: 30 seconds here, 1 minute there. Take that timing literally, as a few seconds can make the difference between bright green, crisp, radiant broccoli with mouthwateringly tender, pink-in-the-middle beef . . . and depressing, faded broccoli mush with beef jerky (and not in a good way). So be organized, swift, and attentive, and reap the benefits. Make sure you use seasoned, not plain, rice vinegar.

2 tablespoons soy sauce

6 tablespoons seasoned rice
   vinegar

2 teaspoons (packed) light
   brown sugar

2 teaspoons toasted sesame oil

1½ pounds flank, sirloin, rib-eye,
   skirt, or strip steak, about
   ¾-inch thick

3 tablespoons canola, soy, or
   peanut oil

½ teaspoon salt

2 tablespoons minced garlic
   (about 6 good-sized cloves)

2 tablespoons minced fresh
   ginger

1 large head of broccoli
   (1½ pounds), tough stem
   ends discarded, cut on the
   diagonal into 2-inch spears

1. Combine the soy sauce, vinegar, brown sugar, and sesame oil in a small bowl and whisk to blend. Set aside.

2. Slice the steak into ¼-inch-thick strips, cutting crosswise, against the grain.

3. Place a large (10- to 12-inch) heavy skillet (or a medium-large wok) over medium heat. After about a minute, add about half of the oil (approximately 1½ tablespoons) and swirl to coat the pan. Turn up the heat to medium-high, and wait another 30 seconds for the oil to get very hot, then add the steak strips in a single layer. Sprinkle with ¼ teaspoon of the salt and 1 tablespoon each of the garlic and ginger.

4. Wait for 1 minute. Then, as quickly and deftly as possible, use tongs to turn over each strip of steak and cook for 1 minute on the second side.

GET CREATIVE

- Add big pinches of red pepper flakes when you salt both the steak and the broccoli.

- Top with toasted peanuts, cashews, or almonds.

- Pass shaker bottles of chile oil and toasted sesame oil at the table, for people to drizzle on top.

- This can also be made with asparagus, or with a combination of broccoli and asparagus.

- Add some diagonally cut carrots and/ or strips of red bell pepper along with the broccoli for a touch of color.

- For a bit of extra-intense flavor, add up to a tablespoon of oyster sauce to the soy sauce mixture.

(This will yield medium-rare strips. If you prefer your meat to be more thoroughly cooked, give them up to 2 minutes on the second side.)

5. Scoop up the cooked steak with tongs or a spoon, and transfer it to a bowl. Include all the cooking juices.

6. Keeping the pan over medium-high heat, add the remaining oil. Wait for 30 seconds, and then swirl to coat the pan. Toss in the broccoli, and sprinkle with the remaining ¼ teaspoon salt. Turn the heat to high, and stir-fry the broccoli for 1 minute.

7. Sprinkle in the remaining garlic and ginger, and stir-fry for another minute.

8. Pour in the reserved soy sauce mixture, and keep the heat high as you stir-fry for 30 seconds. Toss in the cooked meat plus all its juices, and toss briefly to combine. Remove from the heat, and serve right away.

chicken, fish, and meat.

old-fashioned beef stew

Makes 6 to 8 servings

Pure tradition here: an honest bowlful of fork-tender beef, potatoes, onions, and carrots that have created their own rich-tasting sauce. This stew takes up to 3 hours to make, but for most of that time it cooks on its own in the oven, while you're free to do other things. So plan to make this on a day when you're going to be home anyway. Because it keeps and reheats so well, consider making it on a weekend for eating throughout the week. You can save a step by buying pre-cut cubes of stew meat, but I recommend going with larger pieces of chuck (so you know what you're getting) and cutting them up yourself. Look for very small red potatoes, 1½ inches in diameter (sometimes called "creamers"), which need only to be cut in half.

Beef stew keeps well in the refrigerator, in an airtight container, for up to a week. Or you can freeze it in individual portions in resealable bags for up to 2 months. Defrost it in the refrigerator or at the "defrost" power in a microwave oven before gently reheating—either over low heat in a saucepan (stirring occasionally) or in a microwave, in individual bowls or a serving bowl.

3 pounds boneless beef chuck

¾ teaspoon salt

Freshly ground black pepper

2 to 3 tablespoons olive oil
   (possibly a little more)

2 medium red or yellow onions, chopped

3 tablespoons unbleached all-purpose flour

3 to 4 cups beef broth (boxed, canned, or
   reconstituted from bouillon)

1 tablespoon tomato paste

1 tablespoon minced garlic
   (about 3 good-sized cloves)

1 teaspoon dried thyme

2 bay leaves

1 pound (about 15) red creamer potatoes,
   halved

1 pound baby carrots, left whole

1. Adjust the oven rack to the center position and preheat the oven to 325°F.

2. Pat the beef dry with paper towels and put it on a cutting board. Use a sharp knife to trim off and discard any visible outer fat, then cut the meat into a couple of large pieces where it naturally seems to be separating. Cut these larger chunks into 1½-inch cubes (no smaller—if you make them too small, they will cook too quickly and toughen). Sprinkle the meat with the salt and a liberal amount of pepper.

3. Place an ovenproof soup pot or a Dutch oven over medium-high heat. After about a minute, add 2 tablespoons of the olive oil and swirl to coat the pan. Carefully add half of the beef cubes, and cook, undisturbed, for about 3 minutes. (If you crowd the pan with all of the meat, it will steam in its own juices instead of browning.) You will know it is browned properly when it no longer seems to stick to the pan when you nudge a cube with tongs.

4. Use tongs to carefully turn the cubes to another side and continue browning for about 8 minutes, turning the pieces as they cook until they're deep golden brown on all sides. Transfer the browned meat to a medium-large bowl and set aside. If the pan looks dry and the bits left on the surface seem to be burning, add a little more olive oil to the pan. You want a thin film over the entire surface. Add the remaining meat and brown as described. Transfer to the bowl and set aside.

5. Without cleaning the pan, pour in a little more olive oil (just enough to coat the bottom). Add the onions and cook, stirring occasionally, for 5 minutes, or until the onions begin to soften.

6. Sprinkle the flour over the onions and stir to combine. Cook for 2 minutes, stirring occasionally. Then slowly whisk in 3 cups of the broth. (It will make a thick sauce for a moment before thinning out.)

7. Whisk in the tomato paste, garlic, and thyme, and add the bay leaves. Return the browned beef to the pot and check to see that the liquid reaches the top of the meat. If not, add a bit more broth or bouillon. Bring to a boil over high heat.

8. As soon as the liquid reaches the boiling point, turn off the heat. Cover the pot tightly with foil and cover that with a lid, too, if you have one that fits tightly. (You want to capture all the steam as the meat cooks.) Transfer the pot to the oven and cook, undisturbed, for 1 hour.

9. Carefully open the pot (to avoid getting burned by the steam that will escape), and stir in the potatoes and carrots. Cover again with the foil and lid, and return the pot to the oven for another 1 hour of cooking.

10. Remove the pot from the oven and let the stew sit, still covered, for 10 minutes before serving. Remove the bay leaves. Serve hot or warm.

GET CREATIVE

- You can substitute red wine for some or all of the beef broth. Added bonus of doing so: You get to call it "Boeuf Bourguignon."

- Like all stews and braises, this tastes even better the day after you cook it, so if you have time, make it ahead of time, let it cool, cover the pot, and store it in the refrigerator overnight. Before reheating, skim off and discard any solidified fat that has formed on the surface.

- Chopped parsley makes a perfect garnish.

- This is a complete meal on its own, but you can round it out by serving it over or with some cooked egg noodles, lightly buttered, with a green salad alongside.

- If you want to make a couple of meals out of your stew, serve some meat, potatoes, and carrots with a smaller proportion of the liquid for dinner one night; then cut the leftover meat and vegetables into smaller pieces and add some cooked barley for a wonderful second-day soup (with or without additional broth or reconstituted bouillon, as needed).

grandma betty's brisket

Makes 4 to 6 servings

My esteemed mother, Betty, has the right idea: succulent roasted brisket smothered with onions, which melt and mellow during the slow cooking process, flavoring and glazing the meat. Use a heavy pot with a tight-fitting ovenproof lid for this— ideally, one that's not too much larger in diameter than the meat so that the onions remain moist and don't burn. The labor for this is minimal but the oven time is long, so plan to make brisket at a time when you'll be home. It's great the second day, so if you're going to have people over, you can make it well in advance.

The recipe makes enough for a few nights' dinners. Whatever you don't eat, leave unsliced and refrigerate in a resealable plastic bag. You'll find it's even easier to slice when it's cold. You can use the slices for sandwiches or reheat them in the microwave, in a skillet with a few drops of water to moisten them, or in a 325°F oven.

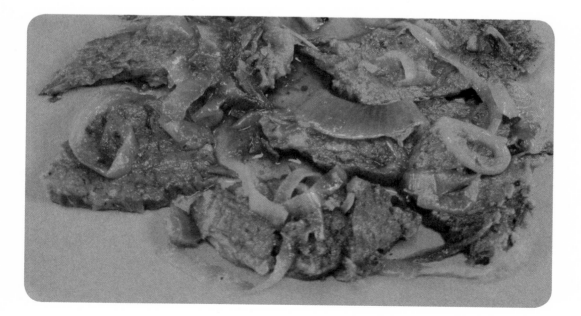

1 teaspoon salt

¼ teaspoon freshly ground black pepper

¼ teaspoon garlic powder

4 large red or yellow onions, sliced
  (not too thin)

One 3-pound beef brisket

2 tablespoons water

1. Adjust the rack to the center position and preheat the oven to 325°F.

2. In a small bowl, combine the salt, pepper, and garlic powder. Mix well, and set aside.

3. Scatter half of the sliced onions in a Dutch oven. Pat the brisket dry with paper towels, then sprinkle the salt mixture evenly over both sides of the meat. Place the brisket, fat side up, on top of the onions and cover with the rest of the onions. Spoon in the water.

4. Cover the pan tightly with foil, then cover it with the lid. (You want to capture all the steam as the meat cooks.) Place the pan in the center of the oven and let the brisket roast, undisturbed, for 3 hours.

5. Remove the pan from the oven, uncover it (being careful not to get burned by the steam), and pierce the meat with a fork. If the fork goes in easily and the meat is tender, it's done. If it still seems a bit tough, cover the pan again with the foil and the lid, put it back in the oven, and check it again every 15 to 20 minutes. Depending on the cut of meat, the total cooking can take as long as 4 hours or more, so be patient. (Grandma Betty reminds us that it is fine for brisket to be a little overdone. Ideally, one should need neither knife nor teeth.)

6. When you take the finished brisket out of the oven, uncover it and let it sit in the pan for at least 10 minutes before slicing it.

7. To serve, transfer the brisket to a cutting board and slice it thin across the grain. Spoon some of the very well cooked (and insanely delicious) onions and pan juices on top of each serving.

GET CREATIVE

- Serve with lightly buttered noodles or Mashed Potatoes (page 186) and a green salad. Alternatively, either Baked Potatoes (page 184) or Deeply Roasted Cauliflower (page 200) is a nice match for brisket, and both share the oven with the brisket while (or after) it cooks. (Any accompanying dish that requires a higher temperature can get oven time while the brisket is resting.)

- Leftover brisket makes great sandwiches. Be sure to pile on some of the onions, along with whatever condiments (mustard, mayo, hot sauce) you like.

- Shred the meat, mix it with the onions, and serve it as a filling for soft tacos or burritos, along with salsa, guacamole (store-bought or homemade—see page 224), and some rice.

- Pile some slices of warm brisket and onions on salad greens to make a hearty dinner salad.

BETTY'S BRISKET WISDOM

Don't remove the layer of fat covering one side of the brisket. It adds flavor and keeps the meat basted during cooking. It mostly dissolves during cooking, and whatever is left can always be cut away after cooking, if you prefer. Cut brisket across the grain in thin slices. If you cut with the grain, you'll end up shredding the meat, which will still taste good but looks less attractive on the plate. You can also "pull" cooked brisket, by shredding it into chunks with two forks. This is great for filling tacos and sandwiches. You can freeze leftover cooked brisket—either whole, for another dinner or two, or sliced, as a stash of sandwich meat.

steak fajitas

Makes 4 servings

I t's always exciting to experience the sensory drama when a hot platter of sizzling fajitas is brought to your table in a Mexican restaurant. Here's a recipe for making the same thing at home. It might be less of a performance piece, but it will taste just as great. Traditionally this is made with skirt steak, but flank and sirloin work equally well. The trick is to cook these fast, hot, and no more than medium-rare—which is nice, because it means minimal stove time for you. A cast-iron skillet is perfect for this.

1½ pounds flank, sirloin, rib-eye, skirt, or strip steak, about ¾-inch thick

½ teaspoon salt

⅛ teaspoon freshly ground black pepper

2 tablespoons olive oil

1 medium red onion, thickly sliced

1 large red bell pepper, cut into ¼-inch-wide strips

1 large yellow bell pepper, cut into ¼-inch-wide strips

1 large green bell pepper, cut into ¼-inch-wide strips

1 teaspoon minced garlic (about 1 good-sized clove)

1. Pat the steak dry with paper towels, and season both sides with ¼ teaspoon of the salt and all the pepper.

2. Place a large (10- to 12-inch) heavy skillet over medium heat. After about a minute, add 1 tablespoon of the olive oil and swirl to coat the pan. Wait another 30 seconds, and then add the steak. Cook, undisturbed, for 1½ to 2 minutes, or until nicely browned. (This will give you a medium-rare result. If you prefer it more well done, you can cook it as long as 2½ minutes.)

3. Use a metal spatula to loosen, lift, and flip the steak, and cook it on the other side for 1½ to 2 minutes for medium-rare (or up to 2½ minutes for medium), adding a little more oil if the pan seems dry. Don't overcook the steak or it will become tough.

4. Transfer the cooked steak to a cutting board or plate, cover it loosely with a tent of foil, and let it rest while you cook the onions and peppers.

5. Without cleaning the pan, return it to the stove over medium heat. After about a minute, add the remaining 1 tablespoon olive oil and swirl to coat the pan. Turn the heat to

GET CREATIVE

• Pass a basket of warmed corn or flour tortillas at the table.

• You can sprinkle the finished dish with lightly toasted cumin seeds.

• Serve with wedges of lime for serious squeezing.

• Top with grated cheese, salsa, sour cream, and/or chopped tomatoes.

• Heap some guacamole (store-bought or homemade—see page 224) on top.

• Top with minced cilantro and/or mayonnaise.

• Top with a dab of sour cream.

• Serve with beans (plain or refried, from a can, heated) and rice.

medium-high, toss in the onion and bell peppers, and cook, shaking the pan and stirring, for only 3 to 5 minutes, or until everything becomes even more brightly colored and barely tender. Toss in the garlic and the remaining ¼ teaspoon salt during the last minute of cooking.

6. Remove the pan from the heat, and let the vegetables rest while you cut the steak crosswise, against the grain, into thin strips. Add the strips of cooked steak to the vegetables in the pan, and mix briefly to combine. Bring the pan to the table and serve right away.

GO THAT EXTRA FLAVOR INCH

You can give the steak a profound dose of flavor by marinating it for 20 minutes or longer in this mixture.

3 tablespoons fresh lime juice

¼ cup olive oil

1 tablespoon minced garlic
(about 3 good-sized cloves)

1 teaspoon ground cumin

1 teaspoon dried oregano

3 tablespoons minced cilantro

¼ teaspoon freshly ground black pepper

½ teaspoon salt

1. Combine all of the ingredients in a small bowl; whisk well. (Alternatively you can put everything in a small jar with a tight-fitting lid and shake to combine well.) Transfer the marinade to a resealable plastic bag, add the steak (either whole, or cut against the grain into ¼-inch-thick strips), and let marinate in the refrigerator, for at least 20 minutes and as long as overnight.

2. Lift the steak out of the marinade, leaving the liquid behind to discard, and cook according to the fajita recipe (but skipping the drying and seasoning of the meat in step 1).

sides.

Spud Simple

Potatoes are the original underground vegetable. Humble, not flashy. Satisfying and substantial. There when you need them. The best friend in the buddy movie of cooking. This gives them a noble quality that makes good cooks want to do as little to them as possible—just enough to showcase their refreshing simplicity with a little butter or salt or olive oil. Parsley or onions, maybe, but not a lot of sauce or fuss. Potatoes provide a delicious edible reminder that less is more.

BUYING AND STORING

When buying potatoes, make sure they have no soft or rotten spots. Look for smooth skin and absolutely no sprouts.

Wait to wash or scrub potatoes until just before cooking them. Store them in a cool, dark, dry place, ideally one with ventilation. The temperature should be about 45°F to 50°F. Don't keep potatoes in the refrigerator, which can turn their starch to sugar and make them sweet.

Although onions and garlic should be stored in the same conditions, you should separate them from your potatoes as much as possible because they produce gases that cause potatoes to rot when stored in close quarters with them.

You can store potatoes for up to 2 months for the heartier varieties, such as russets, and 1 month for small "new" potatoes, such as red creamers, or heirlooms, such as fingerlings. Check in on your stored potatoes every few days, and get rid of any that have softened, shriveled, or sprouted. These conditions are contagious (to other potatoes, not to you).

Vegetable Sides— Front and Center

At my house, vegetables are the stars, and I like to keep their preparation very simple. You'll notice a common theme here: olive oil, garlic or onion or shallot, salt and pepper. It's a light touch in which the vegetables themselves are the variety. Once you discover how accessible this approach is, your "sides" might just become the "center" from time to time. Note that you can expand any of the vegetable sides in this chapter into light vegetarian main dishes, just by serving them over brown rice, couscous, or bulgur (following pages)—or a combination of grains—and topping it all off with toasted nuts, cheese, or a sauce. This is what I call eating a little lower on the food chain, and for so many reasons—from economy and sustainability to health and weight management—it's really the way to go.

how to cook rice

Rice seems like the simplest thing in the world to cook. You just simmer it in the right amount of boiling water until tender, right? Well, yes. At least, theoretically. Problem is, differences in stoves, pots, and individual types of rice make for uneven results. So if you have tried to cook rice (any kind—white or brown, long- or short-grain) according to the package directions and have ended up with either half-raw grains (and possibly a scorched pan) or globs of overcooked mush, I have a plan for you.

But before I get to my plan, you should know that one fine route to reliable rice would be a good electric rice cooker. Full disclosure: I have never used one, but my friends who cook their rice this way swear by their machines. Also, many or most Asian restaurants use rice cookers, with consistently perfect results. So clearly this is one way to go. It takes up space in your kitchen, but it might be worth it if you are a rice lover and want to upgrade to also being a rice achiever.

Now, moving on to my plan (which is kind of unorthodox, but it works). Namely, you boil rice, as you would pasta, in an unmeasured large quantity of water until it is *mostly* cooked. Then you drain the rice, transfer it to a shallow pan, cover it tightly, and bake it until done. This takes about the same amount of time as the old-fashioned stovetop method, but more reliably produces perfectly separate, fluffy, tender grains. The bonus benefits: (1) You are spared having to worry about proportions of rice to water, and (2) after the rice is done, you can leave it right where it is and reheat as necessary in the same pan.

These instructions will work for any kind of rice: white or brown, long-grain or short-. (You didn't ask, but just so you know: my own favorite kind of rice, which I use for just about everything, is brown basmati, which is a fragrant, delicious long-grain rice that will make your kitchen smell incredible. I strongly recommend that brown basmati become your default grain.)

You can make a medium batch (yielding 6 cups cooked rice, or 4 to 6 servings) or a large one (yielding 9 cups cooked rice, or 6 to 9 servings). Use 2 cups uncooked rice for the medium yield, and 3 cups uncooked rice for a large recipe.

Makes about 6 cups cooked rice (medium batch); about 9 cups cooked rice (large batch)

8 to 10 cups water
  (this doesn't need to be exact)
1 tablespoon salt
2 or 3 cups uncooked rice
  (white or brown, long- or short-grain)
1 tablespoon canola, soy, or peanut oil,
  or melted butter

1. Preheat the oven to 350°F. Put the water and salt in a large saucepan, and bring to a rolling boil. Meanwhile, place the rice in a strainer and rinse it several times under cold running water.

2. Add the rice to the boiling water and let it boil rapidly until the rice is just tender to the bite—in other words, *almost* done: 10 minutes for white, 30 minutes for brown. Drain the rice in a colander over the sink, and rinse with warm running water.

3. Brush the oil or melted butter over the bottom of a 9- by 13-inch baking pan (the same size pan will work for both size batches, although if you have a slightly larger one for the bigger batch, use it), and spread the rice out in an even layer. Cover the pan tightly with foil, and bake until a taste test tells you the rice is done to your liking: 15 minutes for white rice, 25 minutes for brown.

4. Serve hot, warm, or at room temperature. (Reheat in a 350°F oven to the desired temperature, if necessary.)

GET CREATIVE

Stir any of these items into the rice just before serving:

- Butter or a flavorful roasted nut oil
- High-quality olive oil
- Minced garlic

- Dried fruit
- Cooked onion
- Minced fresh herbs or scallions
- Toasted shredded unsweetened coconut
- Toasted sunflower seeds or pumpkin seeds
- Your favorite dry spice mix
- Grated citrus zest
- Crumbled feta or goat cheese
- Fajita-Style Peppers and Onions (page 206)
- Cooked peas

Sprinkle (or drizzle or dollop) the top with:

- Grated cheese (Cheddar or a good Swiss, jack, or Parmesan)
- Chopped toasted nuts
- Fresh lemon or lime juice
- Pomegranate molasses (see page xvi)

Two Great Soaking Grains

Talk about easy. Did you know that you can "cook" couscous or bulgur by simply dousing them with boiling water and letting them stand for a little while? Honestly, that's it. They're then ready to serve. Great for when you're short on stove space. Kitchen table grains, both of them, and they're truly delightful-tasting.

The only trick is to use the minimal amount of water, so they'll be firm and fluffy, not waterlogged. After they're softened up, just drizzle with olive oil and sprinkle with a little salt—or dress them up with a touch or two of color and flavor.

You can make these in advance and reheat them in the microwave, in a covered pot in the oven, or in a skillet (first heating a tablespoon of oil, and then sautéing the grains briefly until they're hot).

The cool thing about both of these grains is that they come off as exotic, and all you did was boil water. We all love it when that happens. Buy couscous and bulgur in the bulk bins at any natural foods store or in enlightened grocery stores. They are inexpensive.

In case you are unfamiliar with the genre, couscous is actually a tiny wheat pasta, but it's usually classified as a grain because it looks, feels, and behaves like one. Bulgur is cracked wheat that has been steamed and then dried. So it is a partially cooked product to begin with, which is why a mere soaking is enough to finish the job. Enjoy them both!

couscous

Makes 2 to 3 servings

1½ cups couscous

2¼ cups boiling water

2 teaspoons olive oil or melted butter

¼ teaspoon salt

Place the couscous in a medium-sized bowl, and pour in the water. Cover with a plate and leave alone for 10 minutes. Fluff with a fork, stir in the olive oil or butter and the salt, and it's ready to serve.

bulgur

Makes 2 to 3 servings

1½ cups bulgur

2 cups boiling water

1 tablespoon olive oil

¼ teaspoon salt

Place the bulgur in a medium-sized bowl, and pour in the water. Cover with a plate and leave alone for 30 minutes. Fluff with a fork, stir in the olive oil and the salt, and it's ready to serve.

GET CREATIVE

You can stir any of these things into couscous or bulgur after it's finished soaking:

- ¼ teaspoon minced garlic
- A handful or two of very finely minced fresh parsley, basil, cilantro, and/or mint
- Up to 1 tablespoon very finely minced scallion greens, chives, or dill
- Raisins or dried currants or cranberries
- Chopped toasted walnuts, pine nuts, or pistachios
- A drizzle of toasted nut or seed oil
- Chopped ripe tomatoes

baked potatoes

Makes 4 servings

A baked potato is the mother ship of the entire comfort food fleet. You are blissfully reminded of that when you cut into one and add your favorite touches of butter or sour cream, and you know it will always taste and feel a certain way. You're eating dependability itself, and it's peace-of-mind-inducing as well as soothingly filling. So here's a dependable way to make one.

The best way to serve baked potatoes is to bring them to the table whole and uncut—to let each person cut his or her own and season, fill, or top it right at the table. This last-minute routine will help keep the potatoes maximally hot, which is very important. They're just not the same once they've cooled down. (And once they are baked, don't worry about their becoming overdone—either through waiting in the turned-off oven for you to eat them or by being reheated in a microwave a few days later. They're sturdy things and can withstand multiple heatings.)

This recipe can be vegan, depending on the topping.

4 medium-large russet potatoes (about ¾ pound each)

1. Adjust the oven rack to the center position and preheat the oven to 400°F. Scrub the potatoes under running water and pat them dry with paper towels or a clean dish towel.

2. Place the potatoes directly on the rack in the center of the oven. Let them bake for 50 minutes to an hour, or until the outsides become crisp and the insides are tender enough to be pierced easily with a sharp knife. (Better to overcook them than to have them be underdone.)

3. Remove them from the oven and serve right away. (Or, if the rest of your dinner isn't quite ready, you can wrap them in foil and keep them in the turned-off oven until dinnertime. They'll hold well this way for about 45 minutes.)

- Season with salt and pepper to taste. (Fancy "designer" salts and exotic pepper are great here, too.)

- Top with a pat or dollop of room-temperature butter, sour cream, or plain yogurt.

- Sprinkle snipped chives or minced scallion greens on top.

- To serve a baked potato restaurant-style, cut an X in the top with a paring knife. Holding the potato with a dish towel or an oven mitt if it's too hot to handle, gently squeeze the sides and ends, forcing some of the inside of the potato to pop out. Garnish with butter or sour cream and chives.

- Drizzle with high-quality olive oil.

- Top each potato with a dollop of Roasted Garlic Paste (page 5), for mashing in.

- Cook some bacon (see page 233) and crumble it on top.

- Sprinkle grated Cheddar or jack cheese, or crumbled bleu cheese, goat cheese, or feta, on top.

- Serve hot sauce and/or red pepper flakes on the side.

- Top with your favorite salsa.

- To turn a baked potato into a mini-meal, top it with cottage cheese, leftover cooked vegetables, or freshly cooked eggs. Or serve it with soup and a tossed green salad. You can also expand this recipe into Baked Stuffed Potatoes (page 114).

mashed potatoes

Makes 4 to 5 servings

A very satisfying experience awaits you in this recipe. It's hard to describe the contentment one can experience from boiling potatoes, mashing them by hand with an old-fashioned, hand-held mashing tool, while adding butter and milk (and possibly even real cream). All that satisfaction, and you haven't even eaten them yet! You can mash pretty much any kind of potato, but do it by hand. (If puréed in a food processor, potatoes will quickly become gluey, stretchy, and limp, and there's no fixing them. It's a mistake you don't even want to make once.) Russet (baking) potatoes will yield fluffier results than other types (and might warrant a little extra butter, cream, or milk because their flesh is drier). Yukon Golds, Yellow Finns, red potatoes, and other waxy varieties will give you a denser mash, and you can leave the skins on if you prefer. Once you drain the cooked potatoes, work quickly to keep things hot. It helps to mash them right in the cooking pot, and to warm the serving bowl or individual plates for a minute or so in the microwave right before serving.

3 pounds potatoes, peeled
   (or not) and cut into
   2-inch chunks

1 cup milk (can be part cream)

3 tablespoons butter

1¼ teaspoons salt

Freshly ground black pepper

1. Place the potatoes in a large saucepan and add enough cold water to cover them by a good inch. Bring to a boil, reduce the heat to low, and simmer, uncovered, for 15 to 20 minutes, or until falling-apart tender. (Literally: Cook them until a fork inserted into any of the pieces causes the potato to split.)

2. During the last few minutes of simmering, heat the milk and/or cream either in a saucepan over low heat until bubbly around the edges and warm to the touch (but not boiling, which can cause it to curdle) or for about 45 seconds in a microwave oven. Set aside near the sink (or wherever you'll be working), and have the butter there too.

3. Put a colander in the sink and drain the potatoes thoroughly, then immediately return them to the hot empty pot. Throw in the butter, and begin mashing with the masher. When the potatoes are about halfway mashed, pour in the heated milk or cream plus the salt and some black pepper to taste, and keep mashing, scraping, and stirring. When the mixture is done to your liking (don't try to get it perfectly smooth, or it will have cooled down too much), transfer it immediately to a heated bowl or plates and serve right away.

GET CREATIVE

- For tangier mashed potatoes, substitute buttermilk for some or all of the milk or cream.

- Make green mashed potatoes by stirring in a cup of chopped cooked spinach (or frozen chopped spinach that has simply been zapped in a microwave until hot; squeeze out some of the liquid before adding).

- For subtle garlic mashed potatoes, simmer 4 or 5 peeled garlic cloves with the potatoes while you cook them. Drain the potatoes, then mash the garlic along with the potatoes.

- You can mash any of these items into the potatoes, adding them when you add the milk and/or cream and salt. Or serve a few at the table, for people to customize their own.

  - Roasted Garlic Paste (page 5)—
    1 tablespoon per serving

  - A drizzle of high-quality olive oil

  - A large clove of garlic, minced

  - Crumbled bleu cheese, goat cheese, or other soft, crumbly cheese (2 to 3 tablespoons per serving), or Luxurious Bleu Cheese Dressing (page 51)

  - Grated Cheddar, Parmesan, or Gruyère cheese (however much you want)

  - Sour cream and chives

  - Crumbled cooked bacon (see page 233) or prosciutto

  - Wasabi (1 teaspoon per serving)

  - Horseradish (1 teaspoon per serving)

  - Cooked onion or minced scallion

  - A dash of ground or, even better, freshly grated nutmeg on top

boiled parsley potatoes

Makes 4 to 5 servings

Try this very simple dish on a night when you have little time or patience for kitchen prep. It takes just 15 minutes, start to finish. Red creamer potatoes are easy to find and to work with. They require no peeling or scrubbing—just a quick rinse and perhaps a single cut, and they're ready for the stove. Use little red potatoes, about 1½ inches in diameter. They are lovely on the plate and go well with just about any fish, chicken, or meat entrée as well as many vegetarian dishes. Add the parsley at the very last minute so it stays bright green. These keep well in a tightly covered container in the refrigerator, so save a few for breakfast and reheat them in a microwave or a hot skillet to eat with your eggs.

This recipe is vegan when made with olive oil.

2 pounds (about 30) red creamer potatoes

Salt for the cooking water

A handful or two of flat-leaf parsley sprigs

3 tablespoons butter or olive oil
(or a combination)

¾ teaspoon salt

1. Rinse the potatoes in a strainer or colander under running water, then shake off the excess water. Pat the potatoes dry with paper towels or a clean dish towel, and then cut them in half lengthwise with a very sharp knife. Place them in a large saucepan, add cold water to cover by about an inch, add about a teaspoon of salt, and bring to a boil. Turn the heat down to medium-low, and simmer for 10 to 12 minutes, or until just tender enough for a fork or a sharp knife to pierce them easily. (They should not be falling apart.)

2. During the last few minutes of simmering, rinse a big handful of parsley under running water. Squeeze it tightly over the sink to press out most of the water, then roll it in paper towels to dry it further. Transfer the parsley to a cutting board and mince with a sharp knife. Measure out ⅓ cup, and set this aside.

3. Place the colander back in the sink, and drain the potatoes well. Carefully (so as not to burn yourself) pat the cooking pot dry with paper towels and immediately return the potatoes to the pot. Throw in the butter or drizzle in the olive oil (or use some of both) and toss, sprinkling in the ¾ teaspoon salt as you go. Toss in the parsley, stir, transfer to a bowl, and serve right away.

GET CREATIVE

- Try this with other small waxy potatoes, too, such as fingerlings, Yukon Golds, yellow creamers, or Yellow Finns.

- Use a high-quality olive oil in place of the butter or olive oil.

- Mix the parsley with another minced fresh herb, such as basil, thyme, or cilantro.

- Instead of using regular salt, serve some crunchy "designer" salt at the table.

- Serve with some salsa, sour cream, or guacamole (store-bought or homemade—see page 224) on the side of the plate for dipping.

- Pass a shaker bottle of hot sauce at the table.

roasted fingerlings

Makes 4 to 5 servings

Fingerling potatoes are an heirloom variety (meaning, grown from old-fashioned, non-commercial seeds, favored and thus kept alive by true vegetable gardeners) that has become quite popular in recent years. Easily found in farmers' markets and enlightened produce departments, fingerlings are small, elongated, and knobby, kind of like a wise old person's fingers, which is why they are so named. They have very thin, delicious skin and rich yellow flesh, and were born (or I should say, sprouted) to be roasted at a high temperature in a slick of olive oil. From this process, they emerge fantastically crisp on the outside, creamy on the inside, and indescribably delectable all over.

This recipe is vegan.

2½ pounds (about 24) fingerling potatoes, about 3 inches long

2 tablespoons olive oil

1. Adjust the oven rack to the center position and preheat the oven to 425°F. Scrub the potatoes under running water. Pat them dry with paper towels or a clean dish towel, and then cut them in half lengthwise with a very sharp knife.

2. Line a baking tray with aluminum foil, and drizzle it with the olive oil. (You can use one of the cut potatoes to spread the oil, holding the foil steady with your other hand.)

3. Place the potatoes, cut side down, in a single layer on the oiled surface. Place the tray in the oven, and let the potatoes roast, undisturbed, for 15 minutes.

4. Remove the tray from the oven, and use tongs to turn the potatoes over. Return the tray to the oven and let the potatoes roast for an additional 10 minutes, or until the cut sides are nicely browned and the potatoes are cooked through. Remove from the oven, and serve hot, warm, or at room temperature.

GET CREATIVE

- Season with salt and pepper to taste. (Fancy "designer" salts and exotic pepper are great here, too.)

- Garnish with a sprinkling of minced parsley.

- After you turn the potatoes over, sprinkle them with up to ½ teaspoon dried rosemary or thyme, or up to 2 teaspoons minced fresh rosemary or thyme, before returning the tray to the oven.

- Serve with a small dish of salsa, sour cream, yogurt, ketchup, or mayonnaise, for dipping.

- Drizzle with high-quality olive oil just before serving.

- Pass a shaker bottle of hot sauce at the table.

skillet potatoes with fried onions

Makes 4 to 5 servings

This classic method for making restaurant-style "home fries" involves several steps. First, you boil the potatoes. Then you drain them and brown them in batches in a skillet. Then you sauté onions, and finally you bring it all together in the skillet. All this takes some time, but not a whole lot of work. And it's worth it. If you follow this process (especially cooking the potatoes in batches so they have plenty of room to brown), the end product will be truly, divinely crisp—which, after all, is the whole point of fried potatoes.

You can use any type of potato. A combination of colors will taste great and look beautiful. A shortcut: Use leftover cooked potatoes (4 to 5 cups) to make this dish. Even baked potatoes, although crumbly, will do fine.

This recipe is vegan.

2½ pounds potatoes

3 tablespoons olive oil

¾ teaspoon salt

1 large red or yellow onion, sliced

Freshly ground black pepper

1. Scrub the potatoes (peeling is optional), and cut them into ½-inch cubes. You should have 5 to 6 cups of cubes. Place them in a large saucepan, add water to cover by about an inch, and bring to a boil. Lower the heat to a simmer, and cook, uncovered, for about 15 minutes, or until tender.

2. Put a colander in the sink, and drain the potatoes thoroughly.

3. Place a large (10- to 12-inch) heavy skillet over medium heat. After about a minute, add

1 tablespoon of the olive oil and swirl to coat the pan. Turn up the heat to medium-high, and add half the cooked potatoes in a single layer. Sprinkle with ¼ teaspoon salt, and let them sit, undisturbed, for 5 minutes.

4. Loosen the potatoes with a thin-bladed metal spatula, and turn them over in a single layer on the second side. Let them sit over the heat for another 5 minutes.

5. Scrape from the bottom to loosen the potatoes, and toss them to redistribute in the pan. Cook for another minute, then transfer the potatoes to a plate, scraping out and saving all the tasty browned bits from the bottom of the pan.

6. Wipe out the pan with a paper towel, and repeat the procedure with the remaining potatoes, using another tablespoon of the oil and another ¼ teaspoon salt. Add this second batch to the first one on the plate.

7. Wipe out the pan with a damp paper towel. Return the pan to the stove over medium heat, and wait about a minute. Then add the remaining 1 tablespoon oil, and swirl to coat the pan. Add the onion and the remaining ¼ teaspoon salt, and cook over medium heat, stirring often, for 8 to 10 minutes, or until the onion turns deeply golden.

8. Stir the potatoes into the onions, adding some black pepper. Cook over medium heat, stirring occasionally, for 10 minutes, or until everything is golden. Serve hot or warm.

GET CREATIVE

- For richer flavor, stir in 1 to 2 teaspoons butter when browning the onions.

- Add ½ teaspoon dried thyme when browning the onions.

- Add one of the following, or a combination, to the onions after they have cooked for 1 minute:

  - Up to 4 cups (packed) chopped fresh spinach

  - 1 cup diced bell pepper (any color)

  - 1 small zucchini or summer squash, diced or sliced

  - 1 cup corn (fresh or defrosted frozen)

- Add 1 small minced jalapeño when browning the onions. (Wash the knife, cutting board and your hands with soap and warm water after handling hot peppers.) Or top with hot sauce.

- Add 1 tablespoon minced garlic (about 3 good-sized cloves) to the onions midway through their cooking.

- Garnish with sour cream or yogurt.

- Sprinkle with minced scallions or parsley.

- Toss in some crumbled cooked bacon (see page 233) when you return the potatoes to the skillet.

- Garnish with cherry tomatoes or salsa.

your basic mashed sweet potatoes

Makes 4 servings

Y ou don't need to do much to sweet potatoes, other than getting them cooked. They step up to the plate all on their own, with their reliably sweet, happy flavor. This dish reheats really well, so you can make it ahead of time. You could easily double the quantity for a holiday meal. This recipe works equally well with yellow-fleshed sweet potatoes and the orange-fleshed, red-skinned kind, often referred to (and sold as) yams. (Technically, both kinds are really sweet potatoes. True yams are something else altogether.)

This recipe is vegan.

3 pounds (about 6 medium-sized) sweet potatoes

½ teaspoon salt

1 to 2 tablespoons brown sugar (light or dark)

1 teaspoon fresh lemon or lime juice

1. Set a large pot of water on the stove to boil. Peel the sweet potatoes, and cut them into chunks. Place a large colander in the sink.

2. When the water comes to a boil, add the sweet potatoes and cook for 15 to 20 minutes, or until they are quite soft and a fork can be easily inserted into them. Drain them well in the colander, and transfer them to a large bowl.

3. Add the salt, brown sugar, and lemon or lime juice, and mash until smooth. (A hand-held electric mixer at medium speed or a regular old potato masher works equally well for this.) Serve right away, or refrigerate and reheat (see "Sweet Reheat," below).

SWEET REHEAT

If you want to make these ahead and reheat them (say, for a holiday feast), spray an 8-inch square baking pan (or similar-sized gratin dish) with vegetable oil spray, or grease it with oil or butter. Spread the cooled mashed sweet potatoes in the pan, cover it tightly with foil, and refrigerate for up to 3 days. To reheat, let the pan come to room temperature, still covered. Set the oven rack to the center position, preheat the oven to 350°F, and bake the sweet potatoes, still covered, for about 30 minutes, or until heated through.

GET CREATIVE

- Add up to 3 tablespoons room-temperature butter before mashing the potatoes.

- Replace the brown sugar with honey or real maple syrup.

- Mash in a ripe banana (really good!) instead of the brown sugar.

- Add 1 tablespoon pure vanilla extract before mashing.

- Serve with lemon or lime wedges on the side for squeezing on top.

- Top with toasted walnuts or pecans.

- Spread the sweet potatoes in an 8-inch square baking dish or an oval gratin dish, top with mini-marshmallows (Life is short. Why not?), and put the pan under the broiler. Watch carefully, and remove from the broiler as soon as the marshmallows have melted and are nicely browned on top.

classic asparagus

Serves 3 to 4

Asparagus should be on the crisp side to taste really good. In this method, it gets cooked in a very small amount of water in a wide pan—kind of a one-pan cross between blanching and sautéing. By the time the water has evaporated, the asparagus spears will be perfectly cooked. You do need to watch the pan carefully, though, so they don't overcook or scorch at the end, once the water evaporates. Bonus: This method works well with broccolini and green beans, too.

This recipe is vegan.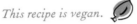

¼ cup water

1 tablespoon olive oil

1 pound asparagus
(about ½-inch diameter),
trimmed (see "Asparagus Tips"
on the opposite page)

Heaping ¼ teaspoon minced
garlic (1 small clove)

¼ teaspoon salt

1. Pour the water and olive oil into a wide, shallow pan, such as a 10- to 12-inch skillet. Lay the asparagus spears in a single layer in the liquid. (If they don't all quite fit into one layer, it's okay to pile them up a little.)

2. Turn the heat to medium-high, and when the liquid reaches a boil, cover the pan and lower the heat to medium.

3. After 2 minutes, begin checking for doneness with a fork. As soon as the asparagus is tender enough to pierce slightly with a small amount of pressure (still resistant, but no longer stone-hard), remove the cover and turn the heat back up to medium-high. Add the garlic and salt, toss to coat, and cook over this higher heat for just 30 seconds. (This allows any remaining liquid to evaporate.) Serve hot, warm, or at room temperature.

GET CREATIVE

- Right before serving, drizzle lightly with high-quality olive oil.

- Squeeze a little fresh lemon juice over the cooked asparagus. You can also garnish with a bit of freshly grated lemon zest.

- Dress the cooked spears with a splash of balsamic vinegar or a drizzle of pomegranate molasses (see page xvi).

- Tarragon, fresh or dried, is the most compatible herb for asparagus. If using dried, add ½ teaspoon when you add the salt and garlic. Or sprinkle on 1 tablespoon minced fresh tarragon just before serving.

- Serve with Poached Salmon with Shortcut "Hollandaise" (see pages 160–61)—and put some of that very delicious sauce on the asparagus, too.

- Take this in an Asian direction by adding 1 to 2 teaspoons minced fresh ginger with the garlic, or by sprinkling the cooked asparagus with sushi ginger and some toasted sesame seeds. You can also sprinkle a little soy sauce and/or a drizzle of toasted sesame oil over the cooked asparagus.

ASPARAGUS TIPS

Asparagus is sold in bundles, usually 1-pounders. Be sure to use it within a few days of purchasing—asparagus really doesn't age well. A shopping pointer: Always check out the tips of the asparagus before buying. If they're dry and tight, the asparagus is fresh. If they're separating, wilted, or at all moist, it's over the hill. Refrigerate asparagus loosely covered. Don't seal it up, airtight, in a plastic bag, or it will soon start to rot—it needs to breathe a little. "Trimming" asparagus translation: Snap off and discard the tough ends. The asparagus will know where its own dividing line is.

absolutely the best broccoli

Makes 4 servings

This two-phase process is a wonderful way to cook broccoli, especially if you're having people over and want to do some of the preparation ahead of time. First you blanch large pieces in boiling water. Then, just before serving, you give it a delicious warm-up in gently heated garlic-infused olive oil for a perfect finish. You can do the first phase—the blanching—up to 5 days ahead, which saves time at the last minute (and blanched broccoli will take up less space in the refrigerator than raw).

This recipe is vegan.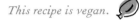

Salt for the cooking water

1 large head of broccoli
(1½ pounds)

2 tablespoons olive oil

½ teaspoon minced garlic
(about half a good-sized
clove)

¼ teaspoon salt

Freshly ground black pepper

1. Put a large pot of cold water to boil over high heat, and add a big pinch of salt. Place a large colander in the sink.

2. While waiting for the water to boil, trim and discard the tough stem end of the broccoli, and slice the rest lengthwise into about 6 hefty spears.

3. When the water boils, lower the heat to a simmer and plunge in the broccoli. Cook for 2 minutes if you like your vegetables tender-crisp, 3 minutes if you like them tender-tender.

4. Drain the broccoli in the colander, shaking it emphatically, and then dry the broccoli by patting it with paper towels or a clean kitchen towel. (You can prepare the broccoli ahead of time up to this point and then keep it at room temperature for up to 2 hours, or in the refrigerator in a resealable bag or tightly covered container for up to

5 days; let it come to room temperature or micro-wave it to warm it slightly before proceeding.)

5. Place a large (10- to 12-inch) heavy skillet over medium-low heat and add the olive oil. While you are waiting for the oil to heat, cut the broccoli into smaller pieces (whatever size and shape you prefer).

6. When the oil has become warm (after about 3 minutes), add the broccoli and heat it in the oil, turning it frequently with tongs, for about 3 minutes. Then add the garlic, and continue to cook for another 3 to 5 minutes (possibly even a little longer), or until the broccoli is heated through, cooked to your liking, and delightfully coated with the garlic and oil. Add the salt, plus some black pepper to taste. Serve hot or warm.

deeply roasted cauliflower

Makes 3 generous servings

Cauliflower is one of those vegetables that is good anywhere and everywhere along the textural spectrum—from raw to mush (as in, boiled to oblivion and mashed with butter, salt, and pepper, mashed-potato-style). This high-temperature treatment allows it to be a bit of both—very well cooked (to the point of singed, but in a good way) and utterly tender, but also crisp and crunchy.

This recipe is vegan.

1 tablespoon olive oil (possibly more)

1 large cauliflower, cored and cut into
  1-inch pieces

¼ teaspoon salt, or to taste

1. Adjust the oven rack to the center position and preheat the oven to 425°F. Line a baking tray with foil, and drizzle it with the olive oil.

2. Arrange the cauliflower pieces on the tray and shake them into a single layer. Put the tray in the oven and roast the cauliflower for 10 minutes.

3. Shake the tray and/or use tongs to redistribute the cauliflower so that more surfaces can come into contact with the hot oil. (This will crisp everything up nicely.) Roast for another 5 minutes, or until a taste test tells you the cauliflower is cooked to your liking. (It will continue to cook a bit more after it comes out of the oven.)

4. Remove the tray from the oven, and let the cauliflower cool for about 10 minutes on the tray. Season with the salt, and serve hot, warm, or at room temperature.

GET CREATIVE

- Spice mixes are really nice on roasted cauliflower. Try sprinkling on a bit of *za'atar* (page 142) about halfway through the roasting process. Or try a store-bought spice blend, such as Cajun blackening spices or curry powder.

- Season with a splash of balsamic vinegar.

- Consider leaving out the salt, or tasting the cauliflower before adding any. You might be surprised at how good it tastes unsalted. That said, it's also fun to garnish this with a very light sprinkling of coarse, crunchy salt.

- Crumble some feta, goat cheese, or bleu cheese over the hot cauliflower after you take it out of the oven, and let it melt to form a cheese topping.

- Sprinkle some toasted breadcrumbs (see page 81) over the cauliflower after it comes out of the oven.

- To make a gratin, transfer the cooked cauliflower to a baking dish, top with toasted breadcrumbs (see page 81) and shredded jack or Cheddar cheese, and put the pan under the broiler briefly to melt the cheese.

- Include a thickly sliced red onion or a thickly sliced carrot on the baking tray and roast it along with the cauliflower.

- Try this same process using broccoli instead of all or some of the cauliflower.

- Roasted cauliflower will keep for up to 5 days in a tightly covered container in the refrigerator, and will respond beautifully to all sorts of sauces, glazes, and salad dressings. You can also just cut it small and throw it into a green salad.

seriously good
green beans amandine

Makes 4 to 5 servings

The classic preparation, only better. The double cooking process involves blanching the beans first, and then coating them in a warm mixture of toasted almonds and garlic-and-butter-infused olive oil. You will want to make this for special occasions. You may also want to make it every night.

Make this vegan by omitting the butter. (You could increase the olive oil.)

Salt for the cooking water

1 tablespoon olive oil

2 teaspoons butter

¾ cup chopped almonds

1 teaspoon minced garlic
  (1 good-sized clove)

1½ pounds green beans, stem
  ends trimmed

¼ teaspoon salt

1. Put a large pot of cold water to boil over high heat, and add a big pinch of salt. Place a large colander in the sink.

2. While waiting for the water to boil, place a large (10- to 12-inch) heavy skillet over medium-low heat and add the olive oil. When the oil has become warm (after about 3 minutes), add the butter and swirl to combine. Turn the heat down to low, add the almonds, and cook, stirring frequently, for 5 to 8 minutes, or until they give off a toasty aroma. During the last couple of minutes, stir in the garlic. Watch carefully and keep stirring, turning the heat down if the almonds or garlic begins to burn. Remove the pan from the heat and set it aside.

3. When the water boils, turn the heat down to low and add the green beans. Simmer for 3 to 5 minutes, or until the beans turn bright green and shiny and are beginning to become tender. (This is subjective, so do a taste test.) When they are

done to your liking, drain them in the colander, shaking it emphatically, and then dry the beans by patting them with paper towels or a clean kitchen towel.

4. Return the pan of almonds to the stove over medium-low heat. Add the green beans, turning them with tongs until they are uniformly coated with the oil and nicely mingled with the almonds. Sprinkle in the salt as you go. Serve hot, warm, or at room temperature.

GET CREATIVE

- Toss a handful of halved cherry tomatoes in with the beans just before serving.

- Canned French-fried onions make a fun, tasty topping.

delightfully spiced carrots

Makes 4 servings

Having written many vegetable-featuring cookbooks over the past very many years, I can say with some confidence that the spices in this recipe are the ones that love carrots the best. And vice versa. Whether eating them cooked or raw, I like my carrots crunchy, so I've designed this recipe around that preference. But perhaps you like them better soft when cooked. If so, you can add an extra, easy step: Simply put a pot of water to boil, and put a colander in the sink. When the water is ready, toss in the sliced carrots and cook for 30 seconds or so. Then immediately drain them in the colander, shake it exuberantly a few times, and proceed with the recipe. You will get your tender result this way.

This recipe is vegan.

1 tablespoon olive oil

1 teaspoon ground cumin

½ teaspoon cinnamon

8 medium-sized carrots
(about 1½ pounds),
cut on the diagonal into
¼-inch-thick slices

½ teaspoon minced garlic
(about 1 small clove)

¼ teaspoon salt

Freshly ground black pepper

1. Place a large (10- to 12-inch) heavy skillet over medium heat. After about a minute, add the olive oil and swirl to coat the pan.

2. Stir in the cumin and cinnamon, and let them cook in the oil for about 30 seconds. Then add the carrots and garlic, turning them with tongs until thoroughly coated with oil and spice.

3. Sprinkle in the salt, and stir well. Cover, and cook, stirring several times, for about 5 minutes, or until the carrots are just tender. (If at any point they appear to be sticking or scorching, add a tablespoon of water.) Serve hot, warm, or at room temperature.

- Garnish with lemon wedges for squeezing at the table.

- Add a teaspoon or two of butter when heating the olive oil and spices.

- Add a pinch or two of red pepper flakes along with the spices.

- Add a tablespoon or two of fresh lemon juice or orange juice along with the carrots.

- Add up to a teaspoon of grated lemon and/or orange zest.

- Add 2 teaspoons honey or brown sugar along with the carrots. (Or just sweeten to taste.)

- Add up to 3 tablespoons minced crystallized ginger along with the carrots.

- Add ¼ cup currants or golden raisins along with the carrots.

- Toss in a few tablespoons of minced fresh mint during the last minute or so of cooking (highly recommended!).

- Sprinkle the cooked carrots with up to ½ cup toasted chopped walnuts or sliced or slivered almonds.

fajita-style peppers and onions

Makes 4 to 5 servings

When cooked minimally over high heat, sweet bell peppers retain much of their crispness and color and become even sweeter and more intense, resulting in the most versatile side-dish-slash-condiment imaginable. A touch of this magical combo can cheer up any plate, at any temperature. Serve it as a side dish or wrap it in a tortilla, and you can accommodate vegetarians alongside meat lovers when whipping up a steak fajita dinner (see page 176). You can also pile these peppers and onions on any burger (see burger chapter beginning on page 125), a Pan-Grilled Boneless Chicken Breast (page 154), an open-faced toasted cheese sandwich, an omelet, pasta, pizza, rice . . . really just about anything. Make a batch and keep it in the refrigerator for up to a week, stored in a resealable plastic bag or a tightly covered container, so you can use it whenever you like.

This recipe is vegan.

1 tablespoon olive oil

1 medium red or yellow onion,
thickly sliced

1 large red bell pepper,
cut into ¼-inch-wide strips

1 large yellow bell pepper, cut into
¼-inch-wide strips

1 large green bell pepper, cut into
¼-inch-wide strips

¼ teaspoon salt

1 teaspoon minced garlic
(1 good-sized clove)

1. Place a large (10- to 12-inch) heavy skillet over medium heat. After about a minute, add the olive oil and swirl to coat the pan. Turn the heat to high, and add the onion. Cook for 3 minutes, or until the onion begins to soften.

2. Add the bell peppers, salt, and garlic, and cook for about 1 minute. Then turn the heat down to medium, and continue to cook and stir (tongs work best) for only about 5 minutes longer. The peppers should be barely cooked. Serve hot, warm, or at room temperature.

GET CREATIVE

• For a kick of heat and flavor, add up to 1 teaspoon chili powder, a pinch of red pepper flakes, a pinch of oregano, or ½ teaspoon ground cumin or toasted cumin seeds (see page 25) along with the onion.

• Once the peppers and onions are cooked, stir in a tablespoon or two of fresh lime juice.

• For an exotic and very special treat, search the aisles of a gourmet store for toasted pumpkin seed oil (or ask someone to give you a bottle for your birthday). Drizzle this on top, and prepare to swoon.

• Top with Peppy Pepitas (page 228) or plain toasted pumpkin seeds.

spinach with garlic

Makes 2 to 3 servings

So simple, and so good. This delicious little dish cooks so fast, you can make successive batches and the first batch will still be hot by the time you're finished with the second. Another reason to make it twice: The first batch might be gone before you get to the second. People walking through your kitchen, armed with forks, know how to make this disappear. You can make this with fresh or frozen (either whole-leaf or chopped) spinach. For this dish, they're pretty much interchangeable.

This recipe is vegan.

1 pound spinach, fresh
(stemming optional) or frozen

1 tablespoon water

1 tablespoon olive oil

½ teaspoon minced garlic

¼ teaspoon salt

1. If using fresh spinach, place it in a colander and rinse well. Shake to remove most, but not all, of the water clinging to the leaves. If using frozen spinach, thaw it in a colander by running it under room-temperature tap water, and then let it drain well, pressing out most of the excess liquid with the back of a spoon. (It doesn't have to be bone-dry—just not soupy.)

2. Place a large (10- to 12-inch) heavy skillet over medium-low heat, add the tablespoon of water and the olive oil, and heat for about 30 seconds. Then add the spinach, and cover the pan. Let it cook, covered and undisturbed, for 30 seconds for fresh spinach or 1 minute for frozen. Then uncover, toss with tongs, and turn up the heat to medium-high.

3. Add the garlic and salt, and cook, stirring with the tongs for about a minute longer, or until the spinach is wilted. Lift out the spinach with tongs, leaving behind any extra liquid. Serve right away.

- Add some black pepper and/or red pepper flakes along with the garlic.

- Drizzle the cooked spinach with a little high-quality olive oil or any roasted nut oil just before serving.

- Drizzle some toasted sesame oil over the cooked spinach and top with toasted sesame seeds.

- Squeeze lemon juice over the cooked spinach.

- Add a handful of raisins or currants along with the spinach.

- Once the spinach is cooked, sprinkle on some lightly toasted pine nuts, chopped toasted walnuts, or chopped apple.

THE SPIN ON SPINACH

The year-round availability of packaged prewashed baby spinach has made it so much simpler to enjoy this great vegetable more easily and more often. I often buy spinach loose, in bulk, rather than packaged, which is usually a less expensive way to go. Look for bulk spinach in the produce departments of many super-markets and at farmers' markets. I like to rewash the packaged prewashed spinach, just as I do the bulk-bought kind. It's a simple procedure if you intend to cook the spinach, because you don't need to spin it dry. The water still clinging to the leaves after you've shaken them a few times becomes part of the cooking process. (However, if your spinach is destined for a salad, spin it very dry.)

braised brussels sprouts
in mustard sauce

Through this dish, I've discovered that many people who think they don't like Brussels sprouts turn out to be wrong. The trick is to slice the sprouts thin and cook them until they're very tender. This makes for a bit more work, but it elevates the sprouts to melt-in-your-mouth status. It's worthy of becoming your Thanksgiving signature. For a change of pace—and a lovely sweet flavor that goes with the sauce—this recipe uses shallots instead of onions or garlic. They're easy to find and easy to cut if you use a very sharp paring knife. You can use any kind of prepared mustard in this recipe. I have made it with everything from Dijon to good old French's yellow.

This recipe is vegan.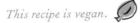

1 pound Brussels sprouts

2 tablespoons olive oil

⅓ cup minced shallots
(about two 3-ounce shallots)

½ teaspoon salt

5 tablespoons water

¼ cup prepared mustard

2 tablespoons light brown sugar

Freshly ground black pepper

1. Use a very sharp knife to cut off and discard the base of the Brussels sprouts. (As you do so, the outer leaves will fall off. Keep and use any that are not bruised!) Then slice a piece from one side, place the sprout cut side down (for slicing stability), and cut the sprout crosswise into about 5 slices (more or less, depending on its size). Repeat until you have cut up all the sprouts in this way.

2. Place a large (10- to 12-inch) heavy skillet over medium heat. After about a minute, add the olive oil and swirl to coat the pan. Add the shallots, and sauté for 2 minutes. Stir in the Brussels sprouts and salt, pour in 3 tablespoons of the water, and spread everything evenly across the bottom of the pan. Reduce the heat to medium-low, cover, and let cook, undisturbed, for 5 minutes.

3. Meanwhile, combine the mustard, brown sugar, and remaining 2 tablespoons water in a small bowl, and stir until blended.

4. Once the Brussels sprouts have cooked for 5 minutes, pour in the mustard mixture, stirring to distribute it well. Turn the heat to low, cover the pan, and cook, undisturbed, for 3 minutes.

5. Stir again, and decide if you like the sprouts cooked to this degree or if you want to cook them a bit more. You can leave the skillet on the stove over low heat for up to 5 minutes longer, in which case the sprouts will brown and become more intensely flavored—it's your call. Serve hot or warm, topped with a generous amount of black pepper.

GET CREATIVE

- Use pure maple syrup in place of the brown sugar.

- Throw in up to ½ cup dried cranberries or golden raisins along with the Brussels sprouts.

- Sprinkle some chopped toasted hazelnuts, walnuts, or almonds over the finished dish.

- Scatter some thinly sliced fresh spinach or arugula (just a handful of leaves) over the finished dish—a beautiful green contrast to the yellow sprouts.

dark leafy greens with very sweet onions

Makes 4 servings

Here's your opportunity to become acquainted with some of those mysterious edible dark green leaves you are being told are so good for you. I recommend using some combination of kale, collard greens, mustard greens, and chard to complement the sweet flavor of the onions. Other possible candidates include spinach, escarole, beet greens, dandelion greens, and turnip greens. Don't be put off by the apparent enormity of the quantity of greens. They cook down dramatically.

This recipe is vegan.

2 tablespoons olive oil

2 medium red or yellow onions, chopped

3 large bunches fresh greens, stemmed if necessary, coarsely chopped (about 12 cups chopped)

½ teaspoon salt

Freshly ground black pepper

1. Place a large (10- to 12-inch) heavy skillet over medium heat. After about a minute, add the olive oil and swirl to coat the pan. Add the onions, turn the heat to high, and sauté for 2 minutes. Then reduce the heat to medium, and cook, stirring often, for another 5 minutes, or until the onions are translucent and soft.

2. Add the greens in three or four batches, sprinkling them very lightly with some of the

salt after each addition. As they cook, turn the leaves with tongs, bringing the wilted ones from the bottom to the top of the pile.

3. When all the greens have wilted to your liking, grind on a generous amount of black pepper, and serve hot or warm.

LARGE GREEN LEAVES TAKE OVER THE WORLD (OR AT LEAST YOUR REFRIGERATOR)

Green leafy vegetables are huge until they're cooked, and they can present a volume challenge for your refrigerator. They're also fairly perishable. Two solutions: Either simply cook and eat them the same day you buy them, thus avoiding the need to store them at all, or, precook them slightly. When you get home from the store, put a large pot of water to boil over high heat, and set a colander on a plate next to the stove. When the water boils, turn the heat down to a simmer. Rinse your bundle of greens, still bundled, under cold water, and then dip the leaves (holding the bundle by the stems with tongs) into the hot water for about 10 seconds. As you remove the leaves from the water, shake as much of the water as you can back into the pot; then let them drain in the colander for a few minutes. Take the colander to the sink, and use your hands to squeeze any excess water out of the leaves. After squeezing, you will have a tight little bundle of partly cooked leaves, with their volume many times reduced (and their refrigerator shelf life many times increased). Transfer the bundle to a resealable plastic bag or an airtight container, and refrigerate for up to several days. When it's time to make this recipe, simply slice the bundle into strips, and proceed.

GET CREATIVE

• Add up to 12 medium-sized stemmed, sliced fresh shiitake mushrooms along with the onions.

• Add ½ teaspoon minced garlic just before you begin adding the greens.

• For more sweetness, use Vidalia or Maui onions (two very sweet varieties) instead of regular onions.

• Use a high-quality olive oil for sautéing, and drizzle a little more on at the end.

• Drizzle the cooked greens with any roasted nut or seed oil.

• Gently stir in up to 1 cup crumbled feta cheese or ricotta salata just before serving.

• This is wonderful served over pasta, such as penne or rigatoni.

• Add a handful of dried cherries or golden raisins along with the greens. Or, at the end of cooking, stir in up to 1 cup drained canned unsweetened sour cherries.

• Sprinkle up to ½ cup toasted walnuts or pine nuts on the finished dish.

• Serve with a big chunk of crusty bread to mop up the juices.

urban-grilled summer squash

Makes 4 servings

The definition of "grilled" is up for grabs. You can use a grill or a grill pan (with raised ridges that sear those telltale stripes onto the food). I extend the definition to include this easy method: simply searing something in a pan and not moving it while it cooks (thus allowing it to acquire a delectable golden-brown crusty underside). It's the grilling method for when you live on the fifth floor and you'd probably get evicted if you cooked on a hibachi on your windowsill. Hence the name "Urban-Grilled." It works with any of the thin-skinned, quick-cooking squash varieties, like yellow pattypan, green or yellow zucchini (a combination of the two looks great), or yellow crookneck. To avoid overcrowding the pan (which would "urban-steam" the squash, rather than grilling it), you can brown it in batches as directed and/or set up two or more pans for browning.

This recipe is vegan.

2 to 4 tablespoons olive oil

2 medium red or yellow onions, thinly sliced

¼ teaspoon salt

1 teaspoon minced garlic (1 good-sized clove)

1½ pounds summer squash, cut into ¼-inch-thick slices or ½-inch cubes

Freshly ground black pepper

1. Place a large (10- to 12-inch) heavy skillet over medium heat. After about a minute, add 1 tablespoon of the olive oil and swirl to coat the pan. Add the onions and half of the salt. Cook, stirring often, for about 10 minutes, or until the onions become very tender and lightly golden. During the last minute or so of cooking, stir in the garlic. Then transfer the mixture to a serving bowl that will be large enough to hold the squash as well, and set aside.

2. Without cleaning it, return the pan to the heat and add another tablespoon of olive oil, swirling once again to coat the pan. Add as much of the squash as will fit in a single layer, and cook without stirring for 1 to 2 minutes, or until very golden on the bottom.

3. Use a thin-bladed metal spatula to carefully loosen each piece and flip it over. Let it cook, undisturbed, on the second side for 1 to 2 minutes, until deeply golden brown on the bottom.

4. Loosen the pieces with the spatula again, and add them to the bowl holding the onion mixture.

5. Repeat the browning process with the remaining squash, adding more oil as needed, in as many batches as necessary.

6. When all of the squash has been cooked, toss it gently with the onions. (Try not to break the squash any more than necessary, but don't fret if you do.) Season with the remaining ⅛ teaspoon salt and a good amount of black pepper. Serve hot, warm, or at room temperature.

GET CREATIVE

- Add ½ teaspoon dried thyme to the onions, or sprinkle the finished dish with 1 tablespoon minced fresh thyme (or minced parsley, or snipped chives).

- Scatter 3 tablespoons minced fresh mint over the finished dish.

- Drizzle a teaspoon of balsamic vinegar over each batch of squash in the pan, just before you transfer it to the bowl. Or drizzle a few teaspoons of pomegranate molasses (see page xvi) over the finished dish.

- Sprinkle up to ¼ cup lightly toasted pine nuts over the squash mixture just before serving.

- Add up to ½ cup crumbled feta or goat cheese when you stir the onions and squash together.

winter squash *au naturel*

Makes 4 servings

Eager to get you acquainted with winter squash (see "Squash for All Seasons," page 218), I've decided to keep it very basic here. You'll simply roast it cut in half, and serve it that way. You can mash it with a fork directly in the skin, and sprinkle in some salt and pepper, maybe melt in a little butter. But start plain and see how you like it (and also see how the particular squash in front of you tastes—the sweetness can vary, depending on growing and harvesting conditions). Believe it or not, the only tricky part about preparing winter squash is cutting it. The combination of its very hard skin and its round shape makes it a knife challenge, so proceed slowly and carefully. (Safest technique: Insert the point of a good sharp knife first, and use a gentle sawing motion to initiate the cutting.) Once you've split the squash, use scissors to cut loose the strands of pulp around the seeds, and then scrape the seeds away with a spoon. Discard the seeds or reserve them to toast—see page 28).

Figure on about ½ pound of squash per serving, and plan accordingly. Ideally, you will find a 1-pound acorn squash for every two servings, or a 2-pound butternut that you can quarter for serving four.

This recipe is vegan.

1 tablespoon olive oil

2 pounds winter squash
    (acorn, butternut, or delicata)

1. Adjust the oven rack to the center position and preheat the oven to 400°F. Line a baking tray with foil, and pour on the olive oil. Use your fingers to distribute the oil so that it coats the area where you'll put the squash.

2. Cut the squash in half lengthwise, and scrape out the seeds. If the squash is very large, cut each half in half again, crosswise this time.

3. Place the squash, cut side down, on the olive oil coating. Put the tray in the oven, and roast the squash until it is tender enough to easily insert a fork or a sharp knife into the flesh: 15 to 20 minutes for delicata, 35 to 40 minutes for acorn or butternut.

4. Remove the tray from the oven, and let the squash pieces rest for about 10 minutes before turning them over. Serve hot or warm, in the skin, with forks for mashing and/or spoons for scooping.

GET CREATIVE

It's fun to have an assortment of condiments at the table and let each person customize his or her squash. Use any of the following:

- Butter, at room temperature

- Salt and pepper

- Balsamic vinegar

- Brown sugar

- Real maple syrup

- Pomegranate seeds and/or pomegranate molasses (see page xvi)

- Wedges of lemon or lime

- Chopped crystallized ginger

- Chopped toasted walnuts or pecans

DELICATA
A SQUASH WORTH ITS STRIPES

The next time you're hunting for produce, check out delicata squash. They're small (averaging about ½ pound) pale yellow ovals with bright orange and deep green stripes—often so beautiful that you might want to keep a bowlful around just to look at. When you cut them open, you'll see a large seed cavity and flesh that tends to be only ½-inch thick, or less. Thus, they cook in about half the time of their winter squash cousins. And their flavor is subtle to the point of ethereal.

SQUASH FOR ALL SEASONS

Most types of squash are available most of the time, yet we still refer to some as summer squash (zucchini, yellow crookneck, pattypan) and others as winter squash (butternut, acorn, delicata). The categories really have more to do with characteristics than with seasons. Summer squash have thin, edible skin and very pale, tender flesh with negligible seeds (all of which traits are especially evident in smaller, younger specimens), and they cook very, very quickly on a stovetop or grill. They're also quite perishable and need to be refrigerated. Winter squash, on the other hand, are encased in hard, inedible skin, tend to have golden-hued, sturdy flesh, and contain a pocket of seeds that you need to remove. (Not unlike when you make a jack-o'-lantern. In fact, pumpkins are a type of winter squash. But you knew that.) Winter squash have a long larder life, meaning you don't need to refrigerate them; they will keep for weeks if stored out of direct sunlight. Winter squash is usually baked unpeeled, in seeded halves, and then the flesh is often scooped out and made into some other fine concoction (such as the soup on page 26). Rarely is it just presented on its own, playing itself, totally unscripted and with no makeup. And this is a shame, because "just plain" winter squash is a delightful thing—sweet from its own natural character, delicate in flavor, and full of excellent nutrients (most notably fiber and vitamins) with very few calories.

party
snacks.

Download *These* Apps

If chips and salsa are your favorite things to serve when people come over to hang out, that's fine. If you're ready to graduate to the next level, go with good bread and a few great cheeses. Next, you might consider adding a bunch of grapes, some thinly sliced apples, some dried cherries or figs, and some olives to the mix. And then you'll be ready to ratchet things up another notch with your own brilliant homemade party snacks and appetizers.

That's where these recipes come in. They'll tell you what you need to know to serve "heavy apps" to your friends. To supplement them, consider other ideas from elsewhere in this book, repurposed as party food—ideas like Roasted Fingerlings (page 190), mini meatballs (see pages 70–71), teriyaki chicken wings (see page 159), and Parmesan Fricos (pages 12–13).

All of these recipes are easy to pull off, and most can be done ahead of time. Make one or two, or make a bunch, and you'll find yourself having one of those evenings where everyone's feeling happy and full, and you unanimously decide not to go out to dinner after all.

pesto

Makes about 1 cup

Fresh pesto is available in grocery stores, but if you have a blender or a food processor, and fresh basil is abundant, it's much cheaper to make your own. This keeps for weeks, or even months, if you keep the top sealed with a layer of olive oil, and you store it in a tightly covered container in the refrigerator. Use it on any dish (and on several of these Party Snacks!) where basil and garlic are already welcome.

3 cups (tightly packed) fresh basil leaves

3 medium cloves garlic

⅓ cup olive oil, plus a little extra

⅓ cup grated Parmesan cheese

Place the basil leaves and garlic in a food processor or blender, and pulverize. Keep the machine running while you drizzle in the olive oil in a steady stream. When you have a smooth paste (seconds later), transfer to a bowl (being sure you scrape every last bit from the blender or food processor) and stir in the cheese. Transfer to a container with a tight-fitting lid, and smooth the top surface of the pesto. Drizzle in enough olive oil to seal the surface, cover, and refrigerate until use.

GET CREATIVE

- Use a high-quality olive oil.

- You can blend ⅓ cup pine nuts or chopped walnuts (raw or lightly toasted) into the basil and garlic.

- Add some salt and pepper to taste.

crostini, any style
(little italian toasts)

Makes 12 crostini; serves 4 as an appetizer

In Italy, toast isn't relegated to the breakfast table. Slices of toasted bread are served as an appetizer, antipasto, or midday snack. Sometimes they're rubbed with garlic and given a drizzle of olive oil and a sprinkling of salt and pepper and maybe some chopped tomatoes and basil. That's bruschetta ("brus-ketta"). Then there are small slices of toasted bread, spread with savory toppings. Those are crostini (you can pronounce that). Here's how to make them, plus a few ideas for things to put on top. It's fun to serve a big platter of them with a bunch of different toppings. Use good bread (somewhat stale is okay, and this is a nice way to use up a day-old baguette), watch it carefully when toasting, so it doesn't burn, and you can't go wrong. A pastry brush comes in handy here.

⅓ cup olive oil

1 teaspoon minced garlic
(1 good-sized clove)

Twelve ½-inch-thick diagonal slices from
1 or 2 French baguettes

1. Adjust the oven rack to the center position and preheat the oven (or toaster oven) to 350°F. Line a baking tray with foil.

2. Combine the olive oil and garlic in a small bowl.

3. Lightly brush the bread on both sides with the olive oil–garlic mixture. Arrange the bread slices on the prepared tray. Bake for about 5 minutes, or until the bread is lightly toasted. (Keep an eye on it, so it doesn't burn.)

4. Remove the tray from the oven, and let the crostini cool for at least 5 minutes before serving. Top with any of the toppings listed at the right.

GET CREATIVE

Top crostini with any of these, or come up with your own ideas. Pretty much anything savory and flavorful will work. Create your own signature crostini, and name them after yourself.

- A spoonful of goat cheese or fresh ricotta sprinkled with a bit of freshly grated black pepper and, if you like, a drizzle of high-quality olive oil

- A small slice of ripe tomato and some minced fresh basil (and a small slice of fresh mozzarella, if you like)

- A dab of pesto (store-bought or homemade—see page 220) and a halved cherry tomato

- Chopped olives

- Olive spread (tapenade) from a jar

- A small pile of well-cooked onions

- Hummus (store-bought or homemade—see page 226)

- Small pieces of cooked asparagus (page 196) and, if you like, a strip of prosciutto

- A slice of tomato, a slice of hard-boiled egg, and a dollop of mayonnaise

- Top with cheese and melt it, as directed for Cheese-Topped Croutons (page 9).

bocconcini skewers
(fresh mozzarella balls with basil and tomatoes)

Makes 10 to 20 skewers

Strikingly simple, this little craft project will only be as good as the few ingredients involved. So choose the freshest mozzarella balls (bocconcini), the sweetest possible cherry tomatoes, and the perkiest basil leaves. There. I've just given you the entire recipe! Obviously, it's a great point of entry for beginners. You can buy cool wooden cocktail picks at any kitchen store and at some specialty grocery stores. Or just use regular toothpicks. How many pieces of cheese, cherry tomatoes, and basil leaves you put on each serving is up to you and depends on their size.

If you're serving this with pesto and you're making it from scratch, you can prepare it well ahead of time (see page 220).

½ pound (about 20) mini mozzarella
   balls, drained

1 small container small cherry tomatoes
   (assorted colors, if available)

About 20 small basil leaves

Pesto for dipping (optional), store-bought
   or homemade (page 220)

1. Skewer 1 or 2 cheese balls, tomatoes, and individual basil leaves on each cocktail skewer.

2. Arrange the skewers on a serving plate. If you like, place a dish of pesto in the center for dipping.

GET CREATIVE

- Drizzle the skewers with high-quality olive oil and sprinkle on some freshly grated black pepper, plus a pinch of dried oregano and/or thyme.

- Wrap the mozzarella balls and tomatoes with small pieces of prosciutto.

guacamole

Makes 4 to 6 servings

Authentic guacamole is a simple thing—just ripe avocado with a few discreet touches of seasoning. Although best known as a dip for chips, guacamole is tremendously versatile as a colorful accompaniment to many savory dishes, especially those featuring eggs, beans, tomatoes, or cornmeal. This is best right after it's made, so try to prepare it at the last minute.

This recipe is vegan.

2 tablespoons fresh lemon juice or lime juice

2 large (about 1 pound) firm, ripe avocados

½ teaspoon salt

¼ teaspoon ground cumin

3 tablespoons very finely minced red onion

3 tablespoons minced cilantro

¼ cup diced fresh tomato or
    tomato-based salsa

⅛ teaspoon cayenne pepper, or to taste

1. Pour the lemon or lime juice into a medium-sized bowl.

2. Cut the avocados in half, remove the pits (see "About Avocados," opposite), and use a soup spoon to scoop the flesh into the bowl.

3. Use a fork to slowly mash the avocado into the juice, adding the salt and cumin as you go. When the avocado reaches your desired consistency (lumps are fine), stir in the onion, cilantro, and tomato or salsa. Add the cayenne. Serve right away.

ABOUT AVOCADOS

Buy avocados that feel heavy and firm. If they're hard as a rock in the store, they'll be perfect in about 3 days (2 days if the weather is hot). If they're only slightly soft and have just the slightest amount of give when gently squeezed, they're ready to use today. If they're much softer than that, they're past their prime. Store avocados in a dark, cool place, but not in the refrigerator (tropical fruit never likes to be refrigerated). To ripen them, store them in a paper bag at room temperature. To remove the pit, carefully cut the avocado in half, running a sharp knife around the pit. Twist the halves to pull them apart. Use a spoon to scoop out the pit. Pull off the skin (it should come off easily) and cut or mash the flesh. To keep it from turning brown, cover the flesh with some fresh lemon or lime juice as soon as possible. (Best to have the juice ready and waiting before you cut the avocado.)

GET CREATIVE

- Add more lemon or lime juice, to taste.

- If you like the grassy, spicy taste of fresh chiles, add up to 1 whole jalapeño pepper, seeded, veins removed, and finely minced; or add some minced green bell pepper if you don't want the spicy heat.

- Stir in up to ½ cup finely chopped peeled, seeded cucumber.

- Add 1 or 2 minced tomatillos for an extra-tangy flavor.

- Top with Peppy Pepitas (page 228).

- In addition to the usual chips, serve this with baby carrots and/or jicama slices or sticks, for dipping.

- Make nachos! Preheat the oven to 350°F. Spread tortilla chips on a tray, and sprinkle them generously with a grated mild cheese, such as jack or white Cheddar. Place the tray in the center of the oven and bake for a few minutes, until the cheese melts. Remove, let cool a little, and serve topped with guacamole and salsa.

hummus

Makes 4 to 6 servings

Y ou can buy some very good prepared hummus in almost any grocery store or deli these days, but it's fun (and much cheaper) to make your own. This homemade version keeps for about a week if stored in a tightly covered container in the refrigerator, especially because you will be coating the surface with a serious slick of olive oil. You'll need a blender or food processor for this. If you use a blender, you may need to work in batches and/or add a bit of water at the start to get the puréeing going.

This recipe is vegan.

Two 15-ounce cans chickpeas (about 3 cups cooked chickpeas)

6 tablespoons sesame tahini

6 tablespoons fresh lemon juice

1 teaspoon minced garlic (1 good-sized clove; or possibly more, to taste)

½ teaspoon salt (possibly more, to taste)

1 teaspoon ground cumin

Olive oil, for the top

⅛ teaspoon cayenne pepper

1. Set a colander in the sink and pour in the chickpeas. Give them a quick rinse and allow them to drain.

2. Put the chickpeas and all the remaining ingredients except the olive oil and cayenne in a blender or food processor, and purée to form a thick paste. Taste the hummus to see if you want to add more garlic or salt.

3. Transfer the hummus to a container with a tight-fitting lid (or put it in a decorative bowl) and smooth the top. Pour a little olive oil on top, and tilt until it coats the entire surface. Cover (with plastic wrap, if using the decorative bowl) and refrigerate until ready to use. Allow to come to room temperature before serving. Sprinkle the top with a light dusting of cayenne, and serve.

DISCOVER TAHINI

Sesame tahini is a flavorful paste made from pulverized sesame seeds. It comes packed in jars and can be found near the peanut butter and other nut and seed butters in the grocery store. When you first open the jar, the oil will likely have separated from the solids. Just patiently stir it back in. Once the jar has been opened, store tahini in the refrigerator, where it will keep indefinitely. In addition to using it in hummus, try it as a spread on its own, or thin it with a little water, add a touch of garlic, some lemon juice, and minced parsley, and use it as a sauce for vegetables or grains—or as a dip.

GET CREATIVE

• Use high-quality olive oil.

• Sprinkle some minced parsley or cilantro and/or a bit of paprika on top of the hummus.

• Reserve a handful of chickpeas to sprinkle on the hummus as a garnish.

• Add up to ¼ cup chopped tomatoes (fresh or dried) before blending. (If using dried tomatoes, soften them in a little hot water first, then drain it off.)

• Use fresh-squeezed orange juice in place of some or all of the lemon juice.

• Add a few tablespoons of finely minced scallion, red onion, or red bell pepper before blending, or sprinkle these on top as a garnish.

• Serve with fresh or toasted pita triangles (or store-bought pita chips) and a platter of raw and cooked vegetables for dipping.

• Use as a topping for crostini (page 221) or Luxury Potato Bites (page 234).

• Use as a sandwich filling (in pita or with regular bread), with cucumbers, tomatoes, and sliced pickles.

peppy pepitas

Makes 8 to 10 servings

Plain hulled pumpkin seeds are among the world's best snacks—delicious and nutritious, not to mention interesting, exotic, and not too filling. This recipe adds sexy, mouthwatering, and mysterious to that list. A slow stovetop toasting in lots of olive oil with whole cumin seeds and chiles infuses them with flavor, and a sprinkling of salt and lime juice takes them over the top. These keep for up to a week, stored in a resealable bag or tightly covered container at room temperature. Or you can store them indefinitely in the freezer, sealed in a heavy resealable bag. So keep this in mind, and make an extra batch or two to freeze. Then you'll always have something impressive to serve your friends for a snack when they drop by on short notice. (They will thaw very quickly at room temperature.)

This recipe is vegan.

¼ cup olive oil

1½ pounds (about 6 cups) hulled
pumpkin seeds

1 tablespoon whole cumin seeds

4 or 5 dried chiles de árbol
(whole pods), or 1 teaspoon
red pepper flakes, or both

¾ teaspoon salt (possibly more)

3 tablespoons fresh lime juice

1. Place a large (10- to 12-inch) heavy skillet over medium-low heat, and add the olive oil. Let it heat for about a minute.

2. Add the pumpkin seeds, cumin seeds, and chiles or red pepper flakes. Use a wooden spatula or spoon to slowly stir until everything becomes evenly coated with the oil. Keep cooking, stirring every few minutes, for a good 20 minutes (possibly even a little longer), until the pumpkin seeds give off a strong toasty aroma and most of them are gradually becoming a light golden brown.

3. Continue to cook on medium-low heat just long enough to stir in the salt and then splash in the lime juice, which will sizzle. Turn off the heat, and wait about 5 minutes for the seeds to absorb the lime juice. Taste, and add more salt if you think it's needed.

4. Remove and discard the whole chiles, put the seeds in a bowl, and serve warm or at room temperature. Or cool completely and transfer to a resealable plastic freezer bag for storage.

GET CREATIVE

• Sprinkle on a few dashes of soy sauce when adding the lime juice.

• Serve these on their own, or use them as a garnish for Latin-style dishes, including guacamole (store-bought or homemade—see page 224), Cuban Black Bean Soup (page 14), Vegetarian Chili (page 100), Steak Fajitas (page 176), Taco Salad (page 58), and as many other things as you can think of.

• These are also great for livening up a green salad, or sprinkling over cooked rice or beans.

CHILES DE ÁRBOL

Dried chiles de árbol (the small, thin red ones) are available in Latin grocery stores, in many supermarkets (often in the Mexican section), or online. They are fairly hot and quite pretty. Because they are left whole in this dish, they don't give off a huge amount of heat—just enough. Dried chiles keep for months and look very attractive in a bowl on the kitchen counter. If you like their flavor but want milder heat, split them open before using them and discard the seeds.

slightly sweet cajun-spiced nuts

Makes 6 to 8 servings

Serve these wonderfully complex glazed nuts on their own or with cheese, and definitely with drinks of any kind. You can also use them, whole or chopped, as a topping for other dishes. Or wrap them in colorful paper or put them in old-fashioned glass jars, and give them as gifts. I originally made this with walnuts, and then tried pecans and cashews. Then, thinking about cost, I tried peanuts, which sell for about a quarter the price of other nuts. They were all fabulous. The large pan is essential for this, because the nuts need maximum contact with the spices in order to become thoroughly coated. Open a window and turn on the stovetop fan before you begin. When you add the vinegar to the hot pan, there will be fumes! These store for up to 2 weeks in a tightly sealed container at room temperature, or indefinitely when sealed in resealable plastic bags and kept in the freezer.

2 tablespoons canola, soy,
   or peanut oil

1 tablespoon butter

2 tablespoons ground cumin

1 tablespoon powdered ginger

1 tablespoon chili powder

1 teaspoon dried thyme

1 pound (about 4 cups) unsalted
   walnuts, pecans, cashews,
   or peanuts

½ teaspoon salt (possibly more)

⅓ cup (packed) brown sugar
   (light or dark)

¼ cup cider vinegar

1. Place a large (10- to 12-inch) heavy skillet over medium-low heat and add the olive oil. Let it heat for about 30 seconds, then add the butter and swirl until it melts.

2. Sprinkle in the cumin, ginger, chili powder, and thyme, and slowly stir the spices into the buttery oil with a wooden spatula or a wooden spoon. Keep the heat steady while you stir for about 2 minutes, or until the spices are fragrant.

3. Add the nuts, spreading them out in the pan. Sprinkle in the salt, and continue cooking and slowly stirring for about 2 minutes.

4. Sprinkle in the brown sugar, and continue to cook and stir for another 2 to 3 minutes, or until the sugar begins to melt and is just starting to adhere to the surface of the pan. (Scrape as you go, and if necessary use a table knife to scrape off the soft sugar coating that will likely have adhered to your wooden stirrer.)

5. Pour the vinegar into the pan. It will sizzle dramatically. (Don't inhale near the pan at this moment.) Keep stirring for another 30 seconds, and you will see that the vinegar is deglazing the pan, loosening up all the tasty stuff that has stuck to its surface. Turn off the heat, and wait about 5 minutes for the nuts to absorb the vinegar.

6. Transfer the nuts to a bowl and let cool until they are at a comfortable tasting temperature. Taste to see if you think they need more salt, and adjust accordingly. Serve right away, or allow to cool and then transfer to a resealable plastic bag for storage.

GET CREATIVE

- You can give the finished nuts an even deeper flavor with a brief final toasting in the oven: Adjust the rack to the center position and preheat the oven to 350°F. Line a baking tray with foil and spray it with nonstick spray. Spread out the spiced nuts on the tray, and bake them for 2 to 3 minutes, or until they turn an even deeper golden brown. Keep an eye on them the entire time, so they don't burn. Remove the nuts from the oven, and allow to cool for at least 10 minutes before serving.

- Toss in ½ cup minced crystallized ginger after the nuts have cooled down.

- Use as a garnish for green salads, cooked grains, or any vegetable side dish where it seems to fit.

- *Make this vegan by omitting the butter.*

bacon-wrapped fruit bites

Makes 12 bacon bites; serves 4 to 6 as a party snack

Prepare yourself for a warm and wonderful one-two punch of flavor—salty, crunchy, and smoky at first, and then blissfully sweet. Dried apricots come in two types: the thin, very tart kind that are halves, and a thicker, plumper, sweeter type that are whole apricots with their pits removed, known as Turkish apricots. For this recipe, you want the Turkish type. Look for them at natural foods stores, good produce markets, and specialty grocery stores. The best setup for this is a rectangular rack (the kind you cool cookies on) set onto (or ideally into) a foil-lined baking tray with sides (often called a jelly roll pan). This will allow the bacon fat to drip down and away from the bites, keeping them crisp. If you don't have these items, just bake the bites directly on a foil-lined baking tray, and then drain them on paper towels before serving.

Vegetable oil spray

6 slices bacon, "regular" or turkey

12 Turkish-style dried apricots or pitted prunes, or a combination

1. Adjust the oven rack to the center position and preheat the oven to 400°F. Line a shallow-sided baking pan with foil, and set a cooling rack on top. Spray the rack with nonstick spray.

2. Cut each slice of bacon in half crosswise to make 12 pieces, each about 4 inches long.

3. Wrap each apricot or prune with a half-slice of bacon, covering as much of the fruit as you can. The bacon will overlap a bit, but it shouldn't go around twice. Place each piece,

seam side down, on the prepared rack. Bake for about 10 minutes, or until the bacon is crisp on the bottom.

4. Use tongs to carefully turn the bites over, and insert a toothpick into each one to secure the bacon ends. Bake for another 10 minutes, or until the bacon is evenly cooked and crisp all over.

5. Remove the baking tray from the oven, and leave the bites on the rack to cool for a few minutes before serving. (The sugar in the fruit will have become very hot.)

BACON BASICS

Bacon is easy to cook—just be sure to ventilate your kitchen as much as possible in the process.

Allow 2 strips (1 ounce) per serving. Lay them flat, in a single layer, in a skillet or frying pan, then put it on the stove over medium heat. Cook for 3 to 5 minutes, turning once or twice with tongs (and being careful not to let them burn!). When the bacon is *almost* as crisp as you want it, transfer it to a plate lined with paper towels, and let it sit for a few minutes to crisp further.

Let grease cool in the pan for a few minutes, and then *very* carefully pour it into a dry can or heatproof jar and put it in the refrigerator, where it will cool and solidify, and then discard it.

A microwave also does a very good job of cooking bacon. Lay strips flat on a plate lined with paper towels, and then place another paper towel on top. Cook on high power for 2 minutes, and then check for doneness. Cook for up to 1 more minute if necessary. (Your microwave might end up smelling like bacon, so mop it out with warm soapy water afterward and then leave it open to air out for a while.)

GET CREATIVE

- Before wrapping the fruit with the bacon, you can stuff it with a bit of cheese (goat cheese, bleu cheese, or even little sticks of Parmesan) or a single nut (an almond, a pecan, or part of a walnut half). Use a sharp knife to cut a slit in the side of the fruit, and slip in your chosen filling. Press the fruit around the filling to seal it completely, and then wrap the bacon around the fruit.

- For a vegetarian alternative, simply stuff the apricots and prunes with nuts or cheese and skip the bacon—and the baking.

- Serve with lime wedges to squeeze on top.

- Serve 2 or 3 warm bites on top of a salad of mixed greens or baby spinach.

- *Make this vegan by simply stuffing the fruit with nuts and skipping the baking.*

luxury potato bites

Makes 24 bites, about 6 servings

Here's proof that humble boiled potatoes can go totally uptown. This is the place to splurge on those expensive ingredients that you love but can afford only once in a great while and in small quantities. (We're talking caviar, crème fraîche, pine nuts, and the like.) A little bit will go far, and your potatoes with assorted toppings will be breathtakingly beautiful, especially if you present them on a dramatic platter of salt. To do this, fill a deep platter or shallow-sided gratin or baking dish with a ¼-inch-deep layer of large-crystal salt. The potato halves will nestle into the salt and not tip over for serving. Or you can skip the salt and trim a tiny slice off the bottom of each potato half to make it sit flat.

This recipe can be vegan, depending on your choice of toppings.

12 small creamer-style potatoes
   (red, white, and/or yellow),
   about 1½ inches in diameter

Choice of toppings (see *get creative*,
   at right)

1. Place the potatoes in a large pot and add enough water to cover them by a few inches. Bring to a boil over high heat and cook for 5 to 10 minutes, or until the potatoes are tender when pierced with the tip of a sharp knife.

2. Put a colander in the sink and drain the potatoes thoroughly, then let them cool until comfortable to handle.

3. Cut each potato in half and use a melon baller or a very small spoon to hollow out a small well in the center of each cut side. (Save the scooped-out potato to throw into a salad or soup—or just to snack on as you work.) Trim off a very thin slice from the rounded side of each half so it will stand upright—or skip this step if serving the potatoes on a platter of salt (see headnote).

4. Fill with your desired toppings and serve warm or at room temperature.

GET CREATIVE

Fill the hollowed-out potatoes with one or more of the following:

- Sour cream or crème fraîche topped with a small amount of caviar or a small piece of smoked salmon and snipped chives.

- Minced anchovies

- Grated sharp Cheddar cheese

- Salsa (tomato or mango) or guacamole (store-bought or homemade—see page 224) and a small sprig of cilantro

- A dollop of pesto (store-bought or homemade—see page 220)

- Lightly toasted pine nuts or chopped walnuts

- Very finely minced red bell pepper (fresh or roasted from a jar)

- Crumbled bacon (see page 233) and bleu cheese

- Hummus (store-bought or homemade—see page 226)

desserts.

The Sweet Truth

I'm always surprised to discover that there are fine cooks who never bake—or make any kind of dessert, baked or otherwise. So clearly it is not necessary to be a dessert maker in order to be considered a good and knowledgeable kitchen culinarian.

However, desserts are a whole lot of fun to prepare, and they make people happy. Dessert knowledge will give you something uplifting to do on a rainy Sunday. It will provide a great collection of ideas for memorable, affordable homemade gifts (think Buttermilk Banana Bread, packed in foil and tied with lots of ribbons, or a tin of Chocolate–Chocolate Chip Mint Cookies delivered in person to someone whose joy is really important to you).

That's the sweet truth about desserts. Most people, even those of us who love baking, wouldn't whip up a nice dessert just for ourselves. We know instinctively that there's something about being baked *for* that makes people feel really loved and cared about. By its very definition, dessert is an edible gift, something designed to share and enjoy with someone else. And that's a very good thing to have in your repertoire.

To get you going on yours, I've chosen ten recipes, carefully selected to give you maximum satisfaction and pride of accomplishment with minimum fuss and preciousness. These recipes give you a nice variety. Only four of them contain chocolate (that's variety in my book). Some are classics, like real Hot Fudge Sundaes, Apple Crisp, and Intensely Chocolate Brownies. Others are a bit more unexpected, like clafoutis, a super-easy French-style batter cake studded with cherries, or a simple bowl of Balsamic Strawberries. I see this as a "greatest hits" of sweet.

Technically speaking, I've tried to steer clear of fancy equipment. That said, you will probably appreciate having a handheld electric mixer, which is really the best way to beat butter to the fluffy state that makes all the difference. As with most of the other highly recommended tools in this book, you can probably find an affordable mixer at a garage sale or thrift store, or from a favorite relative who might be upgrading. In the meantime, all of these desserts can be made by hand. I also highly recommend you become the proud owner of a 9- by 13-inch baking pan, called for throughout this book and especially useful here.

Finally, here's an eleventh dessert idea: Don't forget that you can always just buy a few pieces of perfectly ripe, peak-season fruit, cut it up, and serve it with a few fantastic cheeses and maybe some chunks of equally fantastic chocolate and some toasted nuts. That's an edible gift anyone would appreciate.

hot fudge sundaes

Makes 6 or more servings

You'll be amazed at the difference homemade hot fudge sauce and freshly whipped cream make. This sauce is the genuine article, just like the kind you get in an ice cream parlor and much better than the typical supermarket versions. It takes only about 5 minutes to make. So take the ice cream out of the freezer before you start, and by the time you've made the sauce and whipped the cream, the ice cream will be optimally soft and scoopable. Once you have everything ready, assemble the sundaes quickly so you can enjoy the wonderful, fleeting contrast of hot fudge and cold ice cream while it lasts. Be sure the chocolate chips you use for this are semisweet, not milk chocolate. Or swap in 6 ounces of some other excellent semisweet chocolate, broken or chopped into small pieces.

The sauce will keep in a tightly covered jar in the refrigerator for 2 months or longer. It will become solid, so you'll need to reheat it in the microwave (or by gently warming the jar in a pot of water over medium heat). You can also just eat it cold with a spoon if you're urgently craving a chocolate truffle fix.

1 pint heavy cream (that's the big container, or two of the smaller ones)

½ cup dark corn syrup

1 cup (6 ounces) semisweet chocolate chips

2 teaspoons plus 1 teaspoon pure vanilla extract (some for the sauce, some for the whipped cream)

2 tablespoons butter

3 tablespoons sugar (powdered or granulated)

Excellent ice cream (at least a pint, maybe more; your choice of flavors)

1. Measure out ⅔ cup of the cream and pour it into a medium-small saucepan. Put the remaining unused cream back in the refrigerator for now.

2. Add the corn syrup and chocolate chips to the cream in the pan, and place it on the stove over medium-low heat. Whisk it slowly as it heats and the chocolate melts. Keep cooking and whisking over medium-low heat. Bubbles will begin to form around the sides. When it starts to boil, turn the heat to low and simmer, whisking often, for 3 minutes.

3. Remove the pan from the heat, and slowly whisk in the 2 teaspoons vanilla and the butter. Cover the pan and set it aside.

4. Take the remaining cream out of the refrigerator, and pour it into a medium-large bowl. (Extra space is needed because the cream will double in volume when whipped.) Beat the cream—vigorously—with the largest whisk you have. (You can also use a handheld electric mixer; just be very careful not to overbeat the cream, or you'll have butter.) Be patient, and keep whipping. It will take about 3 minutes for the cream to start frothing. After that point, add the remaining 1 teaspoon vanilla and the sugar. Continue to whip, paying close attention to the condition of the cream as it expands and thickens. You get to decide when it's ready.

5. Put a teaspoon or two of the hot fudge sauce at the bottom of each serving dish. Cover this with a scoop of the ice cream. Spoon on more of the fudge, and top with a dollop of whipped cream.

GET CREATIVE

- Sprinkle on some chopped toasted walnuts or almonds.

- Top each serving with a strawberry or a maraschino cherry.

- Layer slices of banana in with the ice cream.

- Layer in some fresh berries (slice larger ones; leave smaller ones whole), or use frozen unsweetened berries (defrost them in a bowl to collect the juices, which you can drizzle on as a second sauce).

- To make a brownie sundae, put an Intensely Chocolate Brownie (page 246) in a small bowl. Top with a scoop of ice cream, a spoonful of hot fudge sauce, and a dollop of whipped cream.

- Sprinkle crumbled cookies over the ice cream and again over the whipped cream. Use any kind you like; amaretti (Italian almond cookies) are particularly good.

- Garnish each sundae with a small cookie, stuck jauntily into the whipped cream.

balsamic strawberries

Makes 3 to 4 servings

A perfect strawberry, deeply red and exquisitely ripe, should just be eaten. But here's a traditional Italian treatment to enhance those less-than-perfect ones. You simply cut them and let them marinate in sugar for a few hours. Then, shortly before serving, you sprinkle them with sweet-and-tangy balsamic vinegar, and they magically spring to life. This works fine with any good-quality balsamic vinegar.

This recipe is vegan.

2 pints (1 quart) strawberries

¼ cup sugar (possibly more)

3 tablespoons balsamic vinegar (possibly more)

1. Clean the strawberries by wiping them with a damp paper towel. Hull them, and then halve or slice them, depending on their size.

2. Place the strawberries in a shallow pan (a 10-inch glass pie pan works well) and sprinkle with the sugar.

3. Cover tightly with plastic wrap, and let the pan sit for at least 2 hours, stirring or shaking it every now and then. (If the berries are going to sit for much longer than that, refrigerate them, but allow them to return to room temperature before serving.)

4. Within half an hour of serving, sprinkle on the vinegar. (Begin with 3 tablespoons, then taste and add up to a tablespoon more. If the berries taste too tart, add a little more sugar.)

GET CREATIVE

- You can make this with a combination of raspberries and blackberries, in addition to, or instead of, the strawberries.

- Balsamic Strawberries are a perfect topping for a great vanilla gelato or ice cream.

- Top each serving with a little lightly whipped cream (see page 240) or a dollop of crème fraîche.

- Spoon over Buttermilk Banana Bread (page 252) or slices of good pound cake from a bakery, warmed for a few minutes in the oven or toaster oven.

- Serve with small Italian cookies or chocolates.

chocolate–peanut butter crunchy things

Makes about 2½ dozen

This is the only recipe I know of that begins with melting peanut butter, and I can't even remember where I got the idea. I've been making this, both with kids and by myself (that's how much I love it), for years. After the PB is melted, you mix in some chocolate chips, which will become very soft and almost melt too. Then you add some crisp cereal and form little balls, which get chilled in the refrigerator. The PB and chocolate firm up, and the result is a batch of delectable treats somewhere between candy and cookie; lacking a culinary category, I call them Crunchy Things. (The school-age kids I've made this with call them "Doo-Dads." You can call them whatever you like.) You can probably use any kind of peanut butter for this, but I have only made it with the very basic natural kind that is made from just peanuts. A trick to handling peanut butter without it sticking to everything is to lightly coat whatever you're using to measure, move, and contain it (measuring cup, rubber spatula, spoons, plate) with vegetable oil spray.

This recipe is vegan.

1 cup smooth peanut butter

⅔ cup (4 ounces) semisweet
  chocolate chips

2 cups crisp cereal (such as
  Kashi Go-Lean Crunch)

1. Place the peanut butter in a small saucepan or a cast-iron skillet. Put it over medium heat, and stir with a wooden spoon while it softens. This will take only about 1 minute.

2. Remove the pan from the stove and put it on a trivet or a folded dish towel. Pour in the chocolate chips, and stir until they soften into the peanut butter. They don't need to melt all the way; you just want them supple.

3. Pour in the cereal, and mix slowly until all the pieces of cereal are completely (or at least reasonably) coated.

4. Use two spoons to scoop up and form tablespoon-sized hunks of the batter, and put them on a plate. Refrigerate, uncovered, for about an hour, or until firm. You can eat them straight from the refrigerator, or transfer the solid Things to a heavy resealable plastic bag and freeze them. They are good frozen, or just plain cold.

GET CREATIVE

• Add ⅓ cup shredded coconut (sweetened or not, depending on your sweet tooth).

• Add ⅓ cup chopped toasted almonds or walnuts.

• Vary the cereal. Just avoid highly sweetened products, which will make this cloying.

• You can use 2 cups crunchy chow mein noodles (the kind that come in a can) in place of the cereal.

• Substitute butterscotch chips for some or all of the chocolate chips.

• If you're feeling crafty, make Peanut Butter Cups: Buy some fluted candy papers at a baking or cooking supply store. Spoon the batter into the papers and chill as directed.

chocolate–chocolate chip mint cookies

Makes 3½ to 4 dozen cookies

The world's best holiday cookie awaits you. And my definition of a holiday cookie is that when you bite into it, a holiday happens. I believe this is the only recipe I've ever written that uses peppermint extract, but these cookies are worth the price of several bottles. The cookies freeze beautifully when stored in a tin, and even taste good frozen. In the meantime, the peppermint extract has a half-life of about 2,000 years, so keep that bottle around for the next batch, which will likely happen sooner than that. Heads up: You'll need to take the butter out of the refrigerator about an hour before you start baking so it can come to room temperature.

1½ cups (3 sticks) butter, plus a little extra for the cookie sheets

1 cup granulated sugar

1 cup (packed) light brown sugar

1 large egg

2 teaspoons pure vanilla extract

2 teaspoons peppermint extract

3 cups unbleached all-purpose flour

½ cup unsweetened cocoa powder

2 teaspoons baking powder

Scant ½ teaspoon salt

2 cups semisweet chocolate chips (one 12-ounce package)

1. About an hour ahead of time, unwrap the butter and place it in a large bowl. Use a table knife to cut it into 1-inch pieces, and let it stand at room temperature to soften.

2. Adjust the oven rack to the center position and preheat the oven to 350°F. Put a little soft butter on a paper towel, a piece of waxed paper, or a butter wrapper, and lightly grease two cookie sheets.

3. Pour the granulated sugar, and crumble the brown sugar, into the bowl holding the softened butter. Use a handheld electric mixer at high speed (or if you don't have one, use a whisk, with enthusiasm) to beat the butter and sugar together until light and fluffy. Add the egg and beat well. (Use a rubber spatula to scrape the sides of the bowl a few times during this process.) Add the vanilla and peppermint extracts, and continue to beat for another minute or two, until everything is well combined.

4. Combine the flour, cocoa powder, baking powder, and salt in a medium-sized bowl, and whisk slowly to blend. Add this to the butter mixture, along with the chocolate chips, stirring with the spatula until the dough is thoroughly combined.

5. Drop the dough by rounded teaspoons onto the prepared cookie sheets, spacing them 2 to 3 inches apart and flattening each mound slightly with the back of a spoon. (You will need to bake these in batches, so just spoon out as many as will comfortably fit on your cookie sheets.) Bake for 10 to 12 minutes, or until the tops of the cookies are dry and the bottoms are lightly browned.

6. Let the cookies sit on the cookie sheets for about 5 minutes after you take them out of the oven, and then gently transfer them to a cooling rack using a thin-bladed metal spatula. Repeat with the remaining dough.

THE CASE FOR COOKIE SHEETS

If you'd like to become a frequent cookie baker, I suggest you invest in a few cookie sheets (the kind with insulated bottoms and no side rims). They're cheap, easy to store, and most important, if you use them just for cookies and use a separate set of baking trays for savory cooking (such as roasting vegetables), you won't have to worry about your cookies tasting like garlic or whatever you last roasted. If you don't have cookie sheets, line your regular baking trays with foil to prevent this flavor spillover. For most cookies made with butter, you really don't need to grease your cookie sheets, but it never hurts to spray them lightly with vegetable oil spray or grease them with a little softened butter.

intensely chocolate brownies

Makes 8 to 12 or possibly more servings

These are insanely rich, dense, and moist, so you can cut them very small and they'll serve a crowd. And I guarantee you, that crowd will be pleased. They'll keep for several days in a tightly sealed container at room temperature, and they freeze well too. Be sure to allow time to let the butter come to room temperature for about an hour before you start baking.

1 cup (2 sticks) butter, plus a little extra for the pan

1 cup (6 ounces) semisweet chocolate chips

1 cup (packed) light brown sugar

5 large eggs

1 tablespoon pure vanilla extract

½ cup unbleached all-purpose flour

⅛ teaspoon salt

1. About an hour ahead of time, unwrap the butter and place it in a large bowl. Use a table knife to cut it into 1-inch pieces, and let it stand at room temperature to soften.

2. Adjust the oven rack to the center position and preheat the oven to 350°F (325°F if you're using a glass pan). Put a little soft butter on a paper towel, a piece of waxed paper, or a butter wrapper, and lightly grease the bottom and corners of a 9- by 13-inch baking pan. (No need to grease the sides.)

3. Fill a smallish saucepan with about 2 inches of water, and place a heatproof bowl that is large enough to hold the chocolate chips directly on top of the pan. The bowl should rest firmly in place, clutched by the pan's rim, and the bottom of the bowl should not be touching the water. Pour the chocolate chips into the bowl, and put the whole setup on the stove over low heat. Let the water simmer gently until the chocolate chips are all melted (there should be no solid pieces when you give it a stir). Remove the pan from the heat, and carefully, using pot holders or oven mitts, remove the bowl of melted chocolate from the pan. Set it aside to cool a little.

4. Use a handheld electric mixer at high speed (or if you don't have one, use a whisk, with enthusiasm) to beat the butter (by itself, for now) for a couple of minutes, or until it becomes light and fluffy. Crumble in the brown sugar, and continue to beat at high speed (or with your own arm at its personal best) for another 2 minutes or so. Use a rubber spatula to scrape the sides of the bowl a few times during this process.

5. Add the eggs, one at a time, beating well enough after each addition to thoroughly mix it in. Add the vanilla extract, and continue to beat for another minute or two, until everything is very well combined.

6. Keep beating as you slowly drizzle in the melted chocolate. (If you are beating manually, you might want to get someone to help hold the bowl steady for this.) Beat well until the chocolate is completely incorporated. (The constant movement prevents the heat of the chocolate from cooking the eggs.)

7. Sprinkle in the flour and salt, and stir (you can finally stop beating now) until they disappear into the batter. Transfer the batter to the prepared pan, taking care to scrape all of it in with a rubber spatula. Then use the spatula to spread the batter evenly.

8. Bake for 12 to 15 minutes, or until the top springs back a little when lightly touched in the center. (They might seem under-baked, but they will firm up as they cool, and these are moist brownies. That said, if they seem too soft for you, it's okay to leave them in the oven for a few minutes longer, until a toothpick inserted all the way into the center comes out clean. At that point, they'll be cakey brownies, rather than fudgy ones.)

9. Let the brownies cool in the pan for about 10 minutes; then cut them into squares of your preferred size. Let them sit for another 10 minutes or so after you do the cutting, so each piece can solidify. Then remove the squares from the pan and let them cool on a rack. Serve warm or at room temperature.

GET CREATIVE

- For Chocolate Chip Brownies, use an entire 12-ounce bag of chocolate chips. Put half the bag into the batter melted, as directed, and sprinkle the remaining (unmelted) chocolate chips into the batter when you add the flour.

- For Chocolate-Banana Brownies, mash a medium-sized very ripe banana into the butter when you begin.

- For Chocolate-Nut Brownies, stir ½ cup chopped walnuts or pecans into the batter just before spreading it in the pan.

- Use a strainer to sift a little powdered sugar over the top of the brownies after you slice them.

- Serve à la mode with vanilla or coffee ice cream, or as the base of a brownie sundae (see page 240).

cheesecake bars

Makes 24 bars

A full-on formal cheesecake requires a special pan with a removable bottom and, generally speaking, a special occasion. These easy bars with a tasty cookie crust give you the cheesecake effect in a much easier way. They freeze really well in an airtight container. You can just take as many or as few as you'd like out of the freezer and enjoy them an hour later, once they've defrosted. Note that you'll need to start softening the cream cheese about an hour ahead of time.

1½ pounds (three 8-ounce packages) cream cheese

¾ cup (1½ sticks) butter

2½ cups unbleached all-purpose flour

1 teaspoon cinnamon

½ teaspoon plus ⅛ teaspoon salt (some for the crust, some for the filling)

⅔ cup (packed) light brown sugar

4 large eggs

2 tablespoons fresh lemon juice

1 tablespoon pure vanilla extract

⅓ cup granulated sugar

1. About an hour ahead of time, unwrap the cream cheese and place it in a large bowl. Use a table knife to cut it into 1-inch pieces, and let it stand at room temperature to soften.

2. Adjust the oven rack to a medium-low position and preheat the oven to 350°F (325°F if you're using a glass pan).

3. Melt the butter in a microwave-safe bowl in the microwave (30 to 60 seconds on high power), or in a small saucepan over low heat.

4. Combine the flour, cinnamon, and ½ teaspoon of the salt in a large bowl, and stir briefly. Crumble in the brown sugar, and then pour in the melted butter, scraping it all in with a rubber spatula. Use a spoon or fork to mix the butter into the dry ingredients until uniformly blended. Transfer this mixture to an ungreased 9- by 13-inch pan, and pat/press it evenly and firmly into place, forming a crust that coats the entire bottom surface of the pan.

5. Add the eggs, lemon juice, vanilla extract, the remaining ⅛ teaspoon salt, and the granulated sugar to the softened cream cheese. Use a handheld electric mixer (or a sturdy whisk) to beat all these ingredients together. Start slowly, so as not to splash, and then gradually work your way up to high speed as the batter comes together. Keep going until the mixture is uniformly blended. There will still be some small lumps of cream cheese, and that is fine. Pour this mixture on top of the crust, scraping in every last bit with a rubber spatula. There's no need to spread it; it will form an even layer on its own.

6. Bake for 20 minutes, or until the edges are lightly golden, the top looks dry, and nothing jiggles when you shake the pan. Remove the pan from the oven, and immediately use a very sharp knife to cut 24 bars with a gentle sawing motion, so as not to disturb the lovely top surface. Cool completely in the pan before lifting out the squares.

GET CREATIVE

- For a crisper crust, you can bake the crust on its own in the preheated oven for 10 to 15 minutes. Remove it from the oven and let it cool for 10 minutes before pouring in the cream cheese mixture. Once the crust is filled, return the pan to the oven and bake for 20 minutes as directed.

- For a deeper flavor in the crust, you can replace 1 cup of the flour with finely ground almonds. (Pulverize them to a fine powder in a food processor or blender, or look for ground almonds or almond meal in the baking section of the grocery store.)

- Add 2 teaspoons grated lemon zest to the filling mixture for extra flavor. Grate the zest from the lemon before you cut it open to squeeze the juice. Use a microplane grater (page xiii) or the fine holes of a box grater; or shave the lemon peel (outermost yellow part only) with a vegetable peeler, and then chop it with a sharp knife.

- You can top the cooled bars with your favorite jam or marmalade, spread in a thin layer.

- Garnish each square with a slice of strawberry and/ or kiwi.

gingery gingerbread

Makes 24 servings

Fresh ginger makes this a more deeply flavored gingerbread than the kind you might have grown up eating. It's easy enough to grate the ginger, especially if you buy a knob that is very tight and crisp. It should have no wrinkles, and the skin should come off easily with just a little scrape of your fingernail. Peel it, and then use a microplane grater (see page xiii) or the fine holes of a box grater to grate it directly over the bowl, so you catch all of the liquid and solids. The brown sugar can be light or dark; both work very well. Note that you'll need to soften the butter for at least an hour ahead of time.

½ cup (1 stick) butter, plus a little extra for the pan

3 cups unbleached all-purpose flour

2 teaspoons baking soda

1½ teaspoons baking powder

½ teaspoon salt

2 teaspoons cinnamon

1 tablespoon powdered ginger

½ teaspoon ground cloves

3 tablespoons (3 to 4 ounces) grated fresh ginger

⅔ cup (packed) brown sugar

¾ cup molasses

2 large eggs

2 teaspoons pure vanilla extract

1½ cups buttermilk

1. About an hour ahead of time, unwrap the butter and place it in a large bowl. Use a table knife to cut it into 1-inch pieces, and let it stand at room temperature to soften.

2. Adjust the oven rack to the center position and preheat the oven to 350°F (325°F if you're using a glass pan). Put a little soft butter on a paper towel, a piece of waxed paper, or a butter wrapper, and lightly grease the bottom and corners of a 9- by 13- inch pan. (No need to grease the sides.)

3. Combine the flour, baking soda, baking powder, salt, cinnamon, powdered ginger, and cloves in a medium-sized bowl. Whisk slowly to blend, and then stir in the grated fresh ginger, whisking until it's distributed. Set this aside.

4. Crumble the brown sugar into the bowl with the softened butter. Use a handheld electric mixer at high speed (or if you don't have one, use a whisk, with enthusiasm) to beat the butter and sugar together until light and fluffy. Add the molasses and then the eggs, one at a time, beating well after each addition. Use a rubber spatula to scrape the sides of the

bowl a few times during this process. Add the vanilla extract, and continue to beat for another minute or two, until everything is well combined.

5. Add about a third of the flour mixture to the butter mixture, slowly whisking just enough to mostly blend. Then pour in approximately a third of the buttermilk, and stir it in. Continue with another third of the flour mixture, and another third of the buttermilk. Then repeat with the remaining flour mixture and buttermilk. As you do this, switch to stirring with a spoon when the batter thickens, and mix from the bottom of the bowl after each addition—just enough to thoroughly blend without overmixing. (It's okay if the finished batter is not completely smooth.)

6. Transfer the batter to the prepared pan, taking care to scrape all of it in with a rubber spatula. Then use the spatula to spread the batter evenly. Bake for 35 to 40 minutes, or until the top is springy to the touch and/or a toothpick inserted all the way into the center comes out clean.

7. Remove the pan from the oven and allow the gingerbread to cool in the pan for at least 15 minutes before cutting it into 24 rectangular pieces. Serve warm, at room temperature, or cold.

GET CREATIVE

- You can add any or all of these delightful items to the flour mixture when you add the grated ginger:

    - ½ cup chopped dried cranberries or cherries

    - ½ cup minced crystallized ginger

    - ½ cup chopped walnuts or pecans

    - ½ cup golden raisins

- Serve this with:

    - Your favorite applesauce

    - A big spoonful of whipped cream (see page 240)

    - Vanilla or fruit-flavored frozen yogurt, or vanilla, strawberry, or coffee ice cream

    - Freshly cut fruit or defrosted frozen berries

    - Store-bought caramel sauce, warmed briefly in a microwave or in a saucepan

buttermilk banana bread

Makes about 8 servings

Banana bread was invented to use up soft overripe bananas. If, from time to time, you've got a few extra bananas that are turning dark and soft, don't throw them out. In just a few minutes, you can transform them into banana bread batter. You'll need a standard loaf pan for this, about 9 by 5 inches, and about 3 inches deep. You can often find them at garage sales and secondhand stores. Or you can bake two mini-loaves, one to keep and one to bring to someone's house as a perfect little gift. If you go this route, begin checking for doneness after 40 minutes.

You can make this a day before you plan to serve it. Store it, wrapped in plastic wrap or in a resealable plastic bag, at room temperature—or in the refrigerator if you're keeping it for more than a day. You can also freeze it whole, or in slices so you can grab a single serving and toast it. (Okay to put it in the toaster still frozen.)

½ cup (1 stick) butter, plus a little extra for the pan

3 medium bananas, very ripe

¾ cup buttermilk

¾ cup (packed) light brown sugar

2 large eggs

1 teaspoon pure vanilla extract

1½ cups unbleached all-purpose flour

½ teaspoon salt

1½ teaspoons baking powder

½ teaspoon baking soda

1. About an hour ahead of time, unwrap the butter and place it in a large bowl. Use a table knife to cut it into 1-inch pieces, and let it stand at room temperature to soften.

2. Adjust the oven rack to the center position and preheat the oven to 350°F (325°F if you're using a glass pan). Put a little soft butter on a paper towel, a piece of waxed paper, or a butter wrapper, and lightly grease the bottom and corners of a standard-sized loaf pan. (No need to grease the sides.)

3. Peel the bananas, and place them in a medium-sized bowl. Mash with a fork until they form a mostly smooth pulp; then switch from mashing to mixing as you drizzle the buttermilk directly into the bananas. (You can use the fork or a whisk.) Keep mixing until the mixture is completely blended, and then set this aside.

4. Crumble the brown sugar into the bowl with the softened butter. Use a handheld electric mixer at high speed (or if you don't have one, use a whisk, with enthusiasm) to beat the butter and sugar together until light and fluffy. Use a rubber spatula to scrape the sides of the bowl a few times during this process. Add the eggs, one at a time, beating well after each addition. Add the vanilla extract, and continue to beat for another minute or two, until everything is well combined.

5. Combine the flour, salt, baking powder, and baking soda in a second medium-sized bowl. Whisk slowly to blend. Add about half of this dry mixture to the butter mixture, stirring it in with a wooden spoon. Then stir in about half of the banana-buttermilk mixture. Repeat with the remaining dry mixture, followed by the remaining banana-buttermilk mixture, stirring from the bottom of the bowl after each addition, just enough to thoroughly blend without overmixing.

6. Transfer the batter to the prepared pan, taking care to scrape all of it in with a rubber spatula. Then use the spatula to spread the batter evenly. Bake for 50 to 70 minutes, or until a sharp knife inserted all the way into the center comes out clean.

7. Remove the pan from the oven and allow the bread to cool in the pan for at least 15 minutes before removing it. (The best way to do this is to rap the pan sharply on the counter a few times to loosen the bread, and then let it slide out onto a cooling rack.) To avoid crumbling, wait at least 20 minutes longer to slice and serve.

GET CREATIVE

- Add 1 cup chopped nuts and/or chocolate chips to the flour mixture.

- Dress this up by serving it à la mode with any ice cream or frozen yogurt.

- Top with a generous pile of cut-up fresh fruit in season. It's also good topped with Balsamic Strawberries (page 241) or fresh blackberries or blueberries. Whipped cream is always welcome.

apple crisp

Makes 6 servings

Here's a perfect autumn weekend afternoon: You meet some friends at the farmers' market and buy a bunch of apples, head to someone's place, and hang out, peeling, coring, slicing, and chatting. In no time, you've got a pile of sliced apples, which you pack in a pan, top with a simple mixture of oats, flour, brown sugar, cinnamon, and butter, and toss in the oven. A quick stroll to the corner store for vanilla ice cream, and by the time you're back, the place smells like heaven. You and your friends hang out some more, over generous helpings of warm, freshly baked apple crisp à la mode, and life, at least for this moment, is A-okay.

3 tablespoons fresh lemon juice

10 medium apples (any kind
   except Red Delicious)

¼ cup granulated sugar

½ cup (1 stick) butter

1¼ cups rolled oats
   (regular, not "quick-cooking")

1 cup unbleached all-purpose flour

½ teaspoon salt

2 teaspoons cinnamon

¼ cup (packed) brown sugar
   (light or dark)

1. Adjust the oven rack to the center position and preheat the oven to 350°F (325°F if you're using a glass pan).

2. Pour the lemon juice into a large bowl. Peel, core, and slice the apples, and as you cut them, add the slices to the bowl. As the apples accumulate, toss them with the juice every now and then. When all the apples are sliced and tossed, sprinkle in the granulated sugar and gently toss again. Transfer the apple mixture to a 9- by 13-inch pan, and set it aside.

3. Melt the butter in a microwave-safe bowl in the microwave (30 to 60 seconds on high power), or in a small saucepan over low heat.

4. Without cleaning it, use the empty apple bowl to combine the oats, flour, salt, and cinnamon, stirring them together briefly. Crumble in the brown sugar, then pour in the melted butter, scraping it all in with a rubber spatula. Use a spoon or fork to mix the butter into the dry ingredients until uniformly blended.

5. Spread this mixture over the apples in the pan, patting everything down as you go so it forms a solid topping, as evenly distributed as possible.

6. Bake for 35 to 40 minutes, or until the top is crisp and golden and the apples are bubbling around the edges. Let cool for at least 10 minutes. Serve hot, warm, or at room temperature.

GET CREATIVE

- You can make this with different kinds of fruit. Try swapping in pears for some of the apples. In the summer, you can make this with peaches, nectarines, apricots, and/or plums (any combination). The total amount should be 8 to 10 cups of sliced fruit. (With the summer option, sprinkle the cut fruit with 1 tablespoon unbleached all-purpose flour and toss to coat, so it won't end up too wet.)

- Add up to ¼ cup minced crystallized ginger to the topping mixture.

- Add up to ½ cup chopped walnuts or almonds or whole pine nuts to the topping mixture.

- Toss up to ½ cup dried cranberries or golden raisins with the apples before spreading them in the pan.

- *Make this vegan by using canola oil instead of butter.*

cherry clafoutis

Makes 6 servings

Pronounced "cla-foo-TEE," from a word meaning "to fill" in a regional French dialect, this easy farm-style French dessert is a cross between a cake and a jumbo fruit pancake or a filled popover, studded with black cherries. You just beat together a quick crêpe-like batter and pour everything right into the pan. You make it with frozen pitted cherries, which require no work other than opening the bag—not even defrosting. If nice fresh cherries are in season, use them instead of the frozen ones, but you'll need to pit them (cherry pitting gadgets are available in some kitchen supply stores). It's fun to bring the whole pan to the table straight from the oven so your guests can admire this beautiful, dramatic-looking dish.

2 tablespoons butter

1½ cups pitted black cherries (frozen/not defrosted, or fresh)

1⅓ cups plus 1 tablespoon unbleached all-purpose flour

1½ cups milk

3 tablespoons sugar

4 large eggs

1 teaspoon pure vanilla extract

¼ teaspoon salt

1. Adjust the oven rack to the center position and preheat the oven to 350°F. Put the butter in a 9- by 13-inch baking pan, and place the pan in the preheating oven for a minute or so to melt the butter, keeping an eye on it so it doesn't burn. Remove the pan from the oven, and carefully tilt it in all directions to let the butter coat the bottom and the corners. Set it aside.

2. In a small bowl, toss together the cherries and the 1 tablespoon flour, and let this sit for a few minutes while you prepare the batter.

3. Pour the milk into a blender or a food processor fitted with the steel blade. (Or just pour it into a large bowl.) Add the sugar, eggs, vanilla, and salt, and blend (or whisk) until smooth. Sprinkle in the remaining 1⅓ cups flour and process (or whisk) just until the flour is incorporated. (You may need to stop and scrape the sides with a rubber spatula to get all the flour mixed in.) There will be some lumps, and that is fine.

4. Pour the batter into the prepared pan, and then scatter the coated fruit randomly but evenly over the batter.

5. Bake for 30 to 35 minutes, or until puffed and lightly browned around the edges. Serve hot or warm, cut into large squares.

FRUITY CLAFOUTIS

Even though a clafoutis is traditionally made with black cherries, you can use various other fruit, singly or in combination. Just keep the total amount to about 1½ cups. Try offsetting the sweetness of the cherries with some tart raspberries or blackberries, or substitute other types of stone fruit—fresh peaches, apricots, and/or plums, pitted and sliced. In some parts of France, clafoutis is made with grapes or red currants, which are also delicious. In the winter, use frozen unsweetened fruit, adding it to the batter without defrosting it first. You can also use canned fruit (packed in water, not syrup), if you drain it very well first. One more option: Clafoutis can also be made with dried fruit that has been "plumped" by soaking it for an hour or more in fruit juice and/or a fruity liqueur. If using larger pieces of dried fruit, slice them first.

GET CREATIVE

• This looks especially beautiful topped with a dusting of powdered sugar, shaken on through a small strainer.

• Serve with vanilla ice cream or frozen yogurt.

• Sprinkle some toasted sliced almonds over each serving as a garnish.

• Vary the fruit (see "Fruity Clafoutis," opposite.)

index.